KU-023-720

Contents

3

AUSTRALIAN
LITERATURE

BRITISH LIBRARY
LENDING DIVISION

-1 APR 1981

W64-9888

A CRITICAL ACCOUNT
TO 1955

2 *by* 1

CECIL HADGRAFT

NORTHUMBERLAND COUNTY LIBRARY

6

HEINEMANN

LONDON MELBOURNE TORONTO

7 1960

William Heinemann Ltd

LONDON MELBOURNE TORONTO

CAPE TOWN AUCKLAND

THE HAGUE

★

© CECIL HADGRAFT 1960

First published 1960

662,351

NORTHUMBERLAND COUNTY LIBRARY

Printed in Great Britain by
Butler & Tanner Ltd
Frome and London

AUSTRALIAN LITERATURE

Preface

THIS critical account of our literature has no claims to be inclusive. Any reader who wishes for a complete account should refer to Morris Miller's two-volume work, inclusive to nearly 1940, to F. T. Macartney's revision, inclusive to 1950, and to the forthcoming history by H. M. Green.

I have selected those who seem to me the most important and representative writers in poetry, fiction, and the essay up to 1955. The selection of those of last century, it is hoped with some assurance, will be approved. There is no such hope that the selection of those of this century will meet with assent. Had I tried to select purely on the basis of merit, then probably another thirty names would appear. Instead, I have tried to compromise with merit and representative quality.

Some types of literature are not treated—dramatic, travel, descriptive, juvenile, historical, biographical. I thought it more useful to discuss fewer writers in fewer fields so that I might deal with each at greater length.

No criticism today can be definitive. Very few readers then are likely to agree with all the comments on all the writers discussed in this book. I may say that I have not consciously made concessions or adopted bias: I have tried to tell the truth as it appeared to my sense of values.

One last note. But for the comments and help of Eunice Hanger, Tom Inglis Moore, Nicholas Hudson, and one who wishes to rest unnamed, this book would have more errors than it probably has. This is not to suggest that any one of these critics necessarily approves of what I have written. It is merely to offer my heartfelt thanks. I should also like to express my gratitude to the staffs of the Oxley Library and the Mitchell Library.

I have to make grateful acknowledgment to the Senate of the University of Queensland for a grant towards the costs of the research this book necessitated.

C. H.

University of Queensland

PERIOD I
to the 1880s

CHAPTER I

The Earliest Poetry

THE convict colony of New South Wales was founded because most English laws were harsh but many English juries
and judges were not. With a legal system that imposed the death
penalty for over two hundred offences, eighteenth-century juries
were reluctant to condemn an accused on a capital charge: they
preferred to water down their verdict and find him guilty of a
lesser crime involving a lesser penalty. And even when found
guilty on a capital charge, the criminal was very often spared,
his sentence later commuted to transportation.

The English plantations in America received these slaves, and
the plantation owners prospered. But after defeat in the war of
American independence England had to find another repository
for these victims of industrialism and legality. That war ended in
1783. In 1770 Captain James Cook had charted the eastern coast
of what was some fifty years later to be called Australia. Botany
Bay, it was thought, would provide an outlet for England's sur-
plus criminality. It was high time: the coast of Africa was too unhealthy—at least for the officials guarding the convicts—while the
hulks in the Thames were stuffed with verminous wrongdoers.

In January 1788 the First Fleet arrived, eleven little vessels
with a total tonnage of rather more than 3,000 tons. Finding
Botany Bay unsuitable, the father of the new colony, Captain
Arthur Phillip, moved north to Port Jackson. Upon the shore
were decanted about 1,100 human beings, nearly three-quarters of
them being convicts. Their only asset was Phillip himself. With
almost every conceivable disadvantage to harass them, they were
concerned chiefly with remaining alive. That anything like
literature should result from such an inauspicious foundation,
and that within a half-century, is rather surprising. And yet the
first poem appeared in print when the colony was only just past
its majority. It was written by a transported felon. So was the
first novel, twenty years after the first poem. The second batch
of poems was delivered by a government official. Convicts,
officials, visitors—these were the first literary folk in Australia,

and the third group remained the chief contributors during most of the nineteenth century. It was not until the nineties that the native-born began to predominate in literature.

Poetry has been more dependent than fiction on traditional forms, diction, and themes; and so the first poetry written in Australia was not Australian but English. There was not a beginning, but a continuation, a transplantation. More than that—the newcomers were unwilling newcomers, transported as convicts or sent out as officials. It was not until the 1820s that free immigrants started to flow in, and such immigrants were concerned with material advantage. That any or all of these should quickly and naturally assimilate the atmosphere of the new land was not to be expected, still less that they should develop a medium or a diction to express their acceptance. In brief, poets who have written in Australia may be divided into three groups—English poets, Australian poets, and poets. And the classification reflects rough. he chronological development. There are more cross-currents and eddies than this broad generalisation states, of course, but the thesis can be maintained.

The very earliest poets were not minors but minimi. The other poets of last century were minors, gaining in stature but often failing in technique. Those who wrote before Charles Harpur have little more than an historical interest. Their poems are recorded in the history of our literature because they were written by an Englishman in Australia, or by an Australian in England, or by an Australian in Australia. The first of such verses appeared at intervals in *The Sydney Gazette; and New South Wales Advertiser*. They were almost all Royal Birthday odes, products of Michael Massey Robinson (1747–1826), an Oxford man and a genial blackmailer, who was transported to New South Wales in 1798, pardoned, and accorded various official positions in the colony.

These odes began with the *Gazette* of 9 June, 1810, and continued until 18 August, 1821. On the King's and the Queen's birthdays festivities were held in Sydney; on each of these occasions Robinson duly produced a poem and upon the invitation of the Governor recited it. The report of the *Gazette* for 18 January, 1812, contains the following paragraph:

That the *Parnassian Wreath* should at such a season be neglected, would have been, in deed, an umbrage to the Muses; who, to subvert this catastrophe, were pleased to inspire *The Laureat Bard of*

New South Wales with imaginations, which pronounce themselves the work of Nature and Refinement. An *Ode on Her Majesty's Birth Day* was presented to his Excellency by Mr. Michael Robinson, who was received with affable kindness, and requested to be the Reciter of his own performance.

The manner of the Bard's delivery is reported in different issues of the *Gazette* as impressive or vigorous or energetic or solemn. The contents of his offerings are not very varied. Mostly they begin with the glories of Greece, shift to Rome, and end with Albion, notable in war or (when news of Waterloo reaches the colony) in peace and trade; the blessings, thanks to the Monarch, extend even to Australia. Robinson becomes very repetitive in his later odes, and one feels that lines have been lifted from the previous odes and rearranged to compose the latest example. The following lines from the first ode are typical of any others later:

> Such is our MONARCH's mild Behest!
> Such the pure Meed His Wisdom sends
> To bid the Din of Discord rest,
> And Britons harmonise as Friends!

> 'Tis done! and lo! our CHIEF's auspicious Hand
> Spreads Peace and Plenty o'er the smiling Land
> Whilst MERCY bids this fav'rite Legend shine—
> "To err is human, To forgive, divine!"

Robinson also wrote four songs. Here he unbends from his official posture, as befitting an occasion reported in the *Gazette* for 29 January, 1820:

> On Wednesday, being the 26th of the month, a public anniversary dinner was held in George-street, in commemoration of the institution of the Colony. It was attended by a great many respectable persons, of between 60 and 70 in number, and went off with a degree of mirth and hilarity well suited to the occasion.

The last stanza of the song that Robinson composed for the dinner has the right convivial and gratulatory note:

> To her CHIEF, whose paternal and patriot hand
> Diffuses prosperity's smile thro' the land,
> Let this toast be reserv'd, which no party will sever,
> For it springs from one feeling—"MACQUARIE FOR EVER!"

This note, as of a vulgarised Thomas Moore, is found in the other songs.

Robinson's verses, as the extracts serve to show, are the facile versifyings of an educated man able to turn out rimed and metrical lines with a certain fluency. His priority is one of time. This fact and the inaccessibility of his verses may excuse the space here devoted to him.

The first volume of verse to be published in Australia was written by an Englishman. In 1819 Barron Field (1786–1846), friend of Charles Lamb and judge of the New South Wales Supreme Court from 1817, produced his *First Fruits of Australian Poetry*, containing two poems. A second edition containing four additional poems came out in 1823. Both the poems in the first edition are comic, the first in Byron's fashion, the second in Field's.

Botany-Bay Flowers, the first poem, partly in blank verse, partly in couplets, talks of Australian flora in terms of Shakespeare's fairies, and is neat and deft enough. A few lines from it may conceivably have influenced Harpur when he wrote the well-known passage in his *Midsummer Noon*. Today we recall Field's little volume for two things, the claim to priority that he made—

> I first adventure. Follow me who list;
> And be the second Austral Harmonist—

and his lines from the second poem, *The Kangaroo*—

> Kangaroo, Kangaroo!
> Thou Spirit of Australia,
> That redeems from utter failure,
> From perfect desolation,
> And warrants the creation
> Of this fifth part of the Earth.

The additional poems in the second edition reveal Field as growing homesick. He misses the sense of age and of tradition. Nor does he respond to the strange beauty of the new land:

> . . . where Nature is prosaic,
> Unpicturesque, unmusical, and where
> Nature-reflecting Art is not yet born;—
> A land without antiquities . . .

He finds little to inspire him:

> A ship's the only poetry we see.

The prospect of leaving Australia and returning to England is in his mind:

> Lastly, a ship is poetry to me,
> Since piously I trust, in no long space,
> Her wings will bear me from this prose-dull land.

In the year following this edition he had his wish. It is of interest to note this change in Field, from tolerant amusement to weary distaste; but it does not reconcile us to his lack of any poetical gift but metrical competence. He summed himself up in the first poem he wrote:

> I neither Botanist nor Poet truly.

The first poetry by one of the native-born was written in England. William Charles Wentworth (1791–1872), the son of a surgeon, was born on Norfolk Island, a dependency of New South Wales. He was educated for a few years in England as a child, and then returned there in 1816, where he was a student at Cambridge. His poem *Australasia* was placed second in the competition for the Chancellor's prize in 1822, William Mackworth Praed's being placed first. Wentworth's poem was published in England in 1823. The rest of his long life, spent in journalistic, legal, and political activities in Australia and in retirement in England, does not concern us.

His *Australasia*, almost 450 lines in heroic couplets, is remembered by us today for its conclusion:

> And, oh Britannia! should'st thou cease to ride
> Despotic Empress of old Ocean's tide;—
> Should thy tam'd Lion—spent his former might—
> No longer roar, the terror of the fight:—
> Should e'er arrive that dark, disastrous hour,
> When bow'd by luxury, thou yield'st to power;
> When thou, no longer freest of the free,
> To some proud victor bend'st the vanquished knee:—
> May all thy glories in another sphere
> Relume, and shine more brightly still than here:
> May this—thy last-born infant—then arise,
> To glad thy heart, and greet thy parent eyes;
> And Australasia float, with flag unfurl'd,
> A new Britannia in another world!

The sentiment, together with other hopes and aspirations in the poem, finds a response in the Australian heart, and some of the half-hopes, half-prophecies, seem surprisingly justified today.

But all this has not much to do with the poem as the production of a poet.

The diction is pure eighteenth century; the native corroboree, for example, becomes a *Pyrrhic dance*, and Wentworth's childhood fishing is transformed into *ply the treach'rous bait*. Everything is made to seem rather strange and distant, as if seen at one or two removes. It all makes one reluctant to accept, for instance, such a pronouncement as that of P. R. Stephensen in his *Foundations of Culture in Australia*, that "Wentworth's poem is one of the first contributions to *Australian* literature".

The fact is that Wentworth, spending his formative years in Australia, certainly saw the country in a way that was different from that of a visiting Englishman. And he certainly felt about it differently. Wentworth as a man, then, was different in this respect from an Englishman. But it is not a question of Wentworth the man, but of Wentworth the poet. The poem is in one respect, a very important respect, not Australian at all. Wentworth saw Australia as an Australian. But he did not portray it like that: he portrayed the country as seen through the eyes of a reader of English poetry.

It had to take time for an Australian portrayal of Australia to come about. The process was accretional. The literary English way of describing Australia would always be unreal. There had to be an absorption into the poet's vocabulary of words that fitted the Australian setting, that had their Australian associations, and that did not fit other non-Australian things. And there had to grow up an acceptance of the background as the normal inevitable stock for poetry to draw on. For long there was to be in Australian poetry a feeling either of strangeness or of assertive insistence. Australian poets were not to be naturally Australian until the twentieth century. They had, so to speak, first of all to put aside the spectacles of English books, the memories (for their reading from childhood practically gave them these) of non-Australian things. In a word, they first of all had to forget.

To demand this of Wentworth would be ridiculous. He belonged to his era, that is all. The poem is, except for the statements of affection in it, a poem about Australia written by an Australian as though he were an Englishman.

In 1826 there appeared *Wild Notes from the Lyre of a Native Minstrel*, the first volume of verse by an Australian-born poet published in this country. Its author, Charles Tompson (1806–83), was born in Sydney and was a Government official. As a poet he is highly derivative and betrays the influence of Thomson and Gray and Goldsmith. He appears, in short, as a belated Augustan. The following lines from *Retrospect* are typical enough:

> Why do those dreams, to golden memory dear,
> More bright than Life's progressive day appear,
> And Fancy rush, with repercussive spring,
> To where she first essay'd her callow wing?

The traits of stock diction in his models occur very frequently in Tompson:

> . . . woods, and lawns, and meads . . .

while in the drought of summer in Australia we find

> . . . yawning fissures crack the thirsty glade.

He is best in simple forms and simple diction. His most graceful poem is probably Ode V, *To Sylvia*, of which the first two stanzas run:

> Hast thou not seen some captive bird
>   Impatient flit within the wire,
> And seek the bliss of liberty,
>   With anxious fond desire?

> Or hast thou not beheld, in chains,
>   Some poor unhappy pris'ner pine?
> E'en such a wretched slave am I,
>   E'en such hard fetters mine.

Tompson offers a certain variety. He wrote further odes to Sylvia, where Dryden lingers in attenuated memory, and a number of elegies and other poems in different stanza forms and length of line. He produced an imitation of Cowper—*The Storm* —where he falls away from his master into numerous anti-climaxes and dry patches of would-be pathos. He has an appreciable facility and some metrical skill, but he is lacking in intensity, and today appears to us as one of the myriad poetasters thrown up by or derived from the eighteenth century. Had he not been an Australian he would be nothing at all.

The derivative note was inevitable in the first poets of the colony. The new settlement was started by Englishmen, it was very limited in numbers, it was a beginning in locality but a continuation in spirit. The Romantics, slow to make their way in England, were slower to exercise influence in Australia. The standard models were those of the eighteenth century and the orthodox ingredients corresponded—wit and courtly compliment and satire and address. Such were the themes and forms to be expected from poets transplanted physically and emotionally to the strange and unwelcoming land.

CHAPTER II

The Earliest Fiction

THE first novel written in Australia was also printed here—in Hobart in three volumes (1830–1). In this novel, *Quintus Servinton. A Tale, Founded upon Incidents of Real Occurrence,* its author drew upon his own experiences. He was Henry Savery (1793/4–1842), transported to Van Diemen's Land in 1825. He was a convict journalist with some degree of freedom; upon a second offence he was condemned to life imprisonment. In 1842 he died at Port Arthur—according to Henry Melville, owner of the *Colonial Times* (for which Savery wrote articles), by cutting his throat.

In the Preface Savery writes:

> . . . it is no fiction, or the work of imagination, either in its characters or incidents . . . it is a biography, true in its general features . . .

This is written in the character of an editor, supposed to have received the manuscript from Quintus in England: but it is, as we can now see, a good example of the double bluff.

The novel deals with Quintus from his birth in 1772 (the fifth son and eleventh child of his parents), through his experiences as a merchant, his conviction, and his life in New South Wales until almost the granting of his pardon. Quintus is accused of issuing fraudulent bills, and despite protests on his behalf is condemned to death—a sentence later commuted to transportation. He is given the garb of the convict:

> . . . grey cloth jacket, waistcoat and breeches; worsted stockings, and thick heavy shoes; two check shirts, and a broad brimmed, low crowned hat . . .

It is not until a third of the third volume has been covered that Quintus arrives in New South Wales. Here at first he is treated with consideration, but through the jealousy of rivals he loses his position and suffers hardships. He even tries to cut his throat. At length his wife comes to Australia and the ending, after various frustrations, does see the finish of his tribulations.

The novel contains details of the convict system recounted by one who knew them from experience. Savery, like his hero, had been a business man, had been transported for forgery, had met with jealousy and opposition in the colony because of his obvious capacity, and had seen his wife and child come to the colony and again depart. And if, as is possible, Savery cut his throat, then Quintus's own attempt at suicide is a striking fictional anticipation of reality.

The novel transfers to New South Wales a picture of Tasmania during Governor Arthur's regime. But its interest lies also in the story, and this despite the formality of the style, old fashioned even for 1830. It stalks to the verge of the ludicrous and sometimes topples over it:

> ... On the fifth morning after the trial, the Sheriffs visited him with much solemnity, and formally announced that his fate was irrecoverably fixed, and that fourteen revolving suns, would terminate his earthly pilgrimage.

The characters are often "humours" of the line from Ben Jonson to Sheridan, with names like Crabtree, Briefless, and Plausible. With no really organic plot, the novel is a sort of fictional autobiography, a picture of a brash, ambitious, energetic, almost at times irresponsible young man in whom perhaps Savery, repentant, saw his own youth reflected. But despite these flaws the book has power to keep the reader turning the pages. It is worth while remarking the readability of some of these early novels, which with all their faults contrast with the doughy competence of many Australian novels a century later.

One early novel by an anonymous author has only a tenuous connection with Australia. It is *The Guardian*, published in Sydney in 1838 by "An Australian". The consensus of opinion is that the author was a woman of some breeding, born in England or Ireland, probably the wife of some official in Australia. Lady Darling has been put up as a candidate, but the identity still remains uncertain. The Australian affinity is restricted to the place of publication, the author's residence in Australia, and a few references to this country, all of them contemptuous or mocking.

The setting is Ireland. Jessie Errol marries Francis Gambier. An old waiting-woman, to ensure that a murder she has inadvertently acknowledged will not be revealed, tells Jessie that she and her husband had the same father. This fact—that she has

married her half-brother—drives Jessie distracted in the orthodox Gothic manner. She lets fall her infant son, who rolls down
a cliff, and then falls or throws herself into the sea. Today the
revelation of this semi-incestuous relationship fails to move us in
the same way. The potential horror of the theme (if we put
aside Greek drama) stems from the Romantic blood and ghost
and darkness tradition—the Gothic novels of the late eighteenth
century with nightmares and secret sins, Byron and the whispered
rumours of his family life, Shelley and *The Cenci*.

It is altogether an interesting period piece. Much is told by
letters, and these are revealing, or witty, or informative. The
pictures of society are often nearly brilliant, and the conversation
of people of fashion and of waiting-women is admirably rendered.
When the novel is well under way, omens gibber for a moment
and banish. Deaths grow more numerous. These are unmotivated, in the sense that they just occur—the author removes
characters rather cavalierly; a fashionable count, for example,
expires of a bout of immoderate laughter in two brief paragraphs.
Nightmare or prophecy is made to render up its full flavour.
Gambier asleep talks like a Gothic hero awake:

> "—fiend! name her not!—she is not—she is mine for ever. You
> inhale corruption, and damned souls impede your loathsome
> breath . . ."

The transition is from a society novel to a horror romance. *The
Guardian* starts like the end of a Maria Edgeworth and ends like
the start of an Ann Radcliffe. Only the humorous parts can be
taken seriously.

The references to Australia are not many. The future Governor
of New South Wales (he dies before he can assume his position)
says

> he became sick when he thought of going to a country where society
> was divided into parties, dust blown as well as thrown in your eyes,
> children ran under your horses' feet, dogs lay about the streets,
> ladies talked of wool, and dressed like antediluvians; and one
> beautiful spot of land is styled Pinchgut, and another Longbottom.

So much for the general reference. A particular example, specific
enough to be actual, is given by Althorpe, one of the minor
characters:

> "Sydney must be an extraordinary place. I read an advertisement
> in one of the papers I received, stating that a *respectable* servant was

required in a *respectable* family, residing in a *respectable* neighbourhood, a *respectable* distance from the town of Parramatta."

There are a few further sidelong glances down the nose, but
it is clear that, written inside Australia, the novel sees the
country from outside. Its incidental depreciations express the
attitude of a cultivated woman coming into a society very
different from her former one.

The next novel is the first of a family. The period of about
two decades, from around 1840 to 1860, may be characterised
as the Guidebook Period. It contains a sequence of novels, all
providing information about the colonies, generally for prospective immigrants. With this group will be treated a few didactic
novels with a rather different purpose, that of exhortation or
reformation.

Charles Rowcroft (1795?–1850) was first in the field with
Tales of the Colonies (1843). Despite the title, the book is only one
story—the life in Van Diemen's Land of William Thornley, the
narrator. It is a vade-mecum to the colony, and the narrative
is, as it were, the chocolate coating on the pill. Thornley is the
chief person in it, but the most lively and most entertaining is
old Crab, a caricature in the manner of Dickens—testy, complaining, and pessimistic. He has had his fill of the colony, he
insists, and will return to England; but he does not go:

"... you're rather short-handed for what you're about. You see,
when one of the bullock carts turns over, you'll hardly be strong
enough to set it on its legs again."

The method is that of Defoe—details, numbers, costs, instruc-
tions, a sort of diary effect, with every opportunity taken of
pointing a moral if not of adorning a tale. This latter function is
fulfilled by a cascade of incident. Rowcroft leaves nothing out,
and the book seems to burst at the seams.

Rowcroft's other novel with an Australian setting is *The
Bushranger of Van Diemen's Land* (1846). A brig with owner-
captain, an intending immigrant, is captured by escaped convicts. Their leader is a resourceful and dashing figure, Mark
Brandon, plausible but increasingly bloodthirsty. Practically all
the novel is taken up with the search for Helen Horton, elder
daughter of the immigrant. She is taken by Brandon as a
hostage, but is captured by a tribe of Tasmanian aborigines.
Brandon with a couple of followers, her lover (an Ensign) with

a corporal, and her father with some soldiers and later some police all seek to rescue her. The result is an adventure story that found popularity as far away as America.

What was said of Rowcroft's other novel is equally true of this. It is full of such detail as might be unknown to outsiders, it contains a plethora of incident, and despite this queer mixture of instruction and melodrama is quite readable. At the end Helen and a fellow-victim of the natives, fleeing before bushfires and blacks, climb a steep rock. Here Brandon, wounded by the police, has taken refuge:

> . . . they had, by a powerful effort, gained the summit of the rock, and then to their amazement, and not less to their horror, they beheld a powerful eagle, of the vulture species, with its talons firmly fixed on the body and garments of a man, who was lying prostrate on the rock and who was writhing under the creature's monstrous beak and claws!
>
> At the sight of the strangers the gigantic monarch of the mountains flapped its huge wings, and shrieked with its hoarse throat, as it struggled to disengage its claws, which had become entangled in the clothes of the man, who moaned piteously, but seemed to be deprived of all power of motion. And still the great eagle screamed and struggled, and Helen and her companion looked on with horror . . .

So we have an eagle on the rock above, the fire behind, a river below, and the enraged natives ascending. It is like the ending of an instalment in one of the old (or even current) film serials.

It is not so much of a guidebook as the *Tales*. Rowcroft wrote it to show that transportation to the penal colonies was not at all pleasant:

> . . . the circulation of the history, inculcating the certain punishment and remorse which follow crime, may assist in repressing that morbid craving after notoriety which of late years has increased with such lamentable rapidity.

Plus ça change . . . But the stress is more on adventures among dangers, of which the chief, in ascending order, appear to be spiders, scorpions, snakes, and aborigines. These last bulk large in this narrative. Though Rowcroft does put the case for them, on the whole he appears to regard them as an inferior and dangerous species, probably human, to be placated if possible, but likely to attack at any moment, and therefore to be fired on eventually. The novel, then, is a Southern instead of a Western thriller, with black Australians replacing Red Indians.

Very much more reformatory in aim are the next works, and it is difficult to take seriously some criticism expended on them. They comprise the Australian fiction of Mary Theresa Vidal (*née* Johnson) (1818–69), who spent five years in Australia, from 1840 to 1845. Her three volumes on Australian themes form a gradation: the first, a collection of tales, is apparently for Sunday-school children; the second is for servants; the third, for their mistresses.

Tales for the Bush (1845) contains nine cautionary tales, in which the actors are workers or ex-convicts or young servants. Their sins provide examples of retribution. The well-to-do, so it appears, do not afford such material. The principles inculcated are Sunday observance, self-restraint, honesty, respect for one's social superiors, thoughtfulness, and sobriety. It is important to remember that Mary Vidal was the wife of a Church of England clergyman and probably held the views common at the time to the members of that sisterhood. Every principle and every lesson she adduces we must perforce concede; every example she invents we must perforce find side-splitting. Her moralising was apparently an occupational hazard.

In the second book, a novel, *Cabramatta* (1850), the same note of patronising admonition recurs. And the rather childish style persists, though the characters are adult and the book seems intended for adults. John Lester yields to temptation, deceives his master, goes to the bad, becomes a member of a gang of cattle stealers, and is finally sent to Van Diemen's Land. His wife Grace suffers, John repents, and at last they are reunited. It is quite intolerable.

An advance is seen in *Bengala* (1860), both in the ease of narration and the capturing of characteristic dialogue. The main characters are a small group of fairly wealthy families living in the same country area and resembling to an extraordinary degree the gentry of Jane Austen. The book's resemblance to *Emma* is marked in the use of cross purposes, for example, and in the relations between the elderly and sensible John Herbart and the young self-willed Isabel Lang. There is some excitement among the lower orders, but the chief concern is with the social interactions of their betters. One rather unusual ingredient is the love of Father Mornay, a priest, for

Isabel. The author inflicts a remarkable jargon upon him in his distress:

"Avaunt ye, Evil One! Pooh, I am doting. It is no spirit—it is myself."

He finally takes poison. At last, after three almost unreadable chapters full of the worst Victorian rigmarole, she and Herbart marry. Almost the only living character in this volume is an old servant. It is remarkable what an ear the women novelists of the period had for the tone and idiom of those who worked for them.

Quite obviously the guidebook is *Settlers and Convicts* (1847), an Australian equivalent of Defoe's *Plague Year* or *Robinson Crusoe*—the recountal of incidents the author has never experienced and the description of background he has never seen. Long believed to be the product of a mysterious Alexander Harris, the work has been shown by Colin Roderick to be by Samuel Sidney (1813–83),[1] an English publicist who dealt with emigration, livestock, and railways. Sidney was a facile and voluminous writer, and this is but one of his works on the Australian scene. The details of colonial life and experience are so full and they square so well with contemporary accounts that the book might serve as social history. One suspicious circumstance, however, is that, as with Defoe, practically everything that could happen does happen to the imaginary narrator. Sidney apparently gained some of his information from his brother John, who returned to England in 1844 after six years in Australia. The young man who is supposed to tell the story of his adventures is shown as coming to New South Wales about 1825 and leaving about 1840. Starting with little money, he works hard and avoids drink and bad company. At the end of his stay he is the owner of stock, a married man with two children. Practically every aspect of colonial life outside Sydney is described, and he encounters all types from convicts, bushrangers, and free settlers to magistrates. His comments on conditions are often like brief official reports.

Another novel by Sidney, utilitarian like this but with more plot, is *The Emigrant Family* (1849). The Preface unashamedly sets out the aim: it is to be a guidebook and adviser as well as an honest and accurate account of colonial life. These guidebook

[1] John Earnshaw puts a case for Willoughby Bean (*Bulletin* 11.5.55).

novels are like certain more academic examples, the disguised school textbooks. Young students of the classics last century and even later had at their disposal books like *Gallus*, which gave the details in the daily life led by a boy in ancient Rome. To render the dose palatable, incidents and social minutiae were woven into a story. Such textbooks were more or less painless ways of absorbing what used to be called Greek and Roman antiquities. But the novelists like Rowcroft and Sidney and Spence writing about Australia had more exciting material at their disposal and were in addition more skilful than their professorial counterparts.

In Sidney's novel an Englishman and his family come to Port Phillip. On the way to Sydney they are advised by one of the native-born, Reuben Kable, to buy land at Rocky Springs, on the upper Morrumbidgee (*sic*). There is much information about the cost of the land, the methods of stocking, and the conditions to be met with.

The methods used to keep interest alive are the evolution of plot and the introduction of characters; so that love and intrigue and adventure are commonly woven into a story. One can only admire the ingenuity and dexterity of much of this, not in this novel only but in most others of the type. The consequence is that they are still of interest today, and have more than mere historical value. They are weak in character drawing, but often some eccentric or unusual character appears. Martin Beck, descendant of American negroes, is Sidney's best example, the embodiment of an inferiority complex.

There is in this novel, as in some others, not only a tolerant condescension towards things Australian, but at the same time an attempt to be impartial: both the attractive and the crude aspects of the people are noted. There is an unconscious surprise that the good is so good. Miss Smart, for example, the reader is made to feel, can hardly be considered a lady, but Reuben Kable is shown as acceptable—tall, lean, nonchalant, knowledgeable. And the Australian vocabulary is occasionally recorded in the use of such words as *ghibber* and *gunyah* and *bogie*.

Seen from a woman's point of view the colonies and the colonists must have presented a rather different aspect. The mixture of surprise, distaste, tolerance, and even admiration that Sidney displays is found again, but with different flavour, in another guidebook novel, this time by a woman, Catherine

Helen Spence (1825–1910). She made use of her own experiences as teacher and governess in her *Clara Morison: A Tale of South Australia during the Gold Fever* (1854). Most other novels of this type stress convictism, bushranging, and aboriginal life, together or singly. They are by men and for men, and deal with a pastoral or agricultural background. *Clara Morison* is written by a woman for women, and most of the action takes place in towns, and when in towns, indoors.

Had Spence possessed a more pointed style and a greater command of irony, then the theme and its setting might have resulted in an Australian version of Jane Austen or, if that was overmuch to hope for, of Fanny Burney. But the style, clear and straightforward, at times chatty or chirpy, possesses too little nuance to rival the medium of these two. Only occasionally do we find a passage reminiscent of them. Clara's uncle is too mean to offer asylum to her on the death of her father:

> Clara . . . saw that her uncle wished to be spared the mortification of seeing so near a relative reduced to be a nursery governess in his neighbourhood.

So Clara, aged nineteen, emigrates to South Australia in 1850.

Of the two volumes, the first is concerned with the hardships of Clara; the second takes in other characters and other scenes, such as the diggings. The picture of Clara—quiet, proper, respectful of others' opinions, very much the well-bred young woman—and of her misfortunes does not affect our sympathies today quite as it may have done then: we are at times more amused than stirred, and Clara, a picture of virtue in misfortune, takes on a slightly comic colouring. A few minor characters are very delightfully drawn eccentrics, the best being Miss Withering. This acidulous English spinster, omniscient, carping, finding fault with everything in South Australia, leaves rather a silence when she fades from the scene.

Like others of its class, it is a more or less loosely jointed narrative; and it is wonderfully unselfconscious about coincidence. But it carries the reader along. Its readability is partly due to the most natural conversation of ordinary middle-class folk that had so far appeared in any Australian novel.

In her attitude to the people of this new land Spence seems hardly to have made up her mind. Her descriptions of the employers for whom Clara works as a domestic servant are practically all unfavourable. Nor does she seem to have much respect for local critical judgment. One example may serve, a note on the singing of Miss Waterstone ("her charms . . . fully developed, her complexion florid, her voice loud, and her manner imposing"):

> . . . a naturally fine voice, some musical talent, and a slight infusion of taste, rendered her song a very pleasing performance.

The comment here bears as much on the audience as on the performer. On the other hand, when Spence encounters a self-confident Englishwoman affecting superiority, then she finds the colonial types much more tolerable.

This novel has been classed with the guidebooks, but the aim is much less overt than usual. Indeed it is as a story that it provides most interest. It has liveliness, humour, some small irony, much good sense, and at least superficial insight into character. These qualities, together with its ease of style, make it the most entertaining of the class to which it has been assigned.

Australian background is packed into *Tallangetta, the Squatter's Home. A Tale of Australian Life* (1857), by William Howitt (1795–1879), who makes no secret of his intentions: the Preface tells us that ". . . it has been my object to depict the various phases of Australian life and character more fully than could be done in *Two Years in Victoria*". (This last-named book, it may be noted in passing, was used by Charles Reade as source material for *It is Never Too Late to Mend*.) Howitt's novel, like its fellows, is built into the framework of a story, here one that is improbable in the extreme. Sir Thomas Fitzgerald loses his estate because of a lawsuit brought by a relative charging illegitimacy. As neither ambassador presiding (the marriage was solemnised at Florence), nor chaplain officiating, nor marriage certificate confirming is available, the unfortunate Sir Thomas is displaced, and takes his family to Victoria. At length the marriage certificate is produced by a relation, Peter Martin. He has withheld it at the earnest desire of Sir Thomas's mother, who has taken this rather unusual and ambiguous step in order to cure her son of a fever for gambling on the turf.

The book is crowded with incident, but still more crowded with local and contemporary detail. And as though one account might not be memorable enough, Howitt repeats his information; so that we meet bushrangers on more than one occasion and are given several pictures of the diggings. The account at first is of a pastoral paradise, almost a *fête galante*—". . . the warbling crow piped its melodious chant"—and larger fauna in the shape of native companions and emus add a touch of the strange to complete the recipe for the romantic beautiful. As if aware of this, Howitt hastens to redress the balance and enumerate the defects of this Eden—centipedes, flies, heat, scorpions, and snakes. These are detailed by Peggy Wilks, the old servant, one of the more vivid characters. This capacity to strike out minor eccentrics Howitt shares with most of the others. Another oddity is Crouchy, the product of an English sailor and an Abyssinian woman, who is four feet tall, four feet wide, and possessed of inordinate physical strength. This gigantic dwarf is perhaps something that Howitt met on his travels.

Howitt does not introduce or elaborate many native-born characters. He was a visitor to this country and had what was apparently the prevailing attitude of such people to the land and the people born in it. This is glimpsed in an occasional phrase:

> Mrs. Quarrier was a remarkably fine woman, who, though she was born in the colonies and had never quitted them, had all the quiet grace and tact of a lady accustomed to good society.

Howitt's mass of detail almost renders *Tallangetta* a source book: there is everything, from making tea to drought and fire and flood; from selling food to the diggers to escaping from bushrangers; from descriptions of the diggings to a Mormon chapel meeting; from the life of the Old squatter to that of the New. Despite Howitt's former literary experience in England, this volume is one of the most amateurish of its type and perhaps the most crowded.

Quite obviously the guidebook and even more obviously the tract is *Gertrude the Emigrant* (1857). Its author was Mrs. Calvert (1834–72), *née* Caroline Atkinson, the first woman born in Australia to write a novel. One point of interest resides in the use of the Australian idiom, then emerging as *lost*, meaning *helpless* ("I should be lost without mother"), *knock up* with the meaning of *become exhausted*, and some others. And Mrs. Doherty is "a character" in the making, masterful, abrupt, warm-hearted underneath. She takes Gertrude into her service as a sort of servant companion. The remainder of the book tells of life in the bush, with a goanna or a wombat or a group of aborigines every now and then to indicate local fauna, and sheep-dipping, shearing, bush fires, a "coroborry", and the rest to fill in the picture.

As a tract it depends on Gertrude and Tudor, the latter the manager of the holding. After some change of heart by Gertrude and misunderstanding on the part of Tudor the book ends with their union, the marriage of as perfect a pair of prigs as Australian fiction can offer us. Gertrude is gentle, considerate, inflexible. She does not talk as much as Tudor, a non-smoker and non-drinker ("I am aware of the baneful effects of imbibing a narcotic poison into the system"), but spreads influence by quiet persistence. Both as characters are perfectly credible, except perhaps for their dialogue, and all of us must have met people like them. The objection is to the use made of them.

The novel has a great deal of conversation and a comparable amount of incident, the latter often being dismissed in a few paragraphs. If we read the novel at all hurriedly we are pulled up very frequently, for we suddenly become aware that something has happened almost in parenthesis. As a novel it is in no way a precursor, but among the last of its group, and was preceded by much more effective and well-knit examples.

To fit the next novel into this group requires a little stretching. It is didactic, ethical, hortatory. It gives a picture of convictism so far as female prisoners are concerned, and it warns the female reader. But it is not a guidebook in the sense of helping the intending immigrant: any immigrant it might closely concern would be coming to the colony willy-nilly.

This novel is *The Broad Arrow: Being Passages from the History of Maida Gwynnham, a Lifer* (1859). Its author, Caroline Woolmer Leakey (1827–81), wrote under the name of Oliné Keese. She tells the story of a young girl of some breeding who falls victim to the charms of a stock character, a Captain Norwell, dashing and dissolute. He seduces her, tempts her to an unwitting forgery, abandons her when she is accused and convicted of the murder of her child, and at the last repents of his treachery. Maida dies in a prison hospital in Tasmania at the age of twenty-six. Norwell has come out to the colony, only in time to view his victim in her coffin. The sight drives him insane, and the novel ends on this note of gloom and madness.

Now such a theme was unusual in woman's fiction, and Leakey is aware of this:

> I am told the subject is unbecoming a woman's pen. If it be so, and if there be censure attaching to a handling of it, I would face that censure, and deem myself happy in having written the "Broad Arrow," if but one sister, now trembling on the brink of ruin, read it, and enter into my belief—that loss of virtue is (in *most* cases) the first and fatal impulse towards those depths of sin whose end it has been my painful lot to witness in Tasmania.

The aim in mind, then, is obvious—to draw a picture of the fate that can befall the young woman who yields to sexual temptation: first, unchastity; last, Van Diemen's Land. It is intended as a cautionary tale. There is much exhortation, and parts read like miniature and tearful homilies, illustrated by grim accounts of the sufferings of women convicts, of moral degradation and physical squalor and abuse and injustice. But nobody is likely to be convinced that the stage from Maida's yielding to Maida's conviction is very likely or at all typical. It is a very special case, and any potentially compliant young woman might well feel that it could not apply to her.

The style in which all this is conveyed is in many parts comically sentimental. At moments of death it reaches its lachrymose zenith, and then the reader encounters:

> "They will take my babe from me, and I have not even wept over it! No! the scalding drops are fevering my brain, but they will not come forth. My babe! my child!" she continued, in the thrilling accents of despair, "the last comfort is denied thy wretched mother —she may not lay thee in thy grave."

When moral indignation moves the writer's breast, then the style takes on another note, that of the sensational novelette:

> The sated worldling . . . has drunk to the very dregs the purple cup of wantonness, which, while it palled his senses, has not allayed his thirst.

After this, one might imagine, the aptest treatment would be a kindly dismissal of the book. But the paradox of it is that a reader feels nothing of the sort; for the book has an undeniable power. One of its qualities is the capacity to convey atmosphere and to give very memorable descriptions. Often these are brief: one is the account of the religious service at the prison, Port Arthur. The bitter sketch of the audience, the convicts in the convict dress, takes the imagination; the eye sweeps across, at first pausing and then with horror lost in a sea of colour—yellow. A writer who can do this with some frequency is no inconsiderable artist.

Leakey has a second and rarer gift, the power to create a character or to give us some insight into one, to put us, as it were, in some measure into the skin of her creations. Indeed, with the exception of Spence's *Clara Morison*, this is the first novel written in Australia that has any such quality in any degree. It is of interest to note that both authors are women and their best creations are women. Leakey's most successful miniature is Mrs. Evelyn. The picture of the woman—a kindly mother, a devoted wife, convinced of her own good intentions, yet infinitely tactless, obtuse, and towards inferiors so unintentionally wounding—this is admirably done.

More ambitious is Leakey's picture of Maida herself as a convict. Maida is the female counterpart of Marcus Clarke's Rufus Dawes: both are kindly at the start; both suffer injustice; both under the iron mould of the convict system are transformed into unresponsive beings drawing what strength they can from their inner resources. Clarke is more successful, more powerful, more penetrating. But it says much for Leakey that critics should see fit to make the comparison at all. The picture of Maida is an unusual one in Australian fiction. At times she may take on the shape of an allegorical figure, of Resignation or Endurance; but in the main she appears a very lifelike creation, more and more withdrawn, developing a sort of steely resistance, an obduracy, almost, until at last—and here Leakey shows herself all too clearly a creature of her age and conventions—at last Maida yields to the softening influences of religion, and gratefully receives its consolations. The novel remains, despite its weaknesses, the most powerful written by a woman in Australia last century.

All these guidebook or near-guidebook novels have certain traits in common. All give some information about life in the colonies, though not all intend this as guidance for new settlers; all give advice directly or indirectly, and some give moral exhortation. The account of the various colonies, though we now as modern Australians think we have known it all along, can still wake our interest. This may be due to the fact that only one of the writers was born in Australia; they came out as young

or middle-aged people and found the country strange, the inhabitants strange, their habits and pursuits strange. Seeing
things in this way with new eyes, they were aware of the external
with a freshness that long familiarity can dull. There must have
been a demand for such works: some of them were popular and
ran through many editions. The demand arose through interest
in the new land. From the founding of the colony, and before
it, official and non-official accounts had been written and had
found readers. But now there was the added attraction of the
story. A reader enjoyed as well as learned.

Two other points may be noted. Each of these novelists has
in some degree the capacity to give the reader a brief and fairly
lively picture of a minor character, generally an oddity or an
eccentric or even a grotesque. It cannot be proved, but it seems
likely enough that the influence of Dickens is seen here. The
other point is that even the dullest of them can be read with
some interest. They can tell a tale—at least they have that
Victorian gift.

One more novel, this time of a different sort, must be discussed before we turn to the four best-known Australian novels
of last century.

Its author was John Lang (1817–64), the first novelist born in
Australia. The title varies—*The Convict's [Forger's] Wife: a True
Tale of Early Australia* (1855) and *Assigned to His Wife: or, the
Adventures of George Flower, the Celebrated Detective Officer*. It is short,
about one-third or one-quarter the length of the novels we have
just dealt with. Since the story contains just as much incident,
it is obvious that the action must be very fast. The pace in fact
is breathless: chapters are brief and crowded; incidents pile on
incidents; climax on climax's head accumulates.

It is the first Australian mystery or detective novel. Emily
Orford marries in England a waster, Captain Harcourt. (It is
rather odd that this rank has traditionally produced most
villains.) Convicted of forgery, the Captain is transported to
New South Wales, where he runs away from the master he has
been assigned to. Emily, following her husband to Sydney, sees
the placard announcing this, becomes distracted, and retires in
poverty to a small cottage. Enter George Flower, former game-
keeper transported for shooting his sister's seducer, now ex-convict and famous thief-taker. He is the first modern tough
detective in fiction, and anticipates the hard-boiled heroes of

c

Dashiell Hammett and Raymond Chandler by some seventy years or more. Here he does over Nelson, an unsavoury assigned servant:

> "What writing-desk?" said Nelson.
> "*That* writing-desk," said Flower, striking Nelson on the bridge of the nose a blow which swelled up both his eyes and felled him to the earth. "*That* writing-desk," repeated Flower, placing the thick sole of his boot upon Nelson's neck. "Gurgle up the receiver, or I'll squeeze out your poisonous existence."

Flower takes Emily under his protection, and manages to get Harcourt assigned to her. But Harcourt persists in crime, and at last is shot by Flower and his men. So Emily loses a husband, but gains a half-brother, for that is what George Flower turns out to be.

It is all rather delightfully naïve, full of threats and single-handed actions and the authentic melodramatic note. Brade, in the following extract, is the magistrate who has designs upon Emily:

> "You expected an innocent lamb, you wily wolf, and you find yourself face to face with a roaring lion." And seizing Mr. Brade by the arms, Flower pinioned him with his back to the wall, glared hideously at him, grinding his teeth while he foamed at the mouth, and the saliva ran down either side of his finely chiselled chin.

The "finely chiselled chin" is very good.

The novel has all the ingredients to make a film.

Only a representative selection of the guidebook novels has been treated. Even so, the space devoted to the few chosen is greater, proportionately, than can be given to later novels of this century and the next. The excuse is the well-worn plea that those discussed are early, typical, and accessible in only a few libraries.

CHAPTER III

Harpur, Kendall, and Others

THE first in Australia to be seriously considered as a poet, by
virtue of bulk, intention, and a level above that of the
occasional versifier, is Charles Harpur (1813–68). He is generally evaluated on the selection of his poems published in 1883.
Many, however, still remain uncollected. The assiduous piety
of C. W. Salier has stressed these omissions and the changes in
text carried out in the 1883 volume by the editor of it. But it is
not likely that a complete edition would cause much change in
the critical estimate of Harpur.

He wrote also a play, *Bushrangers* (1853), partly in prose,
partly in blank verse, filled with "humours" endowed with names
like Stalwart, Desperate, Wealthiman Woolsack, and Flinch.
These label the wearers. The dialogue is occasionally successful
in a vaudeville fashion, while Bomebard with his mispronuncia-
tions (*magnamalous deeds, blasphybious words*) belongs to a venerable
line of clowns.

The contrast to the evil of the bushrangers and the idiocy of
the officials is provided by Ada and Abel, the innocent inhabitants of an idyllic rusticity. They succour Stalwart, leader of the
gang, when he is wounded. In return, after an inner conflict, he
makes an attempt upon Ada's purity, and is struck by Abel,
whom he later kills. Ada goes insane. Parts of this theme are
reminiscent of Wordsworth's *The Borderers*. (By an odd coincidence Harpur himself later had an adventure with a bushranging gang.)

Harpur was born in Australia and never left it; he saw much
of eastern New South Wales and was acquainted with its various
aspects; he described it or used it as a setting; but he seems little
of an Australian writer. His period and his upbringing explain
it. Harpur's reading in Milton, in the eighteenth-century poets,
and in the Romantics determined his methods and themes. The
lack of earlier poets writing in or on Australia deprived him of
a lead. In consequence he used for the most part the language
and metres and forms of his models, and saw the Australian

scene through the spectacles now of a late eighteenth-century poet, now of a Romantic, gazing on imposing landscapes. Even in his most widely known poem, *Midsummer Noon in the Australian Forest*, there is nothing characteristically Australian. The following passage is typical:

> Only there's a drowsy humming
> From yon warm lagoon slow coming:
> 'Tis the dragon-hornet—see!
> All bedaubed resplendently,
> Yellow on a tawny ground—
> Each rich spot nor square nor round,
> Rudely heart-shaped, as it were
> The blurred and hasty impress there
> Of a vermeil-crusted seal
> Dusted o'er with golden meal.

Harpur is not so imitative as two later poets, Gordon and Kendall. We can, it is true, feel the influence of earlier writers in him, but he very seldom contains lines of former poets watered down. Another point is that, in the mechanics of verse at least, he is more consistent: he has fewer of the metrical lapses of Gordon or the semantic lapses of Kendall. We might then expect Harpur to be a better poet than either of the others. Such a claim on his behalf has been made. But it is extremely difficult to see where it can be supported.

The plain fact is that Harpur preserves a fairly mediocre level. He does not readily lend himself to quotation; if we seek for "gems", we must generally be satisfied with single lines:

> Then hour on hour
> Paused as if clotting at the heart of time.

The key-word is good, but he then proceeds to use it in similar contexts on other occasions. This tactile skill is seen also in:

> a strange horror gathering to his heart,
> As if his blood were charged with insect life.

Occasionally he can extend, like Milton:

> [the past] lies for aye
> Stretched in the sabbath of its vast repose.

His best things are his narratives, *The Creek of the Four Graves* and *The Witch of Hebron*, both in blank verse, and an embryonic bush ballad, *Ned Connor*, in six-lined stanzas, told in a formalised diction very different from that of the later bush ballads. Harpur's narratives hold the attention, and the story has speed and suspense and excitement. His shorter poems, on the other hand, with the exception of one or two sonnets, are no more than competent. Dozens of obscure versifiers of the eighteenth century wrote as well as Harpur.

His reflective blank verse is hardly living. Here is a fair sample from *Fragments from "Genius Lost"*:

> —we at length,
> Even thus admonished, thus in hope and heart
> Subdued and chastened, might be so constrained
> To look between the thunder-bearing clouds
> That darken over this mysterious ball's
> Blind face, for surer, better things beyond
> Its flying scenes of doubtful good, commixed
> With evident evil: yea, conclude at last
> That whereso in the universe of God
> Our better home may be, it is not here.

This reads like a metrical exercise. True, there are five iambics in each line, and the lines do not rhyme: it is blank verse—technically, that is. There is a dead stamp of beat, a lack of variation. Queerly enough, though each line enjambs (only one stop, and that a comma, at the end of a line in the passage), the effect is one of end-stopping. It is Milton in a stupor.

Harpur had hoped to be a laureate:

> "Be then the bard of thy country!"

This is how "the muse of the evergreen forest" addresses him in *The Dream by the Fountain*. Kendall, indeed, praised him as a pioneer and exalted him as his master. It is a trifle pathetic, this early aspiring; but it should not blind us to Harpur's lack of high poetical quality. He can tell a tale of action in blank verse quite effectively, and occasionally in couplets he describes a scene like an Augustan. But his importance is not very much more than historical.

A better poet than Harpur, though not more competent, is Henry Kendall (1839–82). A cursory reader is tempted to say that Kendall was a mild and gentle man who wrote mild and gentle poetry. He was frequently unhappy and often ill, and he was fond of liquor. Whether he drank because he was unhappy and ill, or was unhappy and ill because he drank, is uncertain.

Probably it worked both ways. He had a love of literature and a desire to be literary, and he wilted in uncongenial surroundings. And his poems, like himself, leaned on others. Even a superficial reading will detect the imprint of Tennyson, Arnold, Byron, and Swinburne—to name the most obvious—on metre, treatment, and phrasing. Sometimes unconscious memory led him to transcribe almost a whole line unaltered. It seems as though he had a certain limited stock of words and expressions on which he was obliged to play repetitive variations. In *To a Mountain*, one of his better poems, we find this trait: no fewer than six words (in a poem of about eighty lines) occur two or three times each— *splendid, grand, sublime, awful, exalted,* and *stately.* He even repeated himself.

Against these indications of dependency we may put the facts that unlike some other Australian poets he conquered in later life his weakness for drink, and that he wrote for periodicals some biting and vigorous satires against persons and groups. The following lines come from *The Song of Ninian Melville*, a poem suppressed when the prospective victim threatened legal action:

> In the fly-blown village pothouse, where a dribbling bag of beer
> Passes for a human being, Nin commenced his new career.
>
> .   .   .   .
>
> Common story, this of Ninny! many fellows of his breed
> Prowl about to bone the guinea, up to dirty tricks indeed!
> Haven't now the time to tan them; but, by Jove, I'd like to tan
> Back of that immense impostor that they call the "working man!"
> Drag upon our just employers—sponger on a worn-out wife—
> Boozing in some alley pothouse every evening of his life!
> Type he is of Nin's supporters: tot him up and tot him down,
> He would back old Nick tomorrow for the sake of half a crown!

The insistence on drink is illuminating.

When we think of his name, memories bring back a number of poems—*September, Bell-birds, The Last of His Tribe, Orara,* and one or two others. They are descriptive poems imbued with an emotional tinge, and generally the emotion is one of regret or plaintive resignation. Kendall appears like a man who is searching.

The four poems just mentioned are his best known. *September* has a confusion of impression and meaning, especially in individual phrases; and, as in many of his poems, the diction can range from the puerile to the pretentious, from

> In a darling old fashion

to

> Wild wings, with the halo of hyaline hours.

The diction between these two extremes is without much distinction. The poem has, however, a recurrent music. This last quality is more noticeable in *Bell-birds*, and the faults of diction are fewer. *Orara* is on a more sustained level. It has in addition what is rare in Kendall, a structure.

What Kendall lacks is discipline. Most of his poems meander: he seems to have composed by lines, with no clear vision of the total effect he was to convey. The poems in which he overcomes this fault are those about which we hear little—his sonnets and his short narratives on classical or Biblical themes. These, often reminiscent of Arnold, have some dignity. The rigid structure of the sonnet and the story outline in the short narrative keep him in check. His sonnets can end effectively: the last lines of *Attila*, if a trifle strained, are clinching:

> Night fell, with rain. The earth, so sick of sin,
> Had turned her face into the dark to weep.

Kendall lived near the coast of New South Wales and his poems describe mountain and stream and valley. The influence of his reading was too strong for him to be really Australian, with the result that they are full of the Romantic diction of the Victorians—*dell, lawn, brook, lea, rill*. That these were acceptable in his age imposes no obligation on us to accept. Perhaps it is too harsh to say as Nettie Palmer does that Kendall, "if brought face to face with anything as common as a bush sawmill would have tried to clothe its raw reality in a quasi-poetic phrase"; but despite the claims that have been made for him as a poet of the Australian landscape, it is difficult to find passages where the essential *genius loci* is captured. This defect, and indeed the lack of quality in his poems, are due to the absence of verbal exactness.

From one example we may learn something of his methods:

> The Queen of that wonderful place
> Looked forth from her towers resplendent,
> And started, and dreamed in his face.

Now this is, one may think, singularly unfortunate. But it is not the worst, nor is it infrequent. The adjective *resplendent* is a metre-filling word: it sounded good to Kendall, no doubt, and he put it in. It is of the same type as others he was addicted to, such as *grand, divine, sublime, ineffable, wonderful,* and, rather more modest, *sunshiny.* They are for the most part "poetical" words: they fill the mouth, the line, and presumably the understanding. Kendall's poetry is full of them. His writings reveal the belief that if the words sound well, then the result of putting them together must be poetry.

And now the two riming words—*place* and *face.* Anyone who has read Kendall with any attention will have noticed the unusual frequency of the word *face.* Sometimes it is in the body of the line, but for the most part it is at the end, where it rimes with either *space* or *place,* but mostly with the latter (which in Kendall stands for any locality). The vagueness of denotation that this brief analysis reveals is characteristic of much of Kendall's poetry. A completely adequate transference of emotion is beyond him. An emotional aura is what his poetry for the most part offers us. Even in observation he is indefinite. When a poet uses the general noun and the vague adjective to convey what he saw or heard, we may doubt if he really saw with his eyes or heard with his ears. If he did see and hear, then he was not a skilful user of words.

This criticism of Kendall will appear to some an insensitive depreciation, to others an example of much ado. For surely, the latter will object, he has now retired to his proper niche and is recognised for what he is: a minor poet with some musical skill, thin and often vague, nostalgic and derivative, producing poetry with a plaintive elegiac note, but hardly an individual poet—perhaps indeed writing his best when he is wearing borrowed robes. It is not certain that this is his reputation. There has been indeed a tendency of late years to rehabilitate him, to suggest that imitation is no crime in poetry, that his earliness atones for his weaknesses, and that his music is notable enough to preserve him. Certainly his satires when published will put him in a different light. The vigour and ease in them should reveal a rather unexpected side of Kendall. But his other poems give him no great claims. He remains a minor, significant in his period, but destined to less prominence as the years pass and the bulk of our poetry mounts.

None of the contemporary versifiers reaches the level of Harpur or Kendall, and none has the same note of devotion and of dedication to poetry that gives these two poets their interest and value. Of the many only a few representative examples can be mentioned—amateurs and wits and narrative poets.

Literature owes some debt to what may be called the frustrated *littérateur*, a cultivated man unsuccessful in life, sometimes disliking his profession and writing in his spare moments, generally charming and often weak, dying in early or middle age, to be regretted by his friends and mourned by a destitute family. The pattern does not fit any one man in all particulars, but there are a few to whom it loosely applies.

The first example in Australia is James Lionel Michael (1824–68). The son of a solicitor in London, he studied law inside his father's office and wrote poetry outside it. Coming to Australia in 1850 he spent some time on the diggings and then practised law in Sydney. Later he moved to Grafton, where he died by drowning—possibly by suicide.

His first volume of poetry, *Songs without Music* (1857), contains about one hundred lyrics in a diluted Tennysonian strain, elegiac in tone and mostly on love and roses and religion. They have a reasonable competence. The best are the *vers de société* type—light, airy, and cynical.

The next work was *Sir Archibald Yelverton* (1858). This was reprinted from *The Month*, with a note by the Editor:

> The Editor offers no apology for giving so long a poem as Sir Archibald Yelverton in one issue. Had he not done so, the best poem written in the Colony would never have been published in New South Wales, to the great disgrace of our literary enterprise and literary patronage.

This narrative poem, a romance of some undefined Middle Ages, has an Introduction verse replete with what can only be described as a hearty breezy eeriness. The story contains orthodox ingredients. Sir Archibald, gloomy and stern and no longer young, brings home his young bride Clara. His conduct leads to an estrangement between them, and when Sir Everard Lee comes on the scene he is doubly welcome to Clara. The pair fall in love; Clara is unfaithful to her husband, and a spying chaplain reveals the lapse to Sir Archibald. The betrayed husband, in the approved medieval fashion, walls up his guilty partner in the crypt. When Sir Everard comes again, the gate is shut to behind him; but he is wary, and escapes over the wall.

The poem is of some length and its value lies in Michael's power to sustain the tension. Despite the absurdity of much of the setting, the work is not by any means contemptible.

Into *John Cumberland* (1860), written in a variety of lines and stanza forms, it seems very likely that Michael put much of his own early life and feelings. It is told by the hero, in turn a precocious adolescent, a would-be poet, a young man with religious doubts, and finally a rejected lover who finds his true mate in Fanny, daughter of the village parson. Some parts of this, together with the picture of the corrupt and glittering life of London, lend support to the view that the poem is a highly modified and stylised autobiography.

Michael's training and interests lay in England. None of his poems is Australian in setting or feeling. He has read the usual authors, he reveals their influence, and he catches (as in the two concluding stanzas of *An Old Story*) something of their wit:

> When, perchance, thou shalt regret me,
> And would'st gladly soothe my pain,
> Cruel! struggle to forget me,
> I shall not come back again.
>
> What! thou meltest?—it would grieve thee
> If I really were to go?
> So!—thou wilt not have me leave thee:
> Credit me, I reckon'd so.

An educated man, he can turn his pen to dexterous use, write a passable lyric, imitate a standard form of verse, tell a narrative with competence. His general quality is a graceful ease.

One is tempted, after reading Michael and thinking of other poets of the century, to make a sweeping generalisation. However open to exception, there is something in it—that up to about the nineties, the educated poet in Australia wrote about England, the less educated about Australia. Books, English poets, culture—it is as though these things, once experienced, drew a veil between a poet in this country and his Australian environment. Writing as late as the early nineties, Francis Adams commented on this:

> Mail steamer and cable have brought England too close.
> Her popular literature has swamped all native originality, and exotic and specialised culture is not yet possible in a community vulgarised throughout by the headlong race for wealth.

There was a sort of vicious circle. A literary man would not deal
with Australian themes until Australian themes had been dealt
with. He had to have, so to speak, reassurance that it was
orthodox.

Two wits and satirists were the pastoralist and politician
William Forster (1818–82), who contributed to the *Atlas*, and
Robert Sealy (1831–61), who published *Scraps* (1859) under the
pen-name of Menippus.

Forster satirised Governor Gipps (in *The Devil and the Governor*)
for his land policies. These lines are the kind that Forster could
apparently turn out with ease:

> I can't remain here for ever, 'tis true—
> But I'll leave my successor something to do;
> If I can't turn the squatters out of their stations,
> I can ruin the scoundrels by proclamations.

Another satire, *The Genius and the Ghost*, attacks free immigrants
for their complacency and their scorn of convicts and emancipists.
Parts of it read as though Forster knew Johnson's *London* fairly
well. Here he comments on the wealthy debauchee, flattered
for his money, praised for his high spirits, married for his
position:

> Then turn away where stocks and dungeons bind
> The wretched dregs and rabble of mankind—
> Where the low sons of vulgar drunkenness
> Are taught the guilt of unrefined excess,
> And dare ye still, without a pang of shame,
> Your virtues and morality proclaim?

Topical and effective in their times, the satires of Forster are
now tame enough. They are without much penetrating sting,
and are such as most educated men could throw off after some
practice.

Sealy is more deft. He is a comic poet and parodist, taking for
his victims Tennyson and Hood and Longfellow. His contemporary, Henry Halloran, comes in for some amusing skits. Sealy
is much more colloquial than Forster and employs without hesi-
tation the slang of the period in the shape of words like *gammon*
and *sawder*.

Now and then he writes serious poems, with an ersatz flavour
of the past. The following stanza concludes *To W. M.*, whom

he addresses as one born out of her due time, the age of chivalry, when the lady loses her knight, "fallen on distant plain":

> The bower maidens would wonder all,
> Up-gazing from their tapestrie,
> At your set lip, and tearless eye:—
> But in your chamber turret high,
> For him who fell, I wish you'd sigh,
> And break your heart, unseen, and die.

The jester for once serious, perhaps, and finding it uncommon difficult to be taken seriously.

The verse of men like these, verse comic and satiric, sometimes urbane, generally sophisticated, neat and competent, mostly light and popular, filled the columns of the newspapers of the period then and later. The press was a sort of arena or public sounding-board for topical versifiers. Since those days either the willing-ness of the one or the capacity of the other seems to have vanished.

The next poet was contemporary only in his earlier verse, and continued to write well into this century.

In his long life George Gordon McCrae (1833–1927) wrote and travelled and talked. He was the leading spirit in Melbourne literary circles of his time and was a member of the only well-known literary club Australia has had, the Yorick Club. Much of the work he contributed to periodicals remains uncollected. Of his published poems the best are three long ones. Two of them take the aborigines for theme—*The Story of Balladeadro* and *Mamba: The Bright-Eyed* (both 1867). The first contains about a thousand lines in tetrameter couplets, the second half as many again in the same metrical pattern. Both deal with tribal customs, quarrels, and fighting, subjects to which McCrae had devoted much attention.

The first is a story of love, murder, and revenge. Kolorkor vainly woos Balladeadro. Scorned by the girl's father, he kills the elder and takes the girl captive. Mora-Mora comes to her rescue, and in the final conflict most are killed. Retribution is also the theme of the second poem. The boy Mamba, reared by the woman Borote, is killed by some treacherous warriors after his initiation. Nernepten avenges the evil deed. Both poems are good stories, and as sheer narrative they hold the interest. The descriptions in them were once more highly valued than now. A contemporary review in *The Colonial Monthly* quotes some examples with approval; on the other hand it asks with some justice whether McCrae has not idealised his natives overmuch. It is easy to detect in these poems the influence of Scott. Over them both lies a patina of romantic and poetic associations created by the diction. Words like *lance* and *shield* in conjunction, strongly evocative of a dead age, highly colour a vision of the aborigines; while *warrior, chief, maiden, wizard* inevitably evoke Scott's chivalry. These are tales of the Middle Ages applied to a dark race (or, as McCrae would put it, *sable warriors*).

McCrae's other long poem, *The Man in the Iron Mask* (1873), is more than one-third the length of *Paradise Lost*. It is divided into four Books, each devoted to a fresh prison in which the captive is confined. The even tale of the long imprisonment is related in level effective verse with a flavour of Tennyson's *Idylls of the King*. In the more lush pieces of description the hand of Keats appears. The following lines are as good as any in the poem:

> The great bronze pendule on the chimney-piece
> Ticked solemnly, and slow, and quaintly with
> A half-way hesitation in its swing
> Like the strange, measured accent of regret.

The poems of McCrae's old age fall far below these levels. *The Fleet and Convoy* (1915) hardly seems the work of the same poet:

> Say, shall he behold him more,
> Shall he hail him from the shore,
> When this cruel war is o'er?

His survival will probably depend on his long narratives, a form not very frequent in Australian poetry.

On the grounds of chronology it is convenient to deal in this chapter with Adam Lindsay Gordon (1833–70), though he has affiliations with the balladists as their precursor. He is more robustious than the poets just considered. Some poets, we know, are not like the poems they write: they are kind, but write satires; they are meek, but write poems of violent action. And one could continue on like this to exhaust the unexpected. But Gordon, we feel, was like much of what he wrote. Coming to Australia from England under something of a cloud, he made a living in various ways—as policeman, horsebreaker, journalist, jockey. He gained a reputation for daring, for a sort of devil-may-care attitude to life, though anxiety about the future underlay the façade he presented to his world. The content of his poems reflects this easy, open-air, surface bravado. But the façade cracked under the stress of disappointment and a constitutional melancholy: he went into the bush and shot himself.

Vigorous and objective, the poems have a rhythm that varies from a lilt to a gallop. The influence in them is that of Swinburne. The content, however, is more physical, less scholarly. His philosophy, which he found in the end no adequate prop or stay, is summed up in lines that have become widely quoted:

> Life is mostly froth and bubble,
> Two things stand like stone—
> Kindness in another's trouble,
> Courage in your own.

Through his life he appeared to follow a course of carefree action, in which the element of risk was welcomed:

> No game was ever yet worth a rap
> For a rational man to play,
> In which no accident, no mishap,
> Could possibly find its way.

Gordon's poems were written at speed, and carelessness is evident in a large number of them. There is a resemblance in this respect to Byron, a touch of the conscious amateur who dashes off his verse with a take-it-or-leave-it air. This carelessness in Gordon can result in lapses of taste and ineptness of rhythm. It is interesting to compare him in such instances with his friend and contemporary, Kendall. Kendall probably sinks lower than Gordon, but he also rises higher. When Kendall is at his worst he is vapid, he even writes flat nonsense. Gordon never writes nonsense, he writes sense that is silly, something that we laugh at. It is hard to find a better example than the lines from *Early Adieux*:

> My mother is a stately dame,
> Who oft would chide with me;
> She saith my riot bringeth shame,
> And stains my pedigree.

One is tempted to believe this written in jest, it reads so like a parody. But it is quite serious, as the rest of the poem shows. *Ashtaroth* provides us with metrical ineptness:

> They have pass'd, leaving little to their children,
> Save histories of a truth far from strict;
> Or theories more vague and bewildering,
> Since three out of four contradict.

Not much of Gordon is good poetry. One poem, *The Swimmer*, where the influence of Swinburne is very evident, contains some lines that his master would not have despised:

> See! girt with tempest and wing'd with thunder,
> And clad with lightning and shod with sleet,
> The strong winds treading the swift waves sunder
> The flying rollers with frothy feet.

And in one poem, *The Rhyme of Joyous Garde*, where there are few lapses, Gordon writes at his very best. It is the soliloquy of Lancelot, repentant for his sin of faithlessness to the King. Whether the metrical pattern suits the theme throughout is not certain, but in parts it has a sweep and verve that carry the theme triumphantly:

> And the long, lithe sword on the hand became
> As a leaping light, as a falling flame,
> As a fire through the flax that hasted;
> Slender, and shining, and beautiful . . .

The poetry of the blade.

Gordon came to Australia at the age of twenty, and remained an Englishman in Australia till his death. In Poets' Corner in Westminster Abbey there now stands a bust of Gordon, between Tennyson and Campbell, with the inscription: Poet of Australia. *The Times*, reporting the unveiling (11 May, 1934), headed its column, The Laureate of Australia, and began its account: ". . . outstanding honour was accorded the national poet of Australia . . ." Now Gordon was not national and he did not really describe Australia. His medium was the derivative diction of the period, and except for one or two poems, as, for example, *A Dedication* to his *Bush Ballads*, one would not know from the descriptions alone that he had ever been in Australia. And in the well-known lines from that poem:

> In lands where bright blossoms are scentless,
> And songless bright birds . . .

many are sure that he betrays a distorted or partial vision. He looked to the past, to old stories and themes, as much as to the present, and to England rather than to Australia. He was in spiritual as well as physical exile.

CHAPTER IV

The Three Themes of Fiction

FOUR well-known novels on typical Australian themes were written last century. Three of the four cannot be classed as much more than competent; yet each in its kind is unique. The four cover what were for long the three staple themes of Australian fiction—convictism, pastoral life, and bushranging. They are concerned with things, with movement and action and violence and adventure. And one of them concerns much more.

The earliest of the four is *Ralph Rashleigh* (1844–5). It was written by James Tucker (1808–66), who had been transported to Australia in 1827 for attempted blackmail. From the time he landed until he died, a mental and physical wreck, in Liverpool Asylum not far from Sydney, Tucker was either a convict or a ticket-of-leave man.

A mutilated version of his manuscript was published in England in 1929, the full text in Australia in 1952. The manuscript does not give Tucker's name—for over a century nobody knew who the author was. The tracking down was a triumph of literary detection carried out by its editor Colin Roderick. Indeed, to many readers his Introduction to the limited edition of the novel remains of greater fascination than Tucker's story itself.

The publication of the full text was the occasion for inflated claims. These claims cannot be sustained. *Ralph Rashleigh* gained its temporary fame from its full publication for the first time and from the discovery of its author; its permanent fame as a novel will derive from the setting—the convict system described by a convict.

It is a picaresque novel in the tradition of Smollett about a century before. A few humorous scenes are reminiscent of Fielding. Rashleigh is an English thief and confidence man sentenced to transportation for life. In Australia he is assigned to a schoolmaster in Sydney, then is sent to Emu Plains, west of Sydney; assigned to a settler at Airds, he is forced to accompany a gang of brutal bushrangers; captured and sent to Newcastle, he escapes and lives with the aborigines; then he rescues and preserves a white woman, and is ultimately pardoned. His experiences affect him; in the artless words of Tucker:

> The sufferings of his early career in the Colony produced such an effect of reformation in his mind that he was ever after respected as a man of singular integrity by all that knew him, who united sincerely in lamenting his premature death, which took place in 1844 . . .

It is perhaps unreasonable to look for characterisation of any depth or subtlety in narratives of this kind. Rashleigh is two stock figures in one. From the time of his conviction he is portrayed as a victim, a passive sufferer under brutality, until his escape from Newcastle. He is a sort of magnet for misfortune. But from there until the end, that is, as a free man among the aborigines, he is a stock hero, powerful, resourceful, energetic. We may conclude that Tucker drew most of the first portion from his own experiences as a convict, and that he concocted the rest from what he had read and what he had heard from others and what he drew from his imagination.

But if we cannot expect vital and living characters, perhaps we may have vivid and exciting incident? Now the events related would as realities be exciting or revolting or moving; potentially they are ideal for the novelist of action. But the narrative is not particularly successful. The reasons lie in the very profusion of events and in the manner of narration. The early part of the novel has an *embarras de richesse*. The sequence of events is a crowded one: there is hardly a moment's breathing space except for the occasional pious reflections. The result is a sort of catalogue.

The style is the formal style of reports, a heritage of eighteenth-century official prose. The even tenor of its orotund address and inflated periods reduces everything to a bland, almost urbane, uniformity.

> A meal was now prepared by Rashleigh, to which his three ruffianly companions did ample justice, making during its progress many coarse jests and brutal allusions to the death pangs of their treacherous associate, whose lifeless body hung within a very few feet of the spot they had selected for their repast.
>
> It may easily be conceived that our adventurer had no appetite after the appalling scene of mortal suffering he had so recently witnessed, and he waited most anxiously for the signal to commence their march, so that he might at least be relieved from the sight of the dead ruffian.

D

The reality concealed by this piece of writing is monstrous; but the effect is that of a board meeting. After a few dozen pages of such prose a reader finds his eyes glazing.

The picture of the system that Tucker presents is a shocking one—floggings, near-starvation, work not to be distinguished from slavery, spiritual wickedness in high places, injustice, death. The period of Tucker's life in Australia up to the composition of the book covered nearly twenty years, and it is hardly possible that he observed or experienced no brighter lights in the sombre picture. The explanation lies in the facts of his own life—that of the condemned felon. Since few of us are willing to acknowledge the complete justice of our punishments, he felt himself a victim. The picture, then, is the next best thing to an exculpation —I was bad, true, but I did not deserve this.

Though he condemns the system, Tucker shows very little feeling for those who suffer under it. The emphasis is on the cruelty, not on the sufferers. They are wretched, they suffer, and they escape when they can. But they appear more or less as animals. Very few lawbreakers engage Tucker's sympathies. It is illuminating to read his comment on Foxley the bushranger's use of the word *tyrant*:

> Such, it is to be observed, is the term used by all the convicts of New South Wales to designate any person, whether magistrate, overseer or constable, who may perform his duty more strictly than is agreeable to the exalted notions these worthies entertain of the deference and consideration with which they ought to be treated.

Tucker does not present the men as inevitable products. All appear cruel in their own right, as it were, whether convicts or overseers or magistrates or warders or even parsons. When a humane man is found, it is for the sake of some turn in the narrative: he is demanded by the exigencies of the story, not by the statistics of human nature.

Tucker thought of himself as apart from the usual run of convicts, picturing himself as Rashleigh (arrested by ill luck, convicted by the treachery of a confederate, condemned harshly). By the time of Rashleigh's escape from Newcastle he had come to the end of his own experiences. For the period after Rashleigh's escape he drew partly on his imagination. Rashleigh changes after that, and Tucker projects himself into a vision of heroic proportions. These two parts of the book, then, are an unconscious exoneration and a wish-fulfilment by a small-time criminal. It is the Convict's Lament followed by the Convict's Dream.

To pass from this story to the next is like passing from darkness to sunlight.

The reputation of *The Recollections of Geoffry Hamlyn* (1859) once stood very high. Its author, Henry Kingsley (1830–76), brother of the more famous Charles, was until the advent of Marcus Clarke commonly held to be the only novelist who had written a novel about Australia that was worth reading. Kingsley came out to the goldfields in 1853 and served with the police and worked on stations. The picture of Australia that his novel presents is one of pastoral life. It is a tale of families, the Buckleys, the Brentwoods, and the Thorntons, and the relations between them, told ostensibly by Geoffry Hamlyn.

For about a third of the novel the characters are in Drumston or in its neighbourhood; then they are shifted to Australia. There, in the heart of the bush, by a series of coincidences they all come together again. Bit by bit the tension increases as we learn or suspect that Hawker, husband of Mary (*née* Thornton) and now escaped convict and bushranger, is nearing the area. He gathers his gang, he strikes, and in an action of increasing speed is brought to bay and captured. The evildoers or those who have deserved punishment or have to be got out of the book are gone. There is a temporary dispersal, until in the closing chapters the important characters once more gather in their original homes in England. The long trip and stay in a foreign land are over.

The book is a novel of exile, an aspect well brought out by H. M. Green. The characters start in England, they are English of a few distinct classes, and they go to Australia to make their fortunes. When they have succeeded, they return to England, leaving the villains dead in Australia. They like Australia while they are in it, but they feel no reluctance in leaving it. The Australian background is full enough, what with kangaroos and parrots, aborigines and convicts, bush and drought and fire, but it is felt to be a background. All are English people transplanted to a new land for a period long enough to fill the book with their adventures. Australia is the backdrop to their interactions.

It is among the most class-conscious of Australian novels without being aware of it. The chief characters in it, naturally enough, are gentry and Church and Army. As English gentlemen of substance, they possess their little self-contained world wherever they are, observing with tolerance the odd behaviour of aborigines, convicts, colonials, and the rest outside their circle. And yet this does not become offensive, for there is no conscious snobbery; it is all taken for granted, and in the course of reading it one almost accepts it as the natural order of things—which in its period it must indeed have seemed to be.

Kingsley's background of family, school, and university sufficiently accounts for most of the attitudes in the novel, for the point of view and the assumptions. But Dickens, whom Kingsley read with enjoyment, and Thomas Hughes (of *Tom Brown's Schooldays*), who was a favourite with brother Charles and whom Henry Kingsley must have read, both appear to have influenced the book. Many of the adults are more mature Tom Browns, healthy and hearty, good English schoolboys, candid and uncomplicated. Kingsley's resemblance to Dickens appears in the crowd of characters, with individual and family stories that interact, the sentimentality, the unbearable coyness where young love is concerned, and the melodrama of threats.

A petulant critic might gird at the superficiality of the novel, and could find some warrant. The events are there for their own sake and the excitement and tension they produce. The characters are stock, the heroes orthodox—fine strong fellows, generally six feet tall, honest and reliable, muscular Christians with no complexity of any kind in their frank natures. One exception is the villain Hawker, though even he is mostly to be expected—handsome and plausible, shooting his man near the end and riding off with a laugh; the other is Mary Thornton, who develops in the book from the headstrong girl to the perplexed mother. All in all, though, they are fine animals. Indeed a passage like the following is ambiguous for a moment if the reader is not alert:

> With broad intelligent forehead, with large loving hazel eyes, with a frill like Queen Elizabeth, with a brush like a fox, deep in the brisket, perfect in . . .

To that point one might, despite *brush*, think it a description of one of the characters. But the next word, *markings*, lets us see that the passage is dealing with a collie. It is a mixture of adventure story, when incidents like hunting or fighting blacks and bushrangers or escaping a bushfire are concerned, and fairy tale, when the child is lost in the bush across the river or excursions are held or characters are in love.

Its qualities are those of its kind. It is all so candid, and its artless outlook on life is so engaging, that a critic feels he should forgo his function. It is, after all, a book for boys of all ages and makes little pretence to be anything else. Kingsley can tell a story of incident with zest; he has control over dramatic feeling, for example in the gathering threat to the families from Hawker, and the fearful possibility that young Charles Hawker may kill his father; he has such good nature and such admiration for human decency; he apportions awards and punishments, with very few exceptions, just as we should like to have them in life. All these are things that account for the book's popularity. It is in addition almost an idyll, and events are viewed through a luminous haze. A reader has so few demands made on him that he feels a sort of responsive gratitude. As a novel it is hard to take quite seriously, but as a story it is only too easy to read.

The most powerful novel written in Australia last century is *For the Term of His Natural Life*, a story of the convict system in Tasmania. It is a very long novel in its original form, running to well over one-third of a million words. Often rambling, frequently verbose, it is nevertheless an Australian masterpiece in its kind. The picture it paints is sombre in the extreme, and parts of it today can hardly be read without discomfort.

Its author, Marcus Andrew Hislop Clarke (1846–81), lived the first half of his brief life in England, where the death of his mother and the indifference of his father left him the plaything of youthful whims and not so youthful desires—"I was suffered at sixteen to ape the vices of sixty." On the death of his father he came to Melbourne, aged seventeen, and dissipated his charm in a variety of jobs and his talent in miscellaneous writings. Some of his work, essays and topical productions, remains uncollected. His great novel was the result of a stay in Tasmania, where he pored over the convict records and gathered the facts and figures on which the novel was based. It appeared in 1870–1 as a serial in *The Australian Journal*. It was reprinted a few years later as a book in a shortened and modified version, and in 1929 for the first time in its original entirety. It remains, in either form, pre-eminently Clarke's magnum opus; and the reader must still wonder at the production of such a considerable work by such an unlikely author—spendthrift, feckless, inebriate, and charm-ing—at the early age of twenty-four.

The novel in its serial form opens in Dickensian fashion—an inn, odd characters, the fat proprietor, the coach in the rain, the air of mystery enveloping two of the travellers. In the shortened version a melodramatic and improbable Prologue replaces the early chapters. From there on we are concerned primarily with the life of one man, Richard Devine, who is wrongfully convicted (of murder in the first version, of robbery in the second) and sentenced to transportation for the term of his natural life. He goes under the name of Rufus Dawes. The sufferings he endures are almost beyond belief—privation, brutality, flogging, torture and, not least, despair of gratitude direly earned and hope often and long deferred. In the end, by a series of coincidences, he recovers his rightful estate and the means of proving his innocence. In the revision Clarke ends the novel tragically, and the whole effect is intensified, the note of tragedy is maintained, and the gloom, except for Sylvia's recognition of her preserver, remains unbroken to the last. The revision, about half the length of the original, is thus improved in its ending, but not in its beginning.

The picture that Clarke gives of the convict system in this novel, which is set in a period beginning in 1827, is one of un-relieved brutality. The cruelties are concentrated on the person of Dawes. In consequence the picture is made more hideous than the reality warrants. Clarke was much affected by his researches, and the book is an exposure, however belated, of the horrors that once prevailed. In a descriptive chapter in the original text he speaks of "the curse of convictism", declaring that "the in-famies current, as matters of course, in chain-gangs and penal settlements were of too horrible a nature to be more than hinted at here". It is admitted that he blacks the chimney, but it was in all conscience black already. Though he focuses all types of punishment upon Dawes, and though this may strain belief, one is inclined to feel that the effect, overwhelming in force, justifies the violation. Under the iron flail Dawes changes in a way that Clarke describes with a skill beyond that of the other Australian novelists of the century. It is a picture of hardening and coarsening, with periodic softenings into humanity and tenderness that are followed by further access of grim resolution. It is not so much the creation of a character as the tracing of temperamental changes.

The intense force of the book derives from details and manner of writing. They serve to show the great difference in capacity between an author like Tucker, who had the advantage of knowing the horrors at first hand, and Clarke, who had merely read about them. There are as many horrors in Tucker as in Clarke, but the effect on the reader of Tucker's narrative is inconsiderable compared with that produced by Clarke's descriptions. Here, for example, is a brief extract from the description of Kirkland's flogging, Dawes being the unwilling executioner:

> "Ten!" cried Troke, impassibly counting to the end of the first twenty.
> The lad's back, swollen into a hump, now presented the appearance of a ripe peach which a wilful child had scored with a pin.
> Dawes, turning away from his bloody handiwork, drew the cats through his fingers twice. They were beginning to get clogged a little.

In descriptions or vignettes of persons, again, Clarke stands by himself in his century. And he has a power to capture significant detail, to put down in a few words what the eye sees and retains after a sudden startled look:

> With a long yellow hand, spiked as it were with long yellow fingers tipped with strong black nails . . .

In such descriptions, especially where the grim or the odd or the sinister is concerned, Clarke excels all his predecessors. He is, when dealing with such themes, our first stylist.

His Natural Life is the only one of these four novels that can be said to have a plot. And here, as in other respects, Clarke is like Dickens, with some stories running parallel and meeting at intervals, with reliance on fantastic coincidence, and (in the original novel) with a happy and huddled-up conclusion. The use of coincidence in this novel in both versions is an abuse, and if one were to judge it by structure alone, then it would be faulty. Clarke took his stand on actuality—he could point to documents proving that certain things had happened. But no documents justify a long series of convenient coincidences. Nor does life itself, with all its oddness. But there still remains a plot, ingenious if improbable. The consciousness of this and the expectation of changes of fortune that it awakens add something to the novel that the purely picaresque story cannot have.

In characterisation also Clarke is superior to the others. At the same time, though noticeably better, he is no prolific creator of characters. Rufus Dawes is shown as human nature changing rather than as a living individual human being. At least, however, the changes are credible and skilfully presented. But this does not apply to Maurice Frere. At the start he is a rather coarse, half-brutal young officer. In the system he has become the persecutor of Dawes, hating the victim whom he has wronged. That hate is very natural. But the change does not convince us. As a persecutor Frere is sadistic, possessed by a devilish and implacable malice that does not appear to be the natural development of his particular characteristics. The most successful piece of character drawing in the novel is to be found in the Rev. James North, a self-tortured parson, a drunkard, a man of intense sensibility and conflicting passions, complex and tortuous. His diary, by means of which a few sections of the story are told, has parts of discursive boredom, but it also has parts of bitter self-revelation. It is likely enough that Clarke here looked in his heart and wrote.

It is as a picture of men under the convict system, however, that *His Natural Life* will live. As a narrator of excitement and suspense and horror Clarke still remains the greatest Australian novelist of his type. Only Hay rivals him in suspense, and surpasses him in insight into and creation of character. The following taste of Clarke's quality may serve to give us his essentials. It is the end of the abortive mutiny on the *Malabar*.

Shaking his assailants to the deck as easily as a wild boar shakes off the dogs which clamber upon his bristly sides, the convict sprang to his feet, and whirling the heavy cutlass round his head, kept the circle at bay. . . . Gabbett, his stubbly hair on end, his bloodshot eyes glaring with fury, his great hand opening and shutting in air, as though it gasped for something to seize, turned himself about from side to side, now here, now there, bellowing like a wounded bull. His coarse shirt, rent from shoulder to flank, exposed the play of his huge muscles. He was bleeding from a cut on his forehead, and the blood, trickling down his face, mingled with the foam on his lips and dropped sluggishly on to his hairy breast. Each time that a man came within reach of the swinging cutlass, he received a fresh accession of rage, and his form seemed to dilate and expand with passion. Viewed through the thunderous gloom of a tropical night, the aspect of this monster, surrounded by assailants who dare not approach him, brought to mind those hideously-grotesque pictures of the combats of evil spirits, drawn by the fantastic pencil of Goya. At one moment bunched with clinging adversaries—his arms, legs, and shoulders a hanging mass of human bodies—at the next, free, desperate, alone in the midst of his foes, with his hideous countenance contorted with hate and rage, the giant seemed less a man than a demon, or one of those monstrous and savage apes that haunt the solitudes of the African forests. . . .

Despite the over-writing typical of both author and period, this is effective in its place in the novel. A fastidious taste may reject it as melodramatic. So it is; but, sustained, it has its vocation. Clarke was of his age, and he can still give us, if not always the characters, at least the form and pressure of the period. In this work he is an inferior and savage Dickens.

Of these four novels the thinnest in texture and the easiest to read is Rolf Boldrewood's *Robbery Under Arms*. Thomas Alexander Browne (1826–1915) took the name Boldrewood from Scott's *Marmion*. Brought to Australia as a mere child, he lived practically all his long life in this country, and was by experience and temperament the only Australian of the four. He was, among other things, pastoralist, gold warden, and police magistrate.

It was in intervals in his official duties that he wrote his novels. He was very prolific. As well as a bulk of memoirs, essays, sketches, and tales, he wrote eighteen novels. The best known of these are *The Squatter's Dream* (1878), *The Miner's Right* (1890), and *A Sydney-Side Saxon* (1891). They appeared first as serials, as did his most famous work, *Robbery Under Arms*. This ran in *The Sydney Mail* as a serial in 1882–3 and appeared as a volume in 1888.

The story deals with life in New South Wales in the forties and fifties, with the life, in particular, of the Marstons and the romantic Starlight, gentleman of fortune. It is a story of cattle-duffing, bushranging, and life on the Turon goldfield west of Sydney. The Marston brothers take to cattle-stealing in a spirit of bravado or youthful daring. The step to bushranging is easy. Most incidents that a reader avid for excitement could demand are there—arrests, escapes, hold-ups, night rides, narrow squeaks, betrayals, and a final stand against the troopers.

This sort of story may present a problem today; it presented a problem then, the problem of moral responsibility. The narrator is Dick Marston, survivor of the original gang, youthful, engaging, and dashing. Is he to be presented in heroic colours? And there is Starlight, not so youthful but just as dashing and even more engaging. Boldrewood kills off Starlight, so that problem is summarily solved. As for Dick Marston, he is captured, sentenced to imprisonment, and released years later, a reformed grey-beard, to marry his Gracey and live a model life.

And there are the incidents that Dick relates. This young man defies the law on many occasions—he steals cattle, he breaks jail, he holds up coaches, he shoots an escort—and all in the gay adventurous manner. But wickedness must not prosper. So Boldrewood has him telling the story (memoirs of an ill-spent life, as it were) in Berrima gaol. He must be repentant for the past; despite the thrill of adventure, he must be sorry he ever did these things. So the narrative is spattered with brief pious reflections, miniature moralisings:

> How easy it is for chaps to take the road to hell! for that was about the size of it . . .

and:

> What a thing it is to be perfectly honest and straight—to be able to look the whole world in the face!

and, to draw to an end with these:

> That's the worst of not being straight and square. A man's almost driven to drink when he can't keep from thinking of all sorts of miserable things day and night.

There are dozens of these punctuating the sequence of criminal escapades. It is all very edifying; but we should feel more reassured if the repentant sinner were not in gaol at the time. It is perhaps significant that they become less frequent as the story progresses.

Boldrewood's style for the most part fits the dashing narrative admirably. It serves as one exception at least to Sheridan's generalisation that easy writing makes damned hard reading. He wrote with speed, with apparent ease, and with few corrections in his manuscript. He had, he said, a facile pen. The narrative, in the first person, is enlivened by the oral turns of speech —*can't, don't, he'll*, and so forth, and by the use of colloquialisms and slang. This note is struck in the opening paragraph:

> My name's Dick Marston, Sydney-side native. I'm twenty-nine years old, six feet in my stocking soles, and thirteen stone weight. Pretty strong and active with it, so they say. I don't want to blow —not here, any road—but it takes a good man to put me on my back, or stand up to me with the gloves, or the naked mauleys. I

can ride anything—anything that ever was lapped in horsehide—
swim like a musk-duck, and track like a Myall blackfellow. Most
things that a man can do I'm up to, and that's all about it. As I
lift myself now I can feel the muscle swell on my arm like a cricket
ball, in spite of the—well, in spite of everything.

There is a sort of breezy braggadocio about it all like the story
it tells—boot, saddle, to horse, and away. Boldrewood has, in
short, the admirable quality of readability, a quality very hard
to define, but equally easy to recognise when it occurs. His
outstanding gift is that of the born storyteller.

Boldrewood does not handle this style with perfect consistency.
Often enough the homely Dick Marston lapses into grammatical
formality: the author starts to write as himself instead of in the
person of the imaginary narrator. These passages the reader
suddenly becomes aware of, and he sees then why a section has
not been so interesting as others. Another point is that the
colloquial fits incident, but is not so well fitted for other purposes;
the account of the goldfields, for instance, informative and
accurate as it is, is not so vivid. Near the end, however, style
and theme marry. The account of the last stand of the bushrangers, the death of Starlight, and the mourning of Warrigal
is as effective a piece of writing as Boldrewood ever managed.

Boldrewood had the advantage of material ready-made to
hand. Many of the incidents and persons and places in the novel
had their actual counterparts. The stealing of over a thousand
head of cattle, the trek to Adelaide, and the sale there—this
really occurred in the early seventies. Terrible Hollow is in the
New England district. The Marstons were based on people that
Boldrewood knew, and even Starlight, though based on no one
character, was apparently a composite.

The transfusion of this reality into the novel appears most in
the incidents, which are real enough, natural and naturally told.
The characters, though, are less successful. The most striking is
a major figure, Starlight. He is, to mature eyes, slightly larger
than life. He represents Boldrewood's colonial attitude to gentle
birth, an attitude that lasted until Furphy attacked it viciously
and in so doing left one with the uneasy feeling that he protested
too much. Starlight is grammatical, he is presumed to be of a
family of note, he is soft spoken, suave and polished, but capable
of rage and violence, and then he is efficient and deadly—an
Australian Claude Duval, in short. Most youngsters wish in

their hearts to be like Starlight, if not to be the author of all his deeds. His modern counterpart is, say, Raffles or, in another and legal line of country, the Saint of the thrillers by Leslie Charteris. It would require a greater novelist than Boldrewood to lend full credibility to such a creation.

The novel is an Australian thriller, valued still because it was one of the earliest competent novels in this country and because it is essentially Australian in setting and incident and most characters. There are no implications: all is pure straight narrative; its surface values are those it is to be judged by. And these values are a narrative excellence and the resulting excitement. The novel remains and is likely to remain the best Australian counterpart of the good American Western.

INTERCHAPTER I

H. M. GREEN in his pioneer survey divided our literature into numerous periods, and was mildly rebuked by Morris Miller for various inconsistencies. The problem is certainly no easier now. If one attempts a few broad divisions, however, it is easy enough to decide on the first period.

This runs from 1810, when Robinson published his first poem, to the 1880s. One might say indeed that the eighties serve as a sort of watershed. They are a rather barren time, no poems of much consequence being published then (except some few by Brunton Stephens), and the only novels of any weight being the early ones of Rosa Praed.

And the 1880s do serve as the end of a period. Kendall died in 1882, his *Songs from the Mountains* appearing in 1880; and *Robbery Under Arms*, the last of the four most famous novels of the century, was serialised 1882-3. So both poetry and fiction tend to mark time around those years.

The period, then, contains about seventy years of poetry, about fifty years of fiction. Of the two, the fiction is certainly the more important, what with the twenty years of the Guidebook novels (about 1840-60), and the enclosing forty years of Tucker, Kingsley, Clarke, and Boldrewood. To set against this we have the relatively unimposing poems of Harpur, Kendall, Gordon, and the early Brunton Stephens. The novelists swallowed and assimilated the offerings of the new land—its space, its fauna, and the varied activities it engendered such as convictism, bush-ranging, mining, and grazing. The life of cities and the inner life of persons were only incidentally treated. As for the poets, they were shackled by the old conventions of attitude and vocabulary that they inherited.

The name Colonial Period has been suggested for these seventy years. If poetry alone is considered, then the name is pertinent. But to apply it to a period that includes Clarke's masterpiece seems almost defamatory. It is worth noting, however, that the literature of the period does not much express Australian ideals. It concerns itself with things and events. It reflects little of the dawning and growing hostility to the corruption of the old world, of the dawning and growing faith (however much this was to be disappointed) that Australia could become The Promised Land.

In a word, one might say that the literature of the period was behind its times. It looked at its past, often with hate or shame; at its present, often with satisfaction; but it did not much express the hope of the future.

PERIOD II

from the 1880s to the 1930s

CHAPTER V

Turn of the Century: Poetry

THE Australian poets around the end of the century may be classed in three groups: the robust Bush Balladists; the "aesthetic" group, if the adjective is loosely used; and the more or less public poets.

Into the last of these groups we may put James Brunton Stephens (1835–1902), though the number of commemorative poems he wrote is quite small. A graduate of Edinburgh, he came to Queensland at about the age of thirty, and died a devoted Public Servant. He was a man of taste and learning, and turned a poetic hand to a great variety of themes. His last poem on public affairs was *Fulfilment*, an ode on Australian Federation, 1 January, 1901, a theme that had engaged his interest decades before. The best of his writings in this line is *The Dominion of Australia*, of which the last stanza runs:

> So flows beneath our good and ill
> A viewless stream of Common Will,
> A gathering force, a present might,
> That from the silent depths of gloom
> At Wisdom's voice shall leap to light,
> And hide our barren feuds in bloom,
> Till, all our sundering lines with love o'ergrown,
> Our bounds shall be the girdling seas alone.

This, as good with its mixed metaphors as such writings usually are, is a warm statement of aspiration that almost glows into poetry.

Some of his verse is philosophical. Here he uses science, especially astronomy, for a parallel: the allegory proves a case or illuminates a belief. The most successful is *The Dark Companion*, the title referring to the satellite of Sirius that was discovered in 1862. There is more than a trace of the didactic in these poems, and he underlines the comparisons, as though his readers were not overly intelligent. In such verses, as in his odes, Stephens preserves a sort of stiff dignity.

A large proportion of Stephens' verse is humorous; *My Chinee Cook*, for example, is still remembered. His devices are multifarious: he parodies, he makes puns (and some are very ingenious), he turns a phrase, he saves up his revelation for the end, he is very deft with odd or unusual incidents, and his reading affords him examples to serve as allusions. The most effective story is *The Midnight Axe*, a sort of ghost story set in this country, where the atmosphere does not lend itself to this evocation. The grotesque, said Lafcadio Hearn, is a mixture of the comic and the frightening. This poem is a story of the grotesque, though the comedy in it may be unconscious. It is instructive to compare the poem with Hood's little masterpiece, *The Haunted House*.

The poem by which Stephens is likely to be best remembered is *Convict Once*, a long narrative of slightly over a thousand lines. The metrical pattern, based on the classical elegiac measure, to which English does not lend itself at all readily, Stephens handles with scholarly skill. (Though Stephens intended it thus, the accentual tendency of English and the licences that he takes render the term *elegiac measure* something of a misnomer. It is more natural to take the lines as dactylic hexameters, catalectic in varying degrees.) It is the story of Magdalen Power, a convict now released from her servitude. She tells the story in the first person—her position as governess of three girls; her intrusion into the love between the eldest, Hyacinth, and Raymond Trevelyan, son of an ex-convict; her remorse after a bout of fever; the oath of Hyacinth's father that he will give his consent only when he himself offers marriage to an ex-convict. The ending after that may be foreseen: he does offer marriage to Magdalen, not knowing her former history. The lovers are thus united, and Magdalen, weakened by fever, dies of heart disease. The narration is oblique, clues are not always obvious, and the frequent gaps make parts of the story obscure. But the main outlines are clear enough even on a first reading.

With such a resistant medium, it is not surprising that Stephens should falter. His taste, in addition, sometimes deserts him. He can perpetrate the most prosaic lines:

> There are some things even I cannot do. False I could not declare her.

And, at the other extreme, he can run into a morass of pretentious diction:

> Curse on those undulous pastures, and far vista'd woods unavailing,
> Scant of contiguous umbrage, unmeet for the tomb that I crave.

These are the over-effects of a misdirected scholar. But on occasion the richness seems justified:

> Down in the vines he is sitting; and radiance leaf-softened and
>   golden
> On the broad calm of his brow through the veil of the vintage is
>   shed.
> Blest be each bough that enshrines him! Henceforth I am ever
>   beholden
> Unto the slenderest, tenderest leaflet that shelters his head.

Stephens here captures something of the fullness, the benevolence of fruition, in a love that encounters the object of its search.

The immediacy of the poem derives chiefly from the use of the present tense almost throughout, and from the introspection of Magdalen, never deceived in the motives that drive on her passionate and complex self. And the skill appears as much as anywhere in the variation of pace. It moves slowly as she broods; when once her decision is taken, it gathers pace until the end. As the conclusion grows obvious, gaps in the narrative are left and a few stanzas sum up a whole sequence. It is not unreasonable to say that this strange and strangely told story has in these days not had its full share of recognition.

One long poem, *The Godolphin Arabian*, runs to 3,000 lines. Stephens uses the prose of Eugene Sue as a basis for a free adaptation. It is the story of a horse, told in ottava rima, and showing the influence of Hood and Byron. Adeptness in riming and in punning has a free outlet and reveals itself as extremely fertile and ingenious. Like Byron, he is by turns satiric, ironic, and cynical, and he ranges in vocabulary from the slangy to the colloquial to the mock pretentious. It is admittedly a mere *tour de force*, an exercise in metrical and linguistic virtuosity, but it shows Stephens, from his earliest period of writing (the poem was completed by 1872), as a very adroit handler of words.

The reputation of Stephens, once very high, is not likely to be so high again. The mark of the scholar, of the intellectual, is perceptible in all his verse. It is not that he obtrudes his learning, as O'Dowd does; but he seems very much of a poet made.

George Essex Evans (1863–1909) may be put in the same group as Stephens and with greater justification, for he was indeed much more of a public poet. He celebrated or commented on the events of his day—Federation, the war in South Africa, Queen Victoria, the British Empire, and Toowoomba; the wives of pioneers, nurses, notabilities lately deceased, and the aspirations of man. Many of these poems take the form of odes. In verse of this type, where even Tennyson was not at his best, it would be unreasonable to expect great success from Evans. As characteristic as any are these lines from a stanza in *The Nation Builders*:

> And the pitiless might of the molten skies, at noon, on the sun-cracked plain,
> And the walls of the northern jungles, shall front them ever in vain,
> Till the land that lies like a giant asleep shall wake to the victory won,
> And the hearts of the Nation Builders shall know that the work is done.

He constituted himself a sort of unofficial Australian poet laureate, the singer of a nation dedicated to work, to Empire expansion, and to peace. As a poet of State and national occasions he felt apparently some responsibility for the national outlook. When he saw fit, he reprimanded backsliders, as in *Auri Sacra Fames* and *Ode to the Philistines*. Whether celebrating or scolding he betrays the general influence of Newbolt and Kipling. Though he wrote a few comic poems, he produced no witty or humorous pieces on topical minor events, but reserved his Muse for more important functions.

As a technician he is fond of long lines with five or six or seven feet, and of long feet, anapests and amphibrachs and even paeons. There is a sort of force in them all, stressed by the dead stamp of a rhythm that is at one with his forthright and rather artless outlook. But he has little subtlety of phrasing, an unreliable ear, and a thickened sensibility. It is very hard to find in Evans many stanzas that justify his confident assurance. The following may serve:

> The grey gums by the lonely creek,
>   The star-crowned height,
> The wind-swept plain, the dim blue peak,
>   The cold white light,
> The solitude spread near and far
> Around the camp-fire's tiny star,
> The horse-bell's melody remote,
> The curlew's melancholy note,
>   Across the night.

Such a stanza will pass muster. But Evans is seldom so tolerable in choice of noun and epithet. Much of his poetry is stereotype. If an adjective were not inserted, a reader might fill the gap almost automatically: it is like plucking words from recognised and long-familiar pigeonholes. Such lines as these show what he normally wrote:

> Or where the streaming mist's white rollers climb
> The dark ravine and precipice sublime—
> A filmy sea that twines and intertwines,
> Wreathes the low hills and veils the mighty lines
> Of sovran mountains, crimsoned and aglow
> In crystal pomp, crested with jewelled snow.

Apart from poems of commemoration, which he wrote as it were in public, Evans produced two fairly long narratives which have their own merits. The story in *Loraine* is rather worn: left to die in the desert by his friend, Loraine is rescued by aborigines and at last reaches civilisation. Here he finds that his betrothed has married the false friend and later has died. He returns to the desert to make a fortune from gold, and prepares to ruin and then kill his betrayer. But he finds his enemy dead and the child of the marriage in tears by the bedside. In *The Repentance of Magdalene Despar* a woman wearies of marriage and goes to the bad. At last she commits suicide.

Credit is due to Evans for his handling of difficulties which appear, oddly enough, to be self-imposed. That is to say, he affects long lines with a loose or swinging rhythm, rather complicated stanza forms, and rime sequences that make considerable demands on his resources. But when the demand for a rime is met, the result is often some intrusive absurdity. Despite all this, his narratives at least by sheer iteration build up the illusion of effectiveness. Evans seldom deals with poetry's real business, but he serves as a sort of tocsin.

Some few poems on Australian topical themes and a few others of wider application serve to rank the next poet as a public one. He is William Gay (1865–97). Various influences made his life what it was—Calvinism, consumption, and metaphysics. From the first influence, one that was imposed upon him as a child and young man, he gradually freed himself, and a poem such as *The Sabbath-Breakers* reveals his reaction. The second brought about his early death. He left Scotland for New Zealand in order to check its inroads, lived there for some three years, and then came to Victoria in 1888. The third influence is seen in the cast of many of his poems. He had for philosophical speculation and study a deep fondness, and some of the problems over which he brooded are reflected in the brief collection of his poems.

Gay's nine years in Victoria made him an ardent advocate of Federation. He wrote six sonnets on Australian themes, and four of them are directly or indirectly concerned with that subject. He reproaches Queensland in 1897 for sending no delegates to the Federal Convention of that year, but prophesies she will later join a united Australia:

> Yet will its splendours mount not far on high
> Ere thou from thy unhappy dusk emerge
> And be with us beneath one radiant sky.

And for those who prefer "a faction's petty profit" in Victoria he has a greater scorn. In *Australia Infelix* he inveighs against the prevailing materialism, but rests confident in the work of patriots,

> Who, venturing all to win their country's good,
> Shall toil and suffer for the sacred hour
> That brings the fullness of her nationhood.

In *Australian Federation*, the poem for which he is best known, he offers up a prayer for unity. The continent is one—

> complete she lies
> Within the unbroken circle of the skies,
> And round her indivisible the sea.

Only the dwellers in the continent are divided—

> With petty variance our souls are spent.

Gay concludes with the well-known adjuration—

> O let us rise, united, penitent,
> And be one people,—mighty, serving God!

Through these four sonnets Gay repeats his themes—the selfishness of those opposing Federation, the guilt of Australians at loggerheads within a country made by Nature for unity, an urging to repent, and the future glory of a land to be linked by federal ties. Parts anticipate the poems of O'Dowd. The idealistic vision of Gay reflected the spirit of some of the leaders of the movement. But Gay's own feelings could not have been theirs in the same way. He was a Scotsman, and the consciousness of unity was part of him before he came to Australia. His concern was, in a word, disinterested—he had no axe to grind. His emotion is not that of one brought up in Australia and finding State jealousies absurd or cramping. It is a philosophical importation with him, not an indigenous growth.

Of his other poems the reflective are the best. He became known first for his *Christ on Olympus*, where the Saviour is depicted as urging the older gods to renounce their divinity and win their salvation as men. This remains Gay's most considerable work. He is most effective here and in other poems of similar type where a problem is posed, to be solved by some often unexpected emotional *volte-face* or recognition of human values. As a sonneteer he is in the formal sense one of our most adequate. But he is not Australian so far as the physical background is concerned; he can write, for example, of "the furrowed lea". So he remains a visitor, sympathetic and with insight, but not fully assimilated or assimilating.

In 1884 an ailing bird of paradise alighted in Australia, fluttered from one capital city to another, and left these shores in 1889. A few brilliant feathers remained to tell of his visitation. This was Francis Adams (1862–93), talker, novelist, critic, journalist, essayist, dramatist. To fill all these rôles with distinction would hardly lie within human compass; but Adams during his brief stay was one of the most competent all-rounders in the country.

He was in addition one of the few poets of revolution. In the Preface to his *Songs of the Army of the Night* (1888) he says: " I make no apology for several poems in the First Part which are fierce, which are even bloodthirsty. As I felt I wrote." He goes on to say that he "was [unhappily] born and bred into the dominant class". The injustice that he saw prevailing in England and in the other lands he visited, including Australia, forms the staple of these poems.

The consumption from which Adams suffered exacerbated this bitter sensitiveness. His poems in consequence are filled with vituperation, only occasionally sweetened with a sort of desperate hope. He is a very uneven craftsman. Some of his non-political poems are maudlin, trite, and extremely ineffective. The prose writer, with standards of technique and a contempt for the trivial, and the poet who perpetrated absurdities hardly seem to be one and the same person. Even at his best Adams is, as he has been called, a minor poet; on the other hand it is not always true that he leaves us cold. *London*, for example, has its effect:

> Cruel City, London, London,
>   Where, duped slaves of devils' creeds,
> Men and women desperate, undone,
>   Dream such dreams, and do such deeds:
>
> London, London, cruel city,
>   By day serpent, by night vampire—
> God, in thy great pity, pity,
>   Give us light—though it be fire!

This little poem contains in brief some of the qualities of Adams—his occasional pointed force, his obvious sincerity, his infrequent felicity of phrase; but on the other hand it does not adequately illustrate his recurrent vices—banality, the blandly confident ludicrous, and the stridency of the man writing at the top of his voice. Adams is best in short poems and then when they are couched in the Landorian epigram mould.

It may seem untimely to include Arthur Albert Bayldon in this period. He was born in 1865 and did not die until recently (1958). In addition, most of his poems on Australian themes were published after the turn of the century. On the other hand, his early work, ninetyish in flavour, appeared before 1900, while some of his later is public verse. So he appears linked to the period partly by time, partly by theme.

Born and educated in England, Bayldon came to Australia in 1889. Those who have written on him have detected a withering, after his arrival, of luxuriance in diction and of exuberance in temperament. The suggestion is that the Australian environment or his Australian experiences or the Australian themes or all these produced the change. But there is as much likelihood that he would have changed in the same way even if he had stayed in England. And, again, the withering is not sudden or complete: fifteen years or so after his arrival he could write poems containing luscious phrasing not inferior, or superior, to earlier efflorescences—*fulgent fires, dewy violets, life's turbid tide, lolling lilies, sultry glooms*. This tendency to deliquescence, as it were, links parts of his work with parts of Daley and Quinn.

The other weakness of Bayldon lies in bathos, and this appears in his public verse on Australian themes. Through all his poems Bayldon can hardly write a dozen consecutive lines without lapsing into some absurdity in tone or meaning or expression. For that reason his short poems or his memorials of dead poets are his best. His well-known sonnet *Marlowe* bears out this judgment—the first ten lines with little claim to permanence and the last four redeeming them:

> The revelry of kisses bought with gold;
> The jest and jealous rival and the strife;
> A harlot weeping o'er a corpse scarce cold;
> A scullion fleeing with a bloody knife.

He is a demonstration of the capital difficulty of poetry. Intelligent and persevering, he is yet inferior to, say, Daley; and nobody is going to call Daley anything but a minor poet.

Whether one regards the Australian Nineties as the end of one age or the beginning of another depends on what aspects are stressed. Some poets of the English Nineties left on their period the label *fin de siècle*, with its suggestions of decline and decadence. To think of this applied to the Australian period seems startling in the face of the hearty balladists. But a few poets at least, Daley and Quinn and Arthur Adams, stand aside from this throng. And the first two, derivative in theme and treatment and vocabulary, might have fitted into the English scene without overmuch grooming, to occupy their respective niches.

Both Daley and Quinn, it has been pointed out, were addicted to the fallacy of the "poetical" theme and the "poetical" word. Their poems abound in *lilac*, *gold*, *rose*, *radiant*, *bloom*, *petal*, *wondrous*, *opaline*, and the rest. The melody comes mostly from Swinburne. But the effects in the two poets are rather different: Daley has more than a scent of the hot-house; Quinn's settings are generally in the open air.

Victor Daley (1858–1905) was Irish by birth, and what is popularly associated with the word *Celtic* tinges part of his work. Two of his volumes reveal this—*At Dawn and Dusk* (1898) and the posthumous *Wine and Roses* (1911). If not mystic, he is regretful. He looks to the past, its legends and its youth, love and lost love, wine and roses; and a mist of nostalgia enshrouds it all. In these works Daley was not the contemporary Australian in outlook. There are some Australian themes, but the poems that contain them are not his best.

Daley is a good example of the highly competent minor poet.

His verse is thin in content, melodious in sound, Ninetyish in flavour:

> My songs and sonnets carven in fine gold
> Have faded from me with the last day-beam
> That purple lustre to the sky-line lent,
> And flushed the clouds with rose and chrysolite;
> So days and dreams in darkness pass away.

Which reads like a less intense Dowson or a less skilful Wilde in his *Sphinx* mood. These frequent memories of other poets make Daley sometimes appear a sort of *mélange*: there is the repetitive and alliterative trickery of Swinburne—

> On a golden dawn in the dawn sublime
> Of years ere the stars had ceased to sing—

the juvenilities of Longfellow, only a little more juicy—

> Silently through his Zenana
> Passed he, glanced with cold and careless
> Eyes at women, fair as houris
> Seen in visions bred of hasheesh—

and he knows Tennyson and the old ballads and . . . Oddly enough, he himself is nevertheless recognisable.

Daley's competence seldom permits him to perpetrate the absurdities that are to be found in Quinn. When he falls from his fairly consistent level, it is into conceit and not so often into bathos:

> And, like a peony
> Drowning in wine, the crimson sun
> Sinks down in that strange sea.

And his competence is seen in the structure of his poems: they have a unity of theme, or a point of view, or a point. They seldom meander; so that, however cloying they taste when in bulk, they provide a formal satisfaction.

In a posthumous volume collected in 1947, *Creeve Roe*, we find Daley in his relation to the contemporary scene. The poems, inferior to his others, respond to the demands of politics or economics, but they do provide some indication of Daley's satiric power and rather unexpected humour. He strikes a democratic note, anti-Capital, and opposed to institutional religion. Perhaps the best of them is *O'Callaghan's Apple*, farcical and punning, and indeed not unworthy of Hood in an off moment.

The value of having Daley in full, or nearly so, is that we can see what his possibilities were. The first two volumes show us his skill in words and rime and point; the third shows his satiric gift. All this would have made him an excellent epigrammatist. It was H. J. Oliver who first pointed out Daley's gift in this genre. The best and best-known is *Faith*:

> Faith shuts her eyes,
> Poor self-deceiver!
> The last god dies
> With the last believer.

These little prickles of malice and wit are not very numerous in Daley, but they serve to exhibit the potential talent he had. It is a pity he did not do more of such writing, for it would have admirably suited his capacity—that of the talented dilettante who lacked stamina.

As in Daley, so in Roderic Quinn (1867–1949) we find a poet who wrote one kind of poetry when he was probably better fitted for another. He wrote a lot, and some of it is hardly worth critical discussion. Facile, thin, derivative, it evaporates under analysis. He wrote some bush ballads, but his heart was given to the sweetly melancholy lyric that was written in England by the hundred. Though much of his diction is like that of Daley, he seems more robust. This is due partly to the predominant Swinburnian anapest, partly to the outdoor settings. Quinn is not pulpy: there is a touch of the swashbuckler, of the pseudo-heroic about him. Perhaps he felt this. We may take as self-revelatory the half-jocular lines:

> . . . one, at heart a troubadour,
> May seem a sober citizen.

He thought that what Australian poetry needed was more art. He did not find it in the bush balladists, but England had it in plenty. Unfortunately, for the most part he never mastered art; indeed it may be doubted if he mastered artifice. He seems to be writing on the edge of poetry, to be on the verge of giving us a good poem. A few lines from *The Sea-Seekers* show him near his best:

> A wave of joy and wonder broke
> Across our souls, and in our veins
> An ancient Viking stirred and woke.

But anticlimaxes lay in wait for him. A poem like *The Black Hound* is an exemplary illustration. Three-quarters of it, almost exactly, are adequate; the other quarter is bathos. That is, the first three lines of each quatrain are invariably followed by a fourth line that is ludicrous. This tendency to fail at most inopportune moments is indicative of his lack of ear, of sense of humour, and of technique. No better—or worse—example can be given than this stanza from *At Her Door*:

> The moon to a cloud-cleft stealing
>   Gazed down on the yearning tide;
> The woman opened the streaming door
>   And stood in the rain outside.

Quinn lacks the formal structural competence of Daley. His poems are invertebrate. They seem to have arisen from no perceptible inner compulsion. As if aware of this, he frequently introduces near the end some circumstance that provides an ersatz climax or presents an intrusive and meaningless problem.

He is more concerned with nature than Daley, and the device of making nature correspond in mood with man is a favourite with him. Something of this is found in his two best-known poems, *The Camp Within the West*, which has its own plangency, and *The Currency Lass*, which, despite some Swinburnian absurdities, does produce an atmosphere. This penetration of vision and intensity of feeling extend to pathos. He is then simple and the effect is perhaps the best he ever achieves. *Doing Nothing*, for example, where a woman broods over her dead, has a poignancy superior to that of the anthology piece by Shaw Neilson, *Granny Sullivan*.

Apart from these, perhaps his most successful poem is *Acushla*. The two concluding stanzas run:

> Her feet were fleet, her pretty feet,
>   Upon the hill and hollow;
> She bade me stay, she cried me nay,
>   But still her eyes said "Follow!"
>
> Acushla! Acushla!
>   The cushat dove is cooing;
> To capture her was sweet, indeed,
>   Yet sweeter the pursuing.

This fusion of bucolic and sophisticated is unusual—a sort of country *vers de société*. The restraint, the half-humorous, half-romantic air, the freedom from seriously used "poetical" diction

—this shows us a Quinn who might have become a miniature Locker-Lampson of the Antipodes.

Another poet who does not belong to the balladists or the public poets is more technically competent than either Daley or Quinn. Arthur H. Adams (1872–1936), who belongs to New Zealand poetry as much as to Australian, looked on this continent with a certain chill appraisal. Occasionally he disliked more vehemently—

> The wide sun stares without a cloud:
> Whipped by his glances truculent
> The earth lies quivering and cowed.
> My heart is hot with discontent:
> I hate this haggard continent—

but his attitude mostly was that of the observer—in his case the poetic visitant. Those poems expressing his reactions to Australia —the land, the city, the harbour, the sun, the men—that Adams culled as representative when he was forty and (so he thought) unfitted for further versifying, are few in number, but they are known to us if only through the anthologies. His most famous comment, and the most discussed, is *The Australian*, with its pithy, acute, and deftly turned distichs:

> No flower with fragile sweetness graced—
> A lank weed wrestling with the waste;
>
> Pallid of face and gaunt of limb,
> The sweetness withered out of him.

With all its detachment, this observational verse of Adams is yet, one is tempted to say, more personal than his nominally personal verse: he feels more when he sees than when he feels. His bleak and stoic tone is one not so much of despair, which implies a hope lost, as of endurance. Adams does not expect anything. Some of the chill that he produces even in his admirers may be due to his phrase-making. No other poet of the period equals him in that. But on occasion the polishing seems so obvious that the reader credits him with more skill and less warmth than he really has.

The third group, the largest and most widely recognised, is the Bush Balladists. Gordon was their forerunner (though there is an example by Harpur), Farrell perhaps the first of them as a group, and Paterson their ripe exemplar. In all there were dozens

who wrote bush ballads in small or large amounts and who can
be classed as members. They were in their time regarded as great,
later they were laughed at as not poets at all, and at present they
tend to be considered by most critics as historical indexes
pointing to the taste and sentiment of an age.

A few characteristics appear in common. The period lies
roughly between the middle eighties and, say, 1914, with the
richest harvest in the nineties. The bush ballad is essentially
narrative, it has mostly a swinging metre, it appears in an
apparently unsophisticated diction, and its themes concern the
people of the outback. There are other poems, such as those of
Brady or Dyson, that do not strictly conform, but most readers
would admit them into the group.

The origins have been argued. One theory holds that the
ballad sprang from the bush songs of pre-1860 days. These songs,
sometimes thought of as national spontaneous folk-poetry, were
sung to tunes mostly of the eighteenth century and were parodies
or versions of former poems. Most are anonymous. The best-
known collections are A. B. Paterson's *Old Bush Songs* and the
much larger volume edited by Douglas Stewart and Nancy
Keesing. Many of the poems are humorous expressions of
grievances or wrongs or hardships. The gap between these
anonymous songs and the narrative bush ballads with their
known authors is wide.

Another theory, not perhaps put forward with all seriousness,
is that the ballads are the product of that gift of song which (we
are all supposed to know) is inherent in Scottish folk; in the new
large land this "Scottish power of song . . . leapt to life again".

The obvious explanation is that the ballads were a literary
fashion started by Gordon. In fact there is nothing surprising
in the growth of the ballads: the material was waiting and so
was *The Bulletin*. Those who wrote them were not illiterates, and
the appearance of unsophistication is the result of sophistication.
When we say that a ballad of the period is too literary we simply
mean that it is written in a different style, itself conventional.
The Bulletin remains a repository of these ballads. This weekly
periodical, founded in 1880 and guided by J. F. Archibald,
exercised an enormous influence on Australian writers that extended into the earlier years of the next century. After it had
been going for some years it began to develop a literary policy.
It demanded force and point and brevity in the prose of its

contributors, and in their poetry a national note and a direct reflection of physical actuality. On the other hand it was not narrowly exclusive: it published material from overseas and the lyrics of Daley and Quinn appeared in its pages. A great deal of its contents was written by those who read it. Its essential literary service was to provide the opportunity of publication for writers who otherwise might have lacked it. Its contribution to the creation of a national ethos hardly concerns us. Under these conditions one is tempted to say that the ballads were inevitable. Gordon, it was said, was the originator of the type. He wrote few poems about Australia, and the ones best known are bush ballads—*The Sick Stockrider*, *From the Wreck*, *Wolf and Hound*, and *How We Beat the Favourite* (set in England), all written in 1869. They are characteristic poems of action, exciting, full of movement, with the note of recklessness, and their tendency was to persist. An additional ingredient was to appear later—humour. And the colloquial or slangy note, embryonic in Gordon, was to intensify.

The stress on galloping horses, so marked in these poems of Gordon, is found in *How He Died* (1887), the best-remembered poem of John Farrell (1851–1904). It is the story of Nobbie, who rides for the doctor to save a child injured by a stampede. But the emphasis is more on the sacrifice of the rider, who crawls the last lap of the journey. There is more sentiment and melancholy in Farrell than in most bush balladists; the interest, that is, turns more on the persons than on the action. Apart from his position as the first of the balladists as a group Farrell has little importance. His roughness of rhythm is not a device but a failing, and often plunges the verse into doggerel. His most forcible writing is satire.

With Andrew Barton ("Banjo") Paterson (1864–1941) the bush ballad culminated. He was, for example, more dexterous in rime than most of the rest, and he echoed more truly than Lawson the spirit of the outback, though he very seldom, in contrast to Lawson, depicted the economic and social anomalies of the period and the place.

Paterson was born in the bush, lived there in youth and on holidays, worked in the city, and returned to the bush periodically. To it he gave his love, and about it and its inhabitants he wrote his poems. With few exceptions, and these in comic poems, he portrays the people of the outback as finer people, with more initiative and *nous*, than city-dwellers. He frankly admitted the bias:

> But I "over-write" the bushmen! Well, I own without a doubt
> That I always see a hero in the "man from furthest out".

The outback concurred, and readers in the towns were willing to connive at a gentleman's agreement.

The most cursory reader can recognise Paterson's familiarity with his theme. The life and tribulations of the drover and his feud with the squatter, the pubs, the country race meetings, mustering, hunting, shearing—all in one poem or another find a place. A passage like this is more than a list of technical terms:

> The "ringer" that shore a hundred, as they never were shorn before,
> And the novice who, toiling bravely, had tommy-hawked half a score,
> The tarboy, the cook and the slushy, the sweeper that swept the board,
> The picker-up, and the penner, with the rest of the shearing horde.

Paterson felt that only the bushman could know these things, even perhaps that only the bushman was entitled to write about them. It was perhaps this and some sense of rivalry as well as fondness for a hoax that led to his attacks on Lawson, whose pictures of the pastoral outback were gloomy compared with his own. The things the two men saw had to be different. Paterson's background of public school and university, of comfort and success, predisposed him to see a more cheerful Australia than did the early hardships of Lawson, his search for jobs, his weaknesses, his resentments. Paterson saw the bush from the point of view of a horseman, where Lawson's outlook was that of the swagman out of work.

The idea of mateship, which is generally attributed to Lawson, appears in Paterson in a more individual, more romantic guise, and there is in it adventure or self-sacrifice. Only two or three persons can be concerned. The mateship of numbers, the solidarity of unionism—that aspect Paterson, from the nature of his circumstances and interests, does not treat of. In one of his rare references to it—*A Bushman's Song*—the emphasis is not on the union but rather on the national dislike of the foreigner:

> I asked a cove for shearin' once along the Marthaguy:
> "We shear non-union here," says he. "I call it scab," says I.

I looked along the shearin' floor before I turned to go—
There were eight or ten dashed Chinamen a-shearin' in a row.

It was shift, boys, shift, for there wasn't the slightest doubt
It was time to make a shift with the leprosy about.

Of contemporary events he writes hardly at all. There are
a song of Federation, some poems of the Boer War—which he
mostly treats from a comic or sporting angle—and a few passing
references to such things as the great national borrowing spree
of the seventies and eighties that was to end in the financial
depression of the early nineties:

> It's grand to borrow English tin
>   To pay for wharves and docks,
> And then to find it isn't in
>   The little money-box.

But apart from these rare glimpses of the scene around he looked
back, and saw the past as the true heroic age. So there is implicit
nostalgia in Paterson's poems, recording as they do a pastoral
period with its memories and songs and what may be called its
legends. To this stock of legends Paterson has contributed largely.
His themes are the adventures of the outback, and humour is
the predominant and most successful feeling he colours them
with. This capacity to popularise figures and incidents, to create,
as it were, a sort of folklore, is Paterson's most important contribution.

No other Australian poet has equalled Paterson in popularity,
and the reasons are not far to seek. He tells stories, and they are
often humorous or sardonic. There is action related in swinging
verse; and the background of plain and river and bush—the
open air, in short—makes itself effectively felt. Horses are almost
as important as men, and this presumably appeals to a nation
that is supposed to love horses. Australians are as little of poetry
lovers as any other people; but here they find verse that they
can read with no difficulty. It is about their own country and
their own people and deals with things that, by hearsay at least,
they know something of. A man need not be odd or "sissy"—
some such mechanism as this probably is at work—to read
Paterson.

Whether we can dignify Paterson's rough familiar verse with
the name of poetry is a different matter. Occasionally he does
manage the Australian idiom in such a way that it illuminates

F

his theme, when nothing else in that spot would do as well. The following lines from *Black Swans* show this:

> I watch as the wild black swans fly over
> With their phalanx turned to the sinking sun;
> And I hear the clang of their leader crying
> To a lagging mate in the rearward flying,
> And they fade away in the darkness dying,
> Where the stars are mustering one by one.

Here *mate* and *mustering* are most adequate: an Australian is watching. On many other occasions, however, the material is there, but the writer cannot deal with it. In *The Droving Days* the picture of the plain is deficient:

> Where the air so dry and so clear and bright
> Refracts the sun with a wondrous light,
> And out in the dim horizon makes
> The deep blue gleam of the phantom lakes.

Here *wondrous* makes all the other adjectives suspect. Like the Australian poets before him, though not to the same extent, Paterson takes refuge in the "poetical" word when he feels he has a subject that demands "poetical" treatment. Then appear the stock words, *wondrous, grand, 'twas, old*—this last not in the the sense of *aged*, but in some such incredible phrase as *The same old steed*.

Paterson, in other words, should not be regarded so much as a poet as an historical document. Even today there are many people who can recite him by the yard. Any writer who can do this to his countrymen is not negligible as a force, whatever he may be as a poet. *The Man from Snowy River* is fated to immortality in Australia, and the words as well as the music of *Waltzing Matilda* are now part of our heritage. While this is true we cannot say, as Paterson himself did,

> The old bush life and all its ways
> Are passing from us all unsung.

The picture of the bush drawn by the verse of Henry Lawson (1867–1922) was smudged in charcoal. His background, as was mentioned before, was very different from Paterson's. Lawson was born in a tent on the Grenfell goldfield, ended his formal schooling at thirteen (though he went to night school later), had as hard an early youth as Burns (on a failing selection at Pipeclay), travelled, married, separated from his wife, drank quietly, and

declined at the end into dependence upon the charity of friends.
His knowledge of the outback came from his toil on the selection,
from his travels, and from six months on the track near the
Queensland border.

Lawson felt acutely his lack of early education and easy
opportunity, and he expressed this sometimes as independence,
sometimes as a rather maudlin conviction of future fame. He
was never well-to-do and the struggle embittered him. In his
prose, where he can be seriously considered as an artist, he is too
sincere to let this colour his work very much. In his verse he
vents his disappointment. He takes the literary convention of
writing about the bush and uses it partly, it would seem, to stress
the black as against Paterson's white, and partly, perhaps unconsciously, to express himself.

It is pictures of the bush life—and a fair amount of city life—
that he gives. If bush ballads must have narrative, then Lawson
has not written very many. He describes people and things rather
than relates what happens, and he reflects upon what he has
described. The theme is a very gloomy one. Deaths are frequent
—*The Ballad of the Drover*, where the young man is drowned just
at the last; *Sweeney*, the drunk going off into the rain; *Jack Dunn*,
dying of fever. When the lyric note appears, then it is a young
girl who is going to die. In *The Cattle Dog's Death* it is the dog
that dies. When we meet old friends they are generally destitute,
and they accept a drink with embarrassment and make us feel
guilty for not being destitute also. This distress occurs in the
city, in the slums, and naturally in the prison; man is mostly
responsible for that. In the country Nature is the destroyer,
whether at night after "the sad Australian sunset" or under the
blaze of a merciless sun or in mud to the knees during rain. The
mateship of the outback that is almost Lawson's own literary
creation in his prose does not brighten his verse very much:

> He tramped away from the shanty there, when the days were long
> and hot,
> With never a soul to know or care if he died on the track or not.
> The poor of the city have friends in woe, no matter how much they
> lack,
> But only God and the swagman know how a poor man fares Out
> Back.

The characters are sometimes resigned, sometimes sardonic,
sometimes resentful. Many of them are full of regret for "the

man they might have been". This gloom is pervasive in Lawson; even the humorous poems do not form an exception. It is interesting to read these as a group, gathered together as they are in some editions. The humour, a convention like the other attitudes, is not very successful as humour; but what is more significant is that in such poems one sees beneath the veneer the same statements of grim nature or human complaint or animal misery:

> Desolation where the crow is! Desert where the eagle flies,
> Paddock where the luny bullock starts and stares with reddened eyes.

One link between Lawson's poems and his short stories is the fact that the same themes occasionally serve for both; *The Sliprails and the Spur* and *Ruth*, for example, have their prose counterparts, and the relationship is seen in phrases that are identical. Another link is the democratic note. It is more assertive in the poems, and *For'ard*, *Second Class Wait Here*, *The Army of the Rear*, and others have a militant bitterness not found in the stories. In dealing with women, especially

> where gaunt and haggard women live alone and work like men
> Till their husbands, gone a-droving, will return to them again,

Lawson has the same touch as he has in his prose.

In their kind his poems are not as successful as Paterson's are in theirs. We find, however, an interesting parallel. If we use the term Bush Ballad instead of some wider term such as Australian Ballad, and if we choose a poem to exemplify the type, then we should certainly take Paterson's *The Man from Snowy River*. It is not very good poetry, but it is still a classic. In a different way Lawson provides us with another, *The Teams*. It is not too much to say that from one point of view it is the equivalent in Australian poetry of Gray's *Elegy* in English poetry. The *Elegy*, wrote I. A. Richards, is "the triumph of an exquisitely adjusted tone". Formal, conventional, with the expected adjective, it epitomises the reflection of an age. Of *The Teams* we can say the same, except that it is not reflective but descriptive. This is not to attribute to Lawson the same quivering sensitiveness to a period and its taste as Gray possessed. Lawson's poem has "fixed" the Australian conception of the bullock team. Any Australian who reads poetry has read it, and it has given a slant to his attitude ever since. The picture is an essential part of the older landscape, and we automatically recall it as part of our inheritance. Lawson has given us a sort of norm. It is a better poem now than when it was written, and also a more important one.

The most voluble of the balladists is Will H. Ogilvie (b. 1869), a Scotsman who spent the nineties in this country and continued to write of Australia after his return to his own land. He has produced some dozen and a half volumes of verse, the first in 1898, the last in 1952.

Ogilvie is a writer who suffers from a fatal facility. He is capable of producing rapid fluent verse on almost any subject and in almost any stanza form. It is not then surprising that emotion appears as a thin veneer of sentiment. When he deals with the outback he writes best, but even then the verse has no direct contact with what he writes of. He is false in the same way as an historical novelist who uses some such phrase as: By my halidom, Sir Knight.

When he does not deal with the west he is mildly melancholic and nostalgic. His verses are flooded with a sticky solution of memories, laments for the past, unrequited love, romantic yearning and all the other ingredients in the recipe for poetry. These themes also are not treated with any approach to directness or particularity. He uses metaphor as a refuge and personification as a cloak: even the light of the camp-fire becomes the Rose of the Camp-Fire Light. He tells of a race, but it becomes the Race of My Heart. A girl becomes Beauty or Blue Eyes. The particular becomes generalised, the concrete is veiled with abstraction. Ogilvie is a poet hiding in a mist.

It is interesting to compare him with Lawson. Anyone who has read the latter's *The Sliprails and the Spur* will find it a striking contrast with, say, Ogilvie's *The Parting*. Here is a stanza from the latter:

> He rode with his burden of sorrow
>   To the crest of the Big Divide,
> And he thought of the long lone morrow
>   And bent to the reins and sighed;
> But turned with a great grief laden,
>   And looked back once to the dell,
> And waved a hand to the maiden—
>   And this was the man's farewell.

No-one would claim that Lawson's is a great poem, but at least

it has definition; it is recognisably Australian (which it is supposed to be); and the scene is almost a particular spot. It has
been apprehended directly by the poetic imagination. Now the
opposite is true of the passage from Ogilvie quoted above. It is
vague, generalised, poeticised. It is the conventional horseman
bidding *farewell* (and so presumably he must look back at the *dell*).
The triteness of phrasing and the lack of impact are thoroughly
characteristic of this writer. Ogilvie sees the West through rosy
poetic spectacles. All is unreal; it is in its way something like
medieval allegory and courts of love. To apply the term bush
balladist to Ogilvie seems a crude vulgarism; for his bush is a
grown-up fairyland, and the vigorous swing of the Australian
ballad becomes in his poems the almost formalised movement
(only a little more hurried) in tapestry or bucolic mural.

The danger in Ogilvie is that of the superficial appeal. He
bears on the surface all the characteristics that some people expect
to find in poetry—ease, metre, rime, and a general glaze of
poetical or romantic diction. Indeed his very faults can momentarily be taken for virtues. In one poem, for example, *His Gipps-
land Girl*, a reader can find after the most cursory glance a treasury
of his peculiar attractions: *to war with the World; one red-gold curl;
to work with a will; he strikes each blow for Love; his hopes in the dusk
lay dead*. This verse has, we may say, a vulgar facility. It is
beneath the surface more coarse-fibred than the apparently
coarser work of Paterson and Lawson.

And then, as if to demonstrate the folly of generalisation, he
will sometimes write as a poet instead of as he thinks a poet
should write. *The Overlander*, for example, a rather longer poem
than usual and one written late in life, has good things among
its melodrama and bathos and poor taste:

> I loved the wide gold glitter of the plains
>   Spread out before us like a silent sea,
> The lazy lapping of the loose-held reins,
>   The sense of motion and of mystery
> As the great beasts slid slowly through the grass,
>   One passing one, then letting it re-pass,

where the last two lines, which lie beyond the usual capacity of
Ogilvie, can bear comparison with anything in Paterson.

A great contrast appears in the next poet. The grimness of
the outback is starkly limned in *Where the Dead Men Lie* and
reflected in the temperament of its author, Barcroft Boake

(1866–92), a victim of melancholia, who hanged himself at the age of twenty-six. However worn by repetition, the poem still preserves its bitter force, from its opening—

> Out on the wastes of the Never Never—
> That's where the dead men lie!
> There where the heat-waves dance for ever—
> That's where the dead men lie!
> That's where the Earth's loved sons are keeping
> Endless tryst: not the west wind sweeping
> Feverish pinions can wake their sleeping—
> Out where the dead men lie!

to the indictment of the absentee squatter at its close.

Boake is a poet who serves to show the general justice of anthologies. The poem has been a favourite choice, and rightly so; for not only is it worth quoting, but the others that he wrote are much inferior. They deal with bushrangers, the running down of a brumby, a flight from a trooper, a race, the death of a drover's wife, mustering, a runaway coach. A few are humorous, but most end in a death; this in some poems is unexpected, for it comes after an apparently humorous opening. The change of tone may be deliberate, but coupled with the metrical clumsiness it seems mere dislocation. In one quality possessed by all the vigorous balladists Boake is deficient—and that is movement. Other balladists give the impression of roughness of rhythm; so does Boake. But theirs, so it would seem, is calculated, for it fits the action; Boake stumbles and labours and stammers along. He was reaching competence at his death.

Two poets have some claim to inclusion among the band of balladists, provided the word *bush* is not insisted on. One is Edward Dyson (1865–1931), whose *Rhymes from the Mines* (1896) bears out its title. His experiences as boy and young man on the fields in Victoria provided him with ample material for such poems. His poems about the bush life proper are few, and then it is the selector and the timber feller that he deals with, not the squatter. And such poems are not narrative like the usual ballads, but chiefly descriptive. He contrasts more than once the town and bush life. His *In Town* is like Lawson's *Faces in the Street*:

> Out of work and out of money—out of friends that means, you
>   bet—
> Out of firewood, togs and tucker, out of everything but debt—
> And I loathe the barren pavements, and the crowds a fellow meets,
> And the maddening repetition of the suffocating streets.

Then to redress the balance he gives *The Drovers in Reply*:

> We are wondering why those fellows who are writing cheerful
>   ditties
> Of the rosy times out droving, and the dust and death of cities,
> Do not leave the dreary office, ask a drover for a billet,
> And enjoy "the views", "the campfires", and "the freedom" while
>   they fill it.

But Dyson's mining poems are his most characteristic. They cover the subject—the characters such as the fossicker, the old digger who has lost the track to his find, the preacher near the field, the trucker; incidents and scenes such as the worked out mine, a rescue, a joke against the Chinese that misfired. He stresses the common sharing of hardships and good luck, an aspect that corresponds to the pastoral mateship of the other balladists. The sense of striving, of challenge met and conquered, again is found:

> But the life's not full of trouble, and the fellow is a fool
> Who cannot find some pleasure down below.

Dyson is the spokesman of the digger who yearns for the old life after he has left it. It is not mere desire for wealth that drives on the prospector, any more than it does the squatter. This note of idealism finds its eloquent expression in what are the best lines hat Dyson wrote:

> Is it greed alone that impels our ranks? Is it only the lust of gold
> Drives them past where the sentinel ranges stand where the plains
>   to the sky unfold;
> Is there nothing more in this dull unrest that remains in the hearts
>   of men,
> Till the swag is rolled, or the pack-horse strapped, or the ship sails
>   out again?
> Is it this alone, or in blood and bone does the venturous spirit glow
> That was noble pride when the world was wide and the tracks
>   were all Westward Ho?

The other poet with his own particular interest is E. J. Brady (1869–1952), one of the few Australian singers of the sea. He voyaged on the sea, and he worked as a shipping clerk. And his travels in New South Wales and Queensland were extensive. The outcome has been a large amount of travel writing and general comment. It would have been surprising if it had not also resulted in some bush ballads. Brady wrote some, but they are inferior to his sea poems. Some are nostalgic, looking back

to old days and the excitement they provided; some are rather
descriptions of places and comments on typical aspects of the
outback; a few are narrative, humorous or serious or romantic.
Despite the use of technical terms—of plough or harness or bush
—Brady's diction, decorated as it is with words like *a-ploughing*,
mayhappen, *cerement*, *nepenthe*, frequently seems to belong to an
old-fashioned "aesthetic" generation.

Brady's poems of the sea have greater vigour and greater
freshness. They derive from his own experience, and deal with
the cargoes, the loading, the work of the sailor, and the movement
and exhilaration of the ships. His sympathies lie with the sailor
on the ship, the lumper on the wharf, as opposed to the owner
and the agent and the shipping company. He represents that
aspect of the sea as Lawson does the swagman on the track and
Paterson the rider on the station.

Brady's sea poems have considerable gusto. He writes often
in the first person and frequently in a colloquial form. Sometimes
it is Cockney. Even in complaint there is something of the open
sea, of lands over the horizon. The note of the sea-shanty is heard
in such poems as *Yankee Packet*, with its swing and its chorus and
its half-boastful flavour of half-comic adventures.

In his facility, his dexterity in the use of technical terms, and
his feeling that the sea is a British inheritance, Brady resembles
Kipling:

> While her grinding engine's grieving
> In the rolling and the heaving;
> While the sogging seas are swirling
> With the white-capped surges curling
>   She will thunder on her way:
> With her piston rods a-thumping,
> While her heavy bows are jumping
>   Like a porpoise at his play.

Even if we compare him with modern poets, it is true enough to
say that Brady has a more authentic note of life on the sea than
any other Australian. It does not make him a great poet; but
the sense of experience, of felt experience, transpires through the
verse.

The balladists, it can be seen, form a very mixed bag. But the
general nature of their themes, the rough rhythm, and the easy
and colloquial language all combine to make one balladist rather
like another. There are dozens of ballads that, examined

"unseen", might be attributed to any one of a score of balladists. This quality of anonymity, we may recall, is also a characteristic of much eighteenth-century English verse. The other resemblance between these two such utterly diverse types is the diction—each is conventional, that of the bush ballad no less a stock sort of expression than the so-called poetic diction of a very different age.

This is underlined by the work of two poets who were writing in the period. If we have a theme that the balladists normally deal with, and if we put it in language and verse that are not the bush ballad kinds, then the contrast is most pronounced:

> Athwart their base rough gorges stretched, and past
> Precipitous steeps, one large dry gum-creek, paved
> With smooth round boulders, and worn gravel-stones.
> Its banks were loose and blistered. Noon's strong heats
> Had sucked the stream that once hummed hereabout
> True desert-music. So Paul drooped, forlorn,
> (Prone on a sandstone block) with head that bent
> As bends some battered bulrush, maimed by rains,
> And sapped by sudden storms.

This comes from a poem by Philip Holdsworth (1849–1902). Born in Australia, he has a nationalistic note, with a sonnet to North Head and an address to Australia (*A Rhapsody*) among the poems in his sole volume, *Station Hunting on the Warrego* (1885). The title poem tells of two men who moved west in search of pasture. One dies of thirst and fever, the other is rescued when at the point of death. This is a common ballad theme, but as treated by Holdsworth it hardly seems Australian at all, and this despite the use of native terms like *gunyah* and *warrigal*. It is interesting to note the literary conventions and patterns that set it apart from the bush ballads. Equally interesting to note is what it lacks. Put in a collection of the bush ballads it would stand out like pin-striped morning trousers among moleskins.

Another example, this time Wordsworthian instead of Arnoldian, deals with a bushfire. The author was Thomas Heney (1862–1928), whose second volume, *In Middle Harbour*, appeared in 1890.

> Five years ago, a boy, I went to make
> Holiday with a brother living near;
> He, first a stockman in the north, went out
> Into far Queensland, and thence many times
> Had brought down herds of cattle half gone wild
> In deserts on the Cooper or Paroo.

Bushfires close in and devastate the valley:

> A racing tide of flame, that e'en the smoke
> Irradiated with an angry glow.
> The wind flung down upon us blazing leaves,
> Still glowing embers, and the swirling ash.

After rain they return to the burnt-out homestead:

> Hence to the latest moment of my life
> Mine eyes shall keep remembrance of that gaze
> When, while the horses tore at the loose reins,
> I saw the valley all a hell of flame.

If Wordsworth in tired middle age had been transplanted to Australia, he might have written something rather like this.

Arguments about the bush ballads have not yet ended. Most critics agree that as poetry they are generally not of a very high order, and are inferior to the border ballads some three or four hundred years before them. (Any defence of them on the grounds that they will be remembered is off the point—*Little Miss Muffet Sat on a Tuffet* will have as long a life, and for reasons just as irrelevant to the question of worth.)

We remember and relish them as we do the photos in a family album. They afford pictures of a past, or part of it, couched in a medium that the readers of that past found acceptable. Some of the reality of the Australian background transpires through the verse, and it is doubtful if there is any verse before where this happens. We also, with a sort of half-acknowledged self-deception, see ourselves in them. The picture of Australians as laconic, generous, daring, humorous men is, we know, not true of most of us however it may have fitted some of the real or imaginary characters then. But all the same it is a picture that we should not be unwilling to have outsiders accept.

CHAPTER VI

Turn of the Century: Fiction

§ 1

THE chief novelist of the end of the century was Rolf Boldrewood, whose major work has been discussed in a previous chapter. Apart from him three women occupy the stage, two of whom continued to write into the new century.

The first is Ada Cambridge (1844–1926). Born in England, she came out in 1870 as the wife of the Rev. George Cross. She soon began to write for *The Australasian*, not (she says) "because I found any fascination in such work to dispute the claims of the house and family, but to add something to the family resources when they threatened to give out". Nineteen of her novels appeared in book form, a few as newspaper serials.

She treats her themes in an easy clear style, of which the fullest and maturest example appears in her book of reminiscences, *Thirty Years in Australia* (1903). This volume has a value and an insight beyond any to be found in the novels. In it she wrote of her own experiences, and being in life a sensible and truthful woman, she produced a work of much charm.

In fiction her main concern is love, and she rings the changes from novel to novel. Such facile relationships are set nearly always in middle-class domestic interiors, where wealth or at least comfort reigns, and on the fringes of which aristocratic connections hover deliciously. Poetic justice prevails, and marriages generally conclude the lengthy sequence of minor incidents.

To talk, as some have done, of a range of characters in her work is futile. There are so few characters. It is true she can produce the humorous oddity or minor eccentric, such as Major Duff-Scott in *The Three Miss Kings* (1891), while in *Materfamilias* (1898) the unconscious self-revelation of the narrator telling her story in the first person is amusing if a little obvious; but apart from such successes she is content with pasteboard figures.

The "advanced" views that have been detected in her poetry

do not obtrude themselves in her novels. She dislikes humbug and hypocrisy and despises mere conventional subservience to social demands, and though a clergyman's wife she thinks that all creeds have some value for living. She reflects a contemporary tendency. Occasionally, as in *A Marked Man* (1890), she puts into the mouth of a character opinions that still startle and shock with their realistic bluntness. In this passage Delavel speaks of his dead wife:

"... since she is dead, I *am* glad—I am, I am! I am glad as a man who has been kept in prison is glad to be let out. It is not my fault—I would be sorry if I could. Some day, Hannah—some day, when we have been dust for a few hundred years—perhaps for a few score only—people will wake up to see how stupid it is to drive a man to be glad when his wife is dead."

The settings are Australian, with a few English; but there is no essentially Australian atmosphere. It indicates that her persons are those of a class in Australia who did not differ essentially in outlook and values from the same class at that time in England. They were the class of people she belonged to and whom she knew best. The amusing anomaly is that she accepted their values more completely than she was aware of. She laughs at snobs and gives them their deserts; if characters are too aware of social distinctions, then she portrays them unfavourably. But she herself is as much an unconscious snob as any. She loves her aristocrats, and graces her novels with—to use her own phrases—"born ladies" and "born gentlemen". Some of this may have been due to the demands of her readers; but the tendency is so marked that it seems natural to her. Indeed, perhaps her only concessions to her public lie in romance. Love and kisses she serves up with cream—

[he] laid his lips in solemn passion upon hers, which met them as flowers meet the morning sun——

sometimes with more piquant sauce—

He fell upon her like a ravening wild animal, and nothing was heard for a time but kisses, sobs, and the crooning of her honeyed voice.

The more refined are more restrained—

Reverently, as if taking consecrated bread, he raised her hand to his bowed face.

Her noble English homes seem like another concession, but this is by no means certain—

> Behold the towers and turrets of the ancestral castle . . . And then consider the interior magnificence of the great home—these chambers innumerable, in which Royalty has slept . . .

We may hope that the novels are mere sops to public taste—but we come to feel that they express her, that they serve as indulgences, as compensations, that they are almost her dreamworld.

The most remarkable thing about Ada Cambridge is not what she has written but what critics have written about her. This leaves in the mind of a reader the implication that she is to be considered a novelist of some stature. As social and historical documents unconsciously throwing light on attitudes and outlooks prevalent among certain classes of the period her novels are of value. As novels they have the value that derives from variety or ingenuity in plot.

The best novel of the second writer surpasses any by Ada Cambridge. This is *Uncle Piper of Piper's Hill* (1889), the author of which used the name "Tasma". She was by a second marriage Jessie Couvreur (1848–97). Brought to Tasmania at the age of four, she lived there until 1867, when her first husband took her to Melbourne. She left this country in 1873 for Europe, and wrote all her novels abroad.

Like Ada Cambridge, she wrote about love, but developed her own particular version—that of the ill-matched husband and wife. *In Her Earliest Youth* (1890) contains the cultured and sceptical Pauline Vyner and the pleasure-loving, bibulous, and gambling George Drafton. They are not happily married but eventually, despite the plottings of the suave Sir Francis Seagrave, the pair make a satisfactory compromise. In *The Penance of Portia James* (1891) the girl again is unwilling but is persuaded by her family and bound by a half-understood engagement. Immediately after the ceremony a spectre from the husband's past arrives on the doorstep with her illegitimate child. This revelation drives Portia to flight. In the end, after the convenient demise of the other woman, husband and wife are reconciled by the prospect of looking after the unfortunate child. In *A Knight of the White Feather* (1892) we encounter a woman unhappily married to a man her inferior in culture and a drunkard to boot. But the chief theme concerns John Fullerton, effeminate and cultured, apparently well matched with Linda Robley. Unfortunately he turns out to be a coward. At last, however, he saves their son from drowning at the cost of his own life, and Linda, distracted and remorseful, rejects the dashing Greville, a contrast to her late husband. The fourth example, *A Fiery Ordeal* (1897), starts with a similar situation: Ruth Fenton is married to a gambler, drinker, and waster. After ruining them both he decamps, goes mad and, setting fire to the bush around the homestead where she has gone, is burnt to death. Ruth marries Donald Brewer, her rich and handsome benefactor.

All these four novels, then, are variations on a theme, one expressed in a line by Tennyson—

Thou art mated with a clown.

The wife in each case is superior to her husband. In addition there is always the other man, a contrast to the husband and his superior in some ways at least. But the wife does not always marry him. Two of the novels end in reconciliation, one in abnegation, only one in marriage.

Tasma's best novel is her first, *Uncle Piper*. Uncle Piper, a rich, dogmatic, uneducated, and intolerant vulgarian with a kind heart underneath it all, is not at ease with his varied relatives, though he is devoted to his little daughter Louey and is kindly disposed towards his sister. The rest are a mixed bag: his step-son the Rev. Francis Lydiat, intense and austere; his step-daughter Laura, an example of the New Woman, sceptical and unorthodox; his nieces Margaret, homely but kindly, and Sara, beautiful but selfish and fickle; his brother-in-law Cavendish, snobbish, ineffective, unpractical, resentful; his son George, resistant to persuasion, contemptuous of his father's opinions and attitudes. The ending is romantically and poetically just. The deserving Margaret is happily married, the undeserving Sara is left in petulant suspense, Laura and George (related only by marriage) marry, and general reconciliations occur. The characters are among the best drawn by any Australian woman novelist before 1900.

In the remaining novel, *Not Counting the Cost* (1895), the Clare family travel to Europe to run down Hubert de Merle, a kinsman holding a large ruby that has been bequeathed to the female branch of the family. They meet by the sheerest chance and Hubert, an ominous and embittered hunchback, befriends the now destitute family. But it is only to capture Eila, the daughter. The arrival of her lover from Tasmania frustrates the evil plot.

These six novels by Tasma have a greater solidity than the work of Ada Cambridge. This is due to her comparative success in characterisation. Piper and Hubert de Merle and Madame Delaunay and some others are drawn with skill. On the other hand she is inferior to Ada Cambridge in the handling of a story. She repeats a situation with variations—the inferior husband, the superior wife, the attractive benefactor. The themes are promising enough, but there they end. Tasma sets herself problems and does not know how to deal with them. She then folds her hands and offers up a prayer to the *deus ex machina*. This personage invariably responds, using as his wand the device of coincidence. A bolting horse injures a child and quarrels are forgotten; a child falls ill just in time, and husband and wife are reconciled; the woman betrayed is run over, and so husband and wife can come together and rear the child; a child is swept away, but is saved by the cowardly father; a mad husband fires the bush conveniently near the homestead where wife and benefactor are staying, and is conveniently burnt to death. These novels, though too long, are good for the first half. Tasma is the novelist of lost opportunities.

The most personally interesting of these three women is Rosa Praed (1851–1935), *née* Murray-Prior. Her novels appeared as written by Mrs. Campbell Praed. She was born in Queensland and lived there until 1876, when she went to England with her husband. She returned once to Australia on a visit. All her volumes, some forty-six in number, she wrote outside this country. There are some reminiscences: *My Australian Girlhood* (1902), telling of her childhood and young womanhood, full of descriptions, but less vivid than *Australian Life: Black and White* (1885). She uses it as an emotional chronicle. Her novels comprise nearly all the rest of her work. A few she wrote in collaboration with Justin McCarthy. In her later life she became obsessed with the occult, aspects of which appear in her novels from the start. About half her novels deal with Australian scenes wholly or in part.

In such a bulk of work there had to be repetition. She uses certain themes—the bush, politics (where her father's position as Postmaster General in the Ministry afforded her a vantage point), the English immigrant of good family, occult influences. Now this would be a reasonable stock-in-trade if she had written half the number of novels and if they had been shorter. As it was, she had to pad to fill out. In consequence many pages are tiresome.

The second of her Australian novels, *Policy and Passion* (1881), has aspects that are to be used again in various forms. The chief character, Longleat, is Premier of Leichhardt's Land (Queensland), and is a powerful rough man of obscure antecedents. The book has two chief threads, one the political career of Longleat and his entanglement with a married woman, the other the infatuation of his daughter Honoria for Barrington, an Englishman of culture and social aplomb. Longleat poisons himself when his convict past is revealed; Honoria escapes Barrington's fascination and attempted seduction and marries Dyson Maddox, her Australian admirer. The novel is the best of her Australian works, but it contains faults of probability. The suicide of Longleat, as has been pointed out, is not in the least necessary. He had been transported to Western Australia for shooting the seducer of his sister. A man of Longleat's temper and character would almost certainly have defied his political opponents, would have denied any sense of shame, and declared that he would do the same thing again. And he would have been cheered for it.

Other themes appear in *Mrs. Tregaskiss* (1895), the story of a woman who finds her husband spiritually out of accord with her aspirations. Rosa Praed's own unhappy marriage is the undoubted basis of the theme. At the end of the book husband and wife are reconciled after the death of their child lost in the bush. This theme of dissatisfaction of wife with husband links Rosa Praed with Tasma, whose first marriage ended in divorce.

The other novels are not remarkable. The last two she wrote, for example, show no advance over the ones written at the start of her career. *Lady Bridget in the Never-Never Land* (1915) is a collection of her usual subjects, with the hypnotic theme stressed a little more:

> His black orbs stared with a disquieting fixity—a sort of inhuman power—from out of his foreign-looking face. That stare was his chief weapon in the subjugation of women—they called it magnetic.

Sister Sorrow (1916), in which she draws on her memories of life

G

on Curtis Island, is the most occult of her purely fictional works, the references ranging from astrology—

> "Those born under the star of Sorrow and often forced by destiny into the Mystic Path and maybe shaped by the Higher Powers to heavenly purposes"—

to some form of faith healing—

> He was drawing down vivifying magnetism from the Custodians of the Life Forces.

The theme of personal subjugation by hypnotic influence is the essence of the book. Written at the end of her career as a novelist, it is very long and exhibits how practice has given her a capacity to spin out trivia to voluminous tenuity. *Nulma* (1897) is her second best work, and deals with a favourite subject—the Australian girl and the Englishman and the Australian man. This novel, written about the middle of her writing career, contains a vivid and well-developed picture of a jealous woman, confident at first in her power of fascination, then feeling doubts and suspicions, testing her lover and herself, torturing herself in the process and then, sophisticated woman though she is, resorting to crude deception. Parts of the dialogue, bitter and revealing, could only have been written by a woman.

As a writer Rosa Praed is easier and more competent than Ada Cambridge and Tasma. As a depicter of character she has drawn nothing as good as the amusing collection of oddities in Tasma's *Uncle Piper*. As a builder of plots she affords a rough contrast with Tasma, who is quite interesting when she sets a problem, but irresponsible in the solution. Rosa Praed's novels tend to linger in the first half; then they gather speed and gallop into sentimentality and melodrama.

The claims advanced for her fiction appear too large. They may be due to a confusion between what she was and what she wrote. She lived a long time and she saw many changes; as a girl she knew the bush and the coast, and she lived for a period on an island; she was a figure in the social life of the Queensland capital; she travelled widely; she was accepted in English literary circles and she knew the literary lions of her day. She had many varied interests—politics, the aborigines, fiction, drama, spiritualism, occultism, reincarnation. And the mere bulk of her fiction, over forty novels, is imposing. She was in fact such an extraordinary figure that it is hard to believe she did not write extraordinary or even great novels. But she herself was more interesting than the novels she has left us.

She may have thought so herself. She had been an imaginative young girl yearning for she knew not what, fretted by vague dreams and aspirations, thoughtful and perplexed, delighting in attention, avid of new experiences, willing to submit herself to a personality stronger than her own provided it was not merely physically potent, finding no answers in men and turning then for a solution and a satisfaction to the supernatural. Had she not written novels she might have been a minor Marie Bashkirtseff. Her novels are her tentative autobiography.

Some of the novels of the mid-century, those of the Guidebook Period, were instructive and interesting both. A few attempted to be edifying, with moderate success. The time-hallowed method of allegory to coat the edification was the device used by J. H. Nicholson (1838–1923) some thirty years later. It appeared in his volume *Halek, a Romance*, published in England in 1882 and in Queensland in 1896. It was followed by a companion volume *Almoni* (1904). The titles are significant. Nicholson said they were derived from Hebrew roots, and he used such forms consistently. They give the novels a specious air of the exotic, but they make the narrative harder to follow.

Halek is an allegory of the progress of the soul, from a concern with the materialistic to a sort of inner peace. The hero, who gives his name to the book, is a rather unstable enthusiast who tells the story of his pilgrimage but leaves us at the end rather in the air. He attempts poetry and music and gains fame in poetry.

The novel is a sort of sermon, homiletic in theme, and Nicholson's style hardly suffices to cover the even lack of savour. Such an allegory owes much, probably has to owe much, to similar works. There are echoes of Johnson, especially in the style, which is full of balance and antithesis:

> I knew not that my sorrows were only beginning, and that if the future were never bright, the present were but barely endurable.

This might with no alteration at all have come from *Rasselas*. And the occasional interpolated tale and fable irresistibly remind us of the *Arabian Nights* and the story of the barber's third brother. The movement from one land to another is like Butler's *Erewhon*. But Nicholson lacks Butler's irony. He seldom uses satire. One of the few examples occurs early in the book, where he describes the religious sect, the Black-whites, who worship a black stone:

> The all-in-all of their faith is to believe that this stone is white; and this faith is the all-in-all of their religion.
> Their form of worship is extremely simple. The elders stand in a circle round about the stone, and when they have joined hands, they rush thereon, head first, and continue this exercise until they are stunned by the repeated shocks. When the elders have performed their duties, it is the turn of the young men; then come the women; and lastly, the children walk up to the stone, and touch it with their foreheads, but not so as to hurt themselves.

Such passages are uncommon. Were they more numerous the book would be more lively.

Some passages in the work, if they occurred in *Erewhon*, would certainly be the preludes to dead-pan excoriating satire on some idiot customs of benighted and deluded humanity. But in Nicholson they are quite serious and artless and well-meaning. His allegory is over-long. All allegories, in fact, are probably too long; for a sustained pretence becomes wearing, like a solemn joke too long drawn out. And the lack of satire in *Halek* leaves it, in addition, too bland. In short, if allegory is not satire, then it must, as with Bunyan, be handled by a preacher of genius.

§2

In the eighties and nineties better fiction appeared in the form of the short story than in the novel. Much of this was due to the influence of *The Bulletin*. This periodical, it is agreed, played a major rôle in the formation of Australian literature. Its influence was at its greatest in the concluding years of the nineteenth century and the early years of this. One important contribution it made was the opportunity it offered of publication and payment. The stories it preferred were for the most part terse objective sketches or tales of Australian life, especially bush life. Its contributors knew the people, the scenes, and the incidents they were dealing with, and under suggestions from the editors they developed something of a genre—perhaps it is not too much to call it the Australian short story—with qualities of colloquial narration, a natural dialogue, and a sort of humorous realism. (These points are well made, and the contrast between the *Bulletin* story and the prevalent story emphasised, by Ken Levis in his article in *Southerly*, no. 4 of 1950.)

The earliest competent practitioner in the century was John Lang, already dealt with as the author of *The Forger's Wife* (1855), who wrote a volume of short stories on Australian themes, *Botany Bay* (1859). The best story in it is the account of Fisher's Ghost, dealing with the apparition, the discovery of the body, the arrest and trial of the murderer, the ingenious defence, and the ultimate confession. His writing is surprisingly modern in style, and this tale, probably the first short story of mystery and detection in Australian fiction, can be read still without having to make allowance for oddities or crudities in expression or construction.

Mary Vidal's stories in her *Tales for the Bush* (1845) antedate those of Lang but cannot be put on his level. Their preaching has already been discussed. The only other writer of competent short stories before the nineties is Tasma. She wrote, as we have seen, six novels. They are as novels superior to most of the short stories contained in her *A Sydney Sovereign* (1890). There are five of these, the first inordinately long, on the theme of the constant woman who is gently remorseless in her devotion and at last gets the reward of her long waiting; one on a cynic's sacrifice on a burning ship; one that is cynical and realistic in its treatment of a Frenchwoman helped to a new life in Australia; one improbable tale of a French girl disguised as a man in the outback; and a story of the bush where the selector's mate goes off because he loves the other's wife. This is the fairly well-known *How A Claim Was Nearly Jumped in Gum-Tree Gully*, long recognised as possessing some of the qualities that stamp the yarns of Lawson.

The rich field of horror and injustice during the convict system serves as material for the short stories of Price Warung. This is the pen-name adopted by William Astley (1855–1911). He was a journalist and freelance writer all his life and knew conditions in Victoria, Tasmania, and New South Wales. His strong democratic sympathies were shown in his activities in the Labour cause. Like Marcus Clarke he studied the old penal system and made use of this knowledge in his short stories.

Warung's work lies half-way between pure fiction and documentary writing: he makes up dialogue and names and modifies events; but the names of real persons occur as well, and many of the events have a basis in fact. His sympathies become a bias.

Hating the cruelties he recounts, he extends the hatred to officials, to the System and even, one sometimes feels, to the mere exercise of official authority. He is on the side of the underdog; but the underdog under the System was, as Warung well knew, not invariably a deserving case. So he is obliged to pick and choose—many of his convict heroes or chief characters are educated men of good birth. He is not under the same restriction when dealing with officials, since he considers that all of them, with hardly any exceptions, have been indelibly tainted by the prevalent brutality. A striking example of this attitude appears in *The Pegging-Out of Overseer Franke* in the volume, *Tales of the Early Days* (1894). The wretched victim is stunned; then on regaining consciousness he has his hand used as a target, is flogged, and then is pegged out beside an anthill. This appalling recital Warung offers almost with relish. Nothing, it seems, is too bad for an official. The point made, however, is that brutality brutalises. The ring-leader in the affair is a gentleman convict named Edgar Allison Mann, who is himself aware of this:

> . . . when the back of a gently-born transport had once been stained with the infamous stigma of the lash-point, only two things, if he were not to become utterly bestial, remained for him to do: to kill his tyrant, and—to die . . .
> "Flog me, and by God who looks from the heaven above, you're a dead man, Mr. Franke."

But Mann is flogged, and what he dreads comes to pass—he becomes a beast:

> After they pegged him out, they placed some victuals and water —just outside his reach. It was Mann who suggested that last refinement.

Warung's stories, then, are strong meat, and his method of narration corresponds. He has a capacity to hold interest, to awaken and sustain suspense—to tell, that is, an exciting tale.

The picture of the bush as harsh but rewarding, a sort of testing ground for the human spirit, and one moreover in which the spirit may find itself—this picture finds no place in the short stories of Barbara Baynton (1862–1929). The idyllic note one does not expect—that appears, and then only occasionally, in some novels around the middle of the century. But one might expect a certain amount of the heroic, some picture of the striving, though the striving be vain. Barbara Baynton gives us neither. With a sombre and embrowning eye she shows us people, partly as the outback has made them, partly as they are without its brutalising or stultifying imprint, but all as victims.

The same pessimistic outlook is found in her novel, with its title that is characteristic of her—*Human Toll* (1907). The orphan child Ursula is brought up in a household that she finds hateful. The parson is a sadistic hypocrite, the schoolteachers are cruel and unjust, and the people in the township brutalised. (There is an astonishingly good account of a drunken dance.) Mina the red-headed girl tricks Andrew into marriage. In the end Ursula, Mina, the baby, and a few aborigines are shown us on a remote selection. Frustrated in her attempts to smother her child, Mina pursues the others with an axe. Ursula flees into the bush with the child in her arms. After days of tormented wandering she sees two figures approaching:

> "Ursie!"
> A great sob broke from her; then—
> "Andree!——"

Which may be rescue or the last delirium. Knowing the general tenor, one suspects the second. The novel form does not suit Barbara Baynton: lacking the discipline of limited space, it allows her to become both melodramatic and maudlin.

Her claims rest on six short stories, three of which are among the best and cruellest written in Australia. All have women as their chief characters: the woman in *Squeaker's Mate*, as enduring as a gumtree in drought, but broken at last; the woman coming to the distant station in *Billy Skywonkie* and then finding she is not wanted; and the mother in her most famous story, *The Chosen Vessel*. Baynton hates the bush and even, one is tempted to think, the people who live in it. There are few kindly characters in her writing, practically all being portrayed as malicious or stupid or drunken, and there is no opportunity for redemption. The mateship in Lawson's stories is a thing not found in hers. With their grim and sordid tones they read almost as if they were a deliberate counterblast to the heroic or cheery or humorous accounts of bush life written by other storytellers of the period. Baynton's intense power is probably unrivalled in Australian short stories.

Some writers give personal details without becoming individual. An example of this practice is Francis Adams. In the short stories contained in his collection, *Australian Life* (1892), he mentions incidentally his malady, books, places he has been to, experiences he has had. But he does not put his trademark on his work. The comments are put in because he wants a detail or so, perhaps because he was at the time very greatly concerned with his own affairs. He is competent, he tells a story with some skill, and he has variety—love story, ghost story, adventure, mystery. His ghost story, *The Hut by the Tanks*, is set in the bush and is as worth remembering as the old classic *Fisher's Ghost*.

As a stranger who for the most part stood outside the life he observed, Adams is sometimes ambivalent in his attitude. This is evident when he writes of incidents with the aborigines. On the one hand he can tell a story from the point of view of the stockman whose mate has been wantonly speared by them; on the other he draws his favourite contrast between the natural kindliness—even tenderness—of a man in his normal relations with his fellows, and the same man's brutality towards the aborigines.

The weakness in the stories, at least for a reader of today, is the melodrama. Indeed practically all minor fiction and some major fiction of last century bear the mark of overwriting, whether in dialogue (where characters strike attitudes and exclaim, Ha!) or situation or reaction. Adams wrote always in haste, partly to keep himself alive, partly because he knew that he had so little life left. In consequence we have some careless and facile writing, and often this facility grows tiresome.

Adams is most effective in mechanical and structural effects, where he displays a fertile and often macabre fancy. So that of his variety the ghost story and the mystery are the ones he writes best.

The short-story writer generally knows what suits him—comedy or tragedy. Not many indeed have been eminent at both. It is hard to tell whether Edward Dyson (1865–1931) knew where his real talent lay. If he thought he was as proficient in the serious as in the comic short story then he was mistaken. He remains the comic historian of the humbler worker in various trades. Dyson had experience of mining and of factory life, and in his short stories he gives us accounts of types, of incidents real and imaginary, and especially of language. In his

Foreword to *Fact'ry 'Ands* (1906) he writes: "What may be called the machinery of this book is the outcome of experience in one establishment; the characters and the incidents are gathered from a wide field. ... I claim for them at least that they are true types of a pronounced Australian class not previously exploited for the purposes of the maker of popular fiction." These stories are best when comic. In *Below and on Top* (1898) the stories are serious and for the most part not successful. In *The Golden Shanty* (1929) the title story is ingenious and funny. But the very best of Dyson is found in his comic tales of factory hands. The nearest approach to success in a serious vein is a sort of half-humorous grotesque pathos in *A Saturday at Spots'*, the story of the ill-dressed girl, with religious convictions, who destroys the finery of two of her companions. The packer, Feathers, wise in the ways of women, accuses her:

> Spotty dug a finger in her mouth, and squirmed for a moment, and then her eyes gleamed and she stood erect for a fine effort.
> "They was offensive in the sight of the Lord!" she said. Then she collapsed again, her finger went back into her mouth, she began to cry, and kicking her old skirt out with her knee, she said, with stupid bitterness, " 'N' mine is sich rags."

The humour in his stories may be thought crude, but it has a yeasty heartiness. Some derives from his representation of the language, its pronunciation and turns of phrase, and especially the slang—*a dilly mag, a flash tom on each fin, cop socko*. Some depends on mother wit, as in the comment on a dirty member of the factory:

> He was streaky too, and the packer explained: "Sleepy don't wash it off, 'e just turns it over."

One of Dyson's most effective resources is a gift for the startling and ludicrous metaphor or simile: *weeping like a wet day; all went merry as a married belle; purring like a gorged tiger;* and, less obvious and more pointed: *She was disliked and respected by the whole factory.*

Dyson became more skilful as he continued to write, his plots neater, and at his best, say, in *The Haunted Corner*, he is as funny as Lawson in *The Loaded Dog*. He hardly attained the suave expertness of the later night-watchman stories by W. W. Jacobs, but he is the nearest Australian equivalent. Dyson is probably rather under-rated by us, a state of affairs not common in

Australian criticism. If he had lived and written in America he would be famous.

One writer of short stories has had his full share of literary good fortune. Almost everyone has heard of Mrs. Grundy, but few know of Thomas Morton, the creator of the phrase that enshrines her in the play in which she does not appear. Perhaps as many have heard of the gay Lothario, but probably as few as before know of Nicholas Rowe, the author of the play which that character graces. This capacity to name or make a character that takes on an odd life outside a book is quite unpredictable. The Australian equivalents of such characters are Dad and Dave, whom all Australians have heard of. But their creator, unlike Morton and Rowe, is as well known as his creations. Steele Rudd, the pen-name of Arthur Hoey Davis (1868–1935), is as familiar a name as Henry Lawson. And yet nobody would make claims of much excellence for Rudd any more than for Morton. So Rudd has been lucky. Films and the radio and comic strips have helped him, but the element of caricature in portrayal and dialogue has also played its part.

The books in which the members of the Rudd family and of other similar families appear are numerous. The title of short story has been denied these tales, and with some justice. On the other hand each sketch is complete, and each has a separate incident to itself. They form a series of comic extravaganzas in which mishaps accumulate. The scenes, according to Rudd's statement, are based on his own experiences in the Queensland outback or on the Darling Downs. The humour arises from extravagance of language and accident. And Rudd does not believe in wasting material: if he thinks an incident funny, then he believes it is even funnier if it occurs three or four times. As Rudd continued to write and his books became more and more popular, he tended to greater extravagance and caricature. In the earlier books there is something both humorously and pathetically heroic about Dad; in the later ones he is reduced almost to a burlesque. Rudd is a writer, not very important in himself, who has made a contribution to our folklore.

One writer might be included in the last section as well as in this, since he is known for both novels and short stories. And he belongs to both the nineties and the early years of this century. This is Albert Dorrington (b. 1871), who came to Australia aged sixteen, and spent a busy twenty years writing and travelling.

He knew the seaboard from Adelaide to Cape York, parts of the inland, and even the islands and ports to the north of the continent. All his fiction except the first volume of short stories was written after he left Australia.

The best of his novels is *And the Day Came* (1908). Dorrington is something of a stylist, and when he wishes he can hit out an epigram or a sentence that stings and a witticism that leaves its barb in the memory. There were, of course, stylists before, but beside him they appear a little outmoded. Dorrington reads modern, he seems to belong to our century despite the flavour of the nineties. So that on starting this novel about Nora Hastings, a young woman of the outback, the reader is agreeably surprised. Here, it seems, we have a cultivated and sophisticated writer looking at the bush from a fresh angle. We appreciate the malice—

Few women of her weight had a place in Manton's memory,

or—

All the men she knew lived by the grace of cattle.

But Dorrington cannot keep it up. It is not long before the plot takes his hand and guides it to a different section of the dictionary. Nora is betrayed by the supercilious Manton, is deserted, follows him to England, hands over her child to a woman to be brought up, and finally after Manton's repentance and murder at the hands of a jealous rival finds her son again. We read that

Each word he had uttered ate like a thin flame into her soul.

The boom and hiss of stagey declamation are orchestral—

"Lord Belstrade . . . you titled blackguard!"
She struck him across the face with her open hand.
"Actress!" he said hoarsely. "Let me pass."

The names of two other novels are striking enough—*The Lady Calphurnia Royal* (1909), written in collaboration with A. G. Stephens, the story of an Australian woman, a fabulously wealthy *femme fatale* who pursues a vendetta against the man who killed the Pasha her husband in a duel; and *Our Lady of the Leopards* (1911) relating the adventures of Larry Delaney in a valley in India where a castle encloses the Princess Thanila Atamala, her attendant Paula, and the ape god Huniman.

In the story of adventure Dorrington tells a straightforward narrative in an exciting way. *A South Sea Buccaneer* (1911) contains in the form of short stories the adventures of Bully Hayes, pearler and miner and owner of luggers, one of the precursors of the granite-chinned, iron-fisted heroes of the strips. His habitat is the east coast of Queensland, the Coral seas, and the ports to the north. In the novel *Children of the Cloven Hoof* (1911) the setting is the Queensland outback, where the Bellinger family of father and sons are horse thieves. The story is a murder mystery, in which Eustace Fitzallan is accused of a murder really committed by Martin Bellinger. The sequence of crime, trial, re-trial, and acquittal is of its kind as good as Dorrington's best. But he is most likely to be remembered for his short stories. His earliest collection, *Castro's Last Sacrament* (1900), contains examples characteristic of him. They are quite short, almost sketches at times, melodramatic in action, exotic in setting, startling in climax. The style varies from a heavy and calculated understatement, so obvious as to be equivalent to a shout, to sensational or sentimental phrases and figures. Dorrington remains the best known of the short-story writers of the period who deal with such subjects.

These short-story writers have each of them their own interest, but they all, except Baynton, seem preliminary, in importance if not always in time, to the next figure. Beside Henry Lawson they are smaller or odder or thinner than when on their own. For bulk and a fairly consistent level of excellence he stands very much by himself. In all, he wrote some 300 short stories, of which about half appeared in volumes over a period of nearly twenty years.

He is spoken of as the most Australian of our authors. This is true—provided certain qualifications are made. His characters are drawn from certain small classes. He can give us the squatter, selector, drover, shearer, teamster, digger, the swagman who had been or was or would be any one of these or none, and sometimes a city type like the small larrikin. His women of the bush or of the boarding-house are among his best creations. These belong to a certain period of our national life, and in drawing them Lawson is fair enough. The squatter on the whole he does not much like, but he redresses the balance every now and then by picturing a kindly one (probably one who has been on the track before becoming prosperous). Even the shanty-

keeper or bush publican, so often a blood-sucking parasite prey-
ing upon the shearer—even here Lawson gives the other side and
in *A Bush Publican's Lament* he puts the case for the former object
of his indignant pen. He is, then, just in his portraiture, and at
the same time limited. He draws on what he knows best.
Within those limits he is sensitive to atmosphere and character.
The humour and humours of the types are caught, the turns of
phrase, the outlook—it is a little world, and nowhere but in
Australia at a certain time could it all exist together. In this he is
essentially Australian, and probably nobody else, not Paterson
or Furphy even, rivals him in just that quality.

The fact that as a picture of Australia it is partial has been
stressed by some critics. The criticism is just: that he shows us
the outback in drought, and sometimes in flood; but he does
not give us a good season. And the claim that his characters
belong to the group that made Australia great is rightly
rejected. Lawson grew up amongst struggle, and he lived
amongst failures. The men and women he drew are not those to
make a country great or prosperous. Nations may be praised
for their good and humble men, but they are made by their
strong and ruthless ones. Lawson was the writer of failures.
He knew them, he felt for them, he was in many ways like
them. In the end, perhaps he tended to use them—they became
copy.

Nearly all his stories are quite short. Their manner of narration classes them as what are called "yarns", easy-going, colloquial stories, sometimes pausing (as in life) to answer an
objection or comment, ambling on again, occasionally looking
as if they were going off on a side-track, but brought back by a
listener. The first person narrative is favoured by Lawson, the
story told by a man lounging against a tree or squatting on his
heel or lying beside a small camp-fire. Sometimes it is the story
itself that matters, sometimes it is the way it is told, the reflection
of the storyteller in the yarn, sometimes it is the background.
Very seldom indeed is it the neat slick O. Henry type with the
surprise ending. Nor is it the well-tailored story of a competent
writer like Maugham. Lawson's later stories tend to be longer
than the earlier ones, and the story element is partly replaced by
description or reflection. Some that he wrote in England are like
essays on the outback.

The stories contain the humour and the pathos that we

associate with his name. The humour we think of as Australian, and it is difficult to pin it down. It has a little cynicism, a little cruelty or heartlessness, some understatement (matched on the other hand by exaggeration), and underlying it is a sort of scepticism or suspended belief. This humour is pervasive in Lawson, even in pathetic stories. As for purely funny stories, he did not write a great number, the most famous of them, though slow-moving at the start, being *The Loaded Dog*. The humour has its undercurrent: There seems (to use his own words) a quiet sort of sadness always running through outback humour. But humour is not his most successful ingredient, and often we can detect the particular mannerism in it: ". . . the aforesaid alleged roast or mutton".

His pathos rises from circumstances, the conflict of the characters with the land—hope long unfulfilled, failure after heartbreaking effort, the burnt-out selection, the loss of a child, the descent of the drunk (drink plays an important part in his stories as it did in his own life), the son gone to the bad. Lawson has a gaunt pity for the common man, and, let it be added, for his womenfolk particularly. One of his most effective stories is set in the city—*A Visit of Condolence*—and consists almost entirely of dialogue between young Bill, aged twelve, and the mother of a dead child. With the possible exception of an occasional phrase by the woman, there is not a false note in it. This restraint Lawson does not always command, and a few of his stories are as maudlin as any death scene in Dickens.

As he continued to write, Lawson seemed to become aware of this danger, and he developed a technique for covering it up or, rather, for infusing a flavour into an ending that is not cynicism or offhandedness or lightness but something of all these. A single example will serve. It is found in *Water Them Geraniums*, and deals with Mrs. Spicer, one of the brown, gnarled, worn bushwomen that Lawson is so successful with. They work themselves into a premature old age and death, they are unlovely to look at, and often they are crude and tactless and complaining. Their youngsters are nagged at and sometimes frightened, but they are fed and made pitifully neat when they are sent or brought to visit a neighbouring selection. Mrs. Spicer by this time is, as she puts it, "past carin' ". One morning young Annie comes and tells the neighbour that mother is asleep, and they can't wake her.

Mary wanted to go, but I wouldn't let her. James and I saddled our horses and rode down the creek.

Mrs. Spicer looked very little different from what she did when I last saw her alive. It was some time before we could believe that she was dead. But she was "past carin' " right enough.

The last two words epitomise the method. One learns to recognise the trick, if trick it can be called. But it is still effective. A man does not love a woman, said Jack Yeats, because she is beautiful or talented or charming or anything like that, but because she scratches her ear in a certain way. That perhaps is it. We know Lawson is going to do it, and we accept it: it is the oddity of a friend which has become familiar.

The relation that Lawson stresses most in his stories is that of loyalty, the conception of "mateship". It would be interesting, if speculative, to attempt to trace the genesis of this Australian brand of comradeship, from the convict days to the gold rushes, to the life on the track to unionism, and determine the contribution each made and the influence each exerted. But at least it is certain that Lawson was its articulate voice. Many of his stories revolve round it—the loyalty to one's mate, the sharing, the wryly humorous acceptance of faults, the open quarrel, and the unmentioned defence. It appears in the yarns almost as a convention, a part of the nature of things outback. Mostly it is an implication, a thing accepted. In later writings, as he perhaps became more conscious of what he was achieving, the portrayal became more explicit, and he made comments on it. In one small essay he extends its provenance and Christ appears as the exemplar. Lawson is best on the subject when he is not so aware of its possible extension. Under discussion and explanation the thing becomes an embarrassment.

Being Australians, we value Lawson for our own reasons. Inheritors of a land with a beginning in history that we forget or do not care overmuch to remember, without the romance of the European background, with no battles at hand, with heroes that fought sand or flood or hunger instead of human enemies, we have the uneasy feeling that political and economic forces are the only things we can look back on. And so we are very willing to accept something that does not belong only to economics or politics. Some of the absurdities of the books and beliefs about Ned Kelly derive from our lack of a Robin Hood. And the heroism of Gallipoli was something we had to have for our souls' sake.

Lawson helped here. We value him because he made a myth for us, because he gave us, feeling rootless without long traditions and faceless without national traits, something of a folklore. The main aspect of it was the "mateship" mentioned earlier, with its oblique loyalties and ironic acceptances, filmed with a patina of sentiment not so obvious as to make us feel uncomfortable. This sticking to one's friend is found in every country, it goes without saying; but Lawson's variety of it, resulting from the physical conditions of the outback and the economic conditions of the period, has become almost an Australian patent. We are not very prone, those of us who are adult, to make and accept heroes. We accept instead the legend of a class, and tend to take to ourselves the same characteristics. We have almost a proprietary interest in it. It was Lawson who made this possible by his pen. It is no wonder then that he was loved and probably still is.

Whether Lawson's art is of the highest kind is uncertain. The comparison often made of him with the world's great story tellers can be unfair to him as to us. If, for example, we look at the stories of Katherine Mansfield, we can see what Lawson lacks. Some of her stories are very nearly terrifying. They are like silent earthquakes. We are on firm earth, among the things we know and recognise, things of everyday, when suddenly the earth trembles and opens and nothing is quite secure or certain any more. Our familiar world takes on a quality we did not know it could assume. Such a capacity, so it seems, Lawson did not have. He limited himself, justifiably we may concede, to what he knew, and this leaves in his writings the print of the actual; but profound implication he is not much concerned with.

Indeed, the taking of the actual and giving to it an imaginative deepening and spread so that the little locale and the few people in it assume a universal significance—this is mostly beyond his scope. Nobody can deny his pity and the moving pathos that many stories contain; but the limitation still remains. Possibly his very Australianism, the quality that stamps him so unmistakably, holds him from the ranks of the greatest storytellers, whose characters are, so to speak, international. But in the sphere he made his own he still remains the master.

CHAPTER VII

Turn of the Century: Essays
Literary and Critical

THE essay in Australia, whether as an informal and personal product or as a critical discussion of literary work, is uncommon before the turn of the century. An audience for it was lacking, for one thing; and the opportunity of publication was restricted to newspapers that had other things to deal with. The names of most early essayists, especially the personal essayists, are now for the most part forgotten.

Our first novelist was also our first essayist. Writing under the name of Simon Stukely, Henry Savery contributed thirty essays to *The Colonial Times* of Hobart. These, which ran from 5 June to 25 December, 1829, were sketches of contemporary life and figures. They were collected the next year in a volume, *The Hermit of Van Diemen's Land.*

Savery resembles Goldsmith in *The Citizen of the World*, and probably modelled his satirical pictures on those blandly astonished reactions. But he is more harsh than Goldsmith. He does not give names, but the figures in his descriptions of a business man, a clergyman, a settler, and so forth, have been identified. His ear for dialect is acute, and there is a revealing little monologue by a farmer on the practice of flogging. Perhaps the following is the liveliest scene:

> Presently a fat middle-aged female in great dishabille, approached the shop from a neighbouring public-house . . . "Give me some tea and sugar."
> "What have you to put them in, my good woman?"
> "None of your good woman for me, d— your eyes," at the same moment stooping to draw off a dirty stocking from a dirtier foot, "here's a leg'll bear looking at—and here's something'll hold the tea and sugar," handing over the stocking, into which the sugar was first placed, and then tying it in the middle with the woman's garter, so as to form a division for the sugar, she received the change and left the shop.

One later figure of interest is a gifted amateur of the class to which James Lionel Michael belonged. This is Daniel Deniehy

(1828–65), almost exactly contemporary with Michael, and like him in some respects—giving early promise of brilliant performance, trained in the law, unstable, dying young. He resembled de Quincey in appearance, memory, knowledge, and conversational powers; but whereas de Quincey conquered or at least survived his indulgence, Deniehy succumbed. Drink was his ruin, and he died of a stroke at Bathurst.

Deniehy wrote some verse, but he is better known for his prose. He is both personal essayist and critic. Most of his writings appeared in *The Freeman's Journal* and *The Southern Cross*, of which paper he was editor for a few years. His articles deal with politics, literature, and society. He is a facile and humorous writer, often with a power of trenchant and sardonic phrasing. It is generally agreed that his best piece is the skit, *How I became Attorney-General of New Barataria*, a comment on the appointment of Lyttleton Holyoake Bayley as Attorney-General in 1859 after he had spent two months in N.S.W. It is, however, an allusive work, and the modern reader requires knowledge of the political and legal background of the period together with a key to the persons. Deniehy himself, for example, appears as Twank. The most readable of his remains are essays such as those on Leigh Hunt and on Federation. A collection or a selection of his writings would fill a gap.

The first piece of literary criticism published in Australia as a separate work is *Australian Literature*, originally a lecture delivered by William Walker (1828–1908) in the Windsor School of Arts on 20 July, 1864. He seems to feel that the material for discussion is rather scanty. In consequence he spends the first half of his lecture on writings such as newspapers, magazines, and chronicle histories. Then he turns to creative writing, and quotes from essayists.

Walker has his doubts about Australian fiction, and when he approves, his reasons for doing so are not calculated to appeal to all modern critics:

> Australia has not yet produced any novelist of note, if we except Miss Atkinson, who, to the credit of her country and her sex, has published two works of fiction of a highly moral cast.

Walker's lecture, full of generalisations and platitudes, must have been rather dull to listen to, and he was justified at its conclusion in making his apologies.

Walker was anticipated in literary criticism by Frederick

Sinnett (1831–66)—though not in a work published separately. Sinnett contributed two articles to the *Journal of Australasia* in 1856. These articles, entitled *Fiction Fields of Australia*, are full of good sense, and they may still serve as advice to Australian novelists today, more than a century after they were written.

In brief, Sinnett discusses whether the Australian scene offers a suitable field for fiction. He decides that it does, just as any country does. The basic human qualities and emotions are much the same in Australia as in England. The environment is different, but this, Sinnett urges, should be incidental:

> Most Australian stories are too Australian . . . in the kind of novel we want to see written . . . we want to see a picture of universal human life and passion, but represented as modified by Australian externals.

It would be well if a placard bearing these words were hung in the study of every budding Australian novelist. Even at that time it appeared to Sinnett that writers overloaded their pages with background. He goes on to say that the first essential of a good novel is characters; and the second, characters; and the third, characters.

The first attempt to cover the whole literary field up to the time of writing was made by G. B. Barton (1836–1901) in *The Poets and Prose Writers of N.S.W.* (1866). Unfortunately it resolves itself into hardly more than an anthology. Barton chose selections from fourteen writers, beginning with Wentworth. There are some comments, but no continuous survey. It would have been interesting to see how a contemporary regarded the situation. His other volume, *Literature in N.S.W.* (1866), deals mostly with newspapers.

Two years later appeared the first study in any detail of an Australian literary figure. This was Sheridan Moore's *Life and Genius of James Lionel Michael*. Like many such studies done at close quarters it is laudatory. Despite the qualifications that he adds, Moore portrays Michael as a sort of Admirable Crichton. Here is a passage that reveals the attitude:

> Michael was not only a fair scholar, a good modern linguist [he spoke French and Italian, and understood German and Spanish], but a sound Art-Critic, embracing Painting, Sculpture, Music, and the Drama, a good Naturalist, well read in History, a pleasing public Lecturer, a skilled amateur Analytical Chemist, and finally a high-toned Metaphysician and Theologian.

A well-known if not very significant piece of early critical writing is Marcus Clarke's Introduction to Adam Lindsay Gordon's *Sea Spray* (1876). It deals more with Australian scenery than with Gordon, and contains the famous passage where Clarke declares that the dominant note of the Australian bush is Weird Melancholy:

> In the Australian forests no leaves fall. The savage winds shout among the rock clefts. From the melancholy gum strips of white bark hang and rustle. The very animal life of these frowning hills is either grotesque or ghostly. Great gray kangaroos hop noiselessly over the coarse grass. Flights of white cockatoos stream out shrieking like evil souls. The sun suddenly sinks, and the mopokes burst out into horrible shrieks of semi-human laughter.

It is interesting to compare that passage with some of the descriptions in, say, Kendall.

Clarke also wrote a number of essays or chats for *The Australasian*, which were published in a volume, *The Peripatetic Philosopher* (1869). There are about sixty of these midget essays, which are amusing comments on Melbourne life. The themes range widely; some are informative, some speculative, some personal in the Elian fashion. Occasionally they throw a light on contemporary attitudes. In *Swagmen* we find:

> The Wimmera district is noted for the hordes of vagabond "loafers" that it supports, and has earned for itself the name of "The Feeding Track" . . . I have no desire to take away the character of these gentlemen travellers, but I may mention as a strange coincidence, that, was the requested hospitality refused by any chance, a bushfire invariably occurred somewhere on the run within twelve hours.

It is worth comparing this comment with later views, with Lawson on the one hand and Ada Cambridge in her reminiscences on the other. Although the essays are so short and often so light, something of a personality comes through them—a personality with restraint and capacity and style.

Two things worth noting characterise the prose sections of *Fernshawe* (1882) by Patchett Martin (1851–1902). One is the odd mixture of balance and excess. He says, for example,

> . . . there are few Australian poets, and those few have achieved little fame and less remuneration,

and he seems to consider this not altogether unjust. But at the same time he can compare Brunton Stephens with Byron in metrical skill. The second point is that here for the first time is struck the note of adulation of Adam Lindsay Gordon. This persisted for fifty years, till the early thirties of this century, in fact, when Gordon was honoured in Westminster Abbey. Martin's unhesitating praise runs:

> In the whole range of English literature there have been few poets possessed of a finer lyrical faculty than Adam Lindsay Gordon.

It all seems very odd; for today that is one of the last qualities we should claim for Gordon.

Even last century, however, praise of Gordon was not always unqualified. Francis Adams in his *Australian Essays* (1886) gives us the first cool critical appraisal of Gordon. He is influenced strongly by the criticism of Matthew Arnold, even using many of Arnold's phrases; he condemns Gordon, for instance, for having an inadequate "criticism of life". In his essay Adams emphasises certain faults in Gordon—his lack of metrical variety, the frequent sameness of theme and tone, the lack of sustained effect, and the fatal fluency that degenerated into jingle. Quaintly enough, in a later work, *The Australians* (1893), he conforms to the usual pattern and praises Gordon far beyond his deserts. As if to make up for this, he has little time for most other Australian writers, Clarke being an exception. There is a considerable resemblance between his conclusions and the strictures passed by the American Hartley Grattan about fifty years later.

Adams is sometimes virulent in his essays, especially when he is confronted by urban social distinctions and pretensions to culture. Whatever we may think of the content, his style is lively and often pungent. He writes in the second volume in very short paragraphs, and this, together with the lack of transitions, produces a rather staccato effect. Here is a brief sample:

> Intellectual life, any more than spiritual life, then, there is little or none, and the social life suffers accordingly.

> Its crude provincial hedonism is more depressing than it is easy to imagine.

> In Melbourne there is plenty of vigour and eagerness, but there is nothing worth being eager or vigorous about.

Some of the liveliness may derive from this device. And he is a phrase maker: *the English Dives and the Indian Lazarus; England . . . the witless mother of nations*—phrases like these are part of his stock-in-trade. Adams is one of the few essayists and critics of last century whom we can care to look at—a bright, competent, and occasionally penetrating practitioner in a genre where Australian writing was then lacking.

So far we have encountered critics who are sane. They may sometimes appear to us to be wrong-headed, but we can attribute most of that to their habit of looking at Australian literature from the point of view of patriots. Now we meet an inhabitant of the lunatic fringe.

In 1887 Sydney Candish published, presumably at his own cost, a book called *Candish's Defence*. He had previously written a poem called *Love*, which had received unfavourable notices. One reviewer indeed had called Candish a Milton in motley. Candish rushed to his own defence, and promptly decided that attack was the best method. He did not merely refute the criticism, he claimed pre-eminence among poets.

He says with a rather disarming self-confidence: "I consider myself the highest critic of poetry in Australia." His method is to take excerpts from his own poem and to print them beside passages from Milton and Pope, and then to invite the reader to consider "whether the nobility in *Paradise Lost* is superior to mine". "I claim above Milton sweetness, grace, sonorous tone, and more highly or chastely finished lines." We may leave him with an extract from his poem, where he is writing of the influence of woman:

> The stars that glitter in the firmament
> Grow pale in rivalry with her bright eyes,
> Electrifying with their flashing speech
> The nervous system of the manly race.

Much of the literary criticism so far deals especially with Adam Lindsay Gordon. It might even be thought that a critic's reliability could be judged by his estimate of Gordon: if he gives a reasoned account, then he is likely to be a reasonable critic; if he absurdly overpraises Gordon, then he is an absurd critic. Unfortunately the criterion is quite useless. Gordon seemed to be a figure about whom critics could lose their heads while remaining perfectly sane in every other particular.

Up to the appearance of Byrne's *Australian Writers* and the start of the Red Page of *The Bulletin*, both in 1896, Australian criticism is subject to these startling excesses. It ranges from the vituperative to the ecstatic. On the one hand a critic writes of John Farrell: "Byron-and-water—Henry Kendall-and-water—Lindsay Gordon-and-water—and some of it very dirty water!" On the other hand the *Melbourne Review* confidently asserts:

> No English poet has appeared since 1860 who is Kendall's superior. Rossetti and Swinburne and Arnold and Morris are indulgently treated if in deference to the enthusiasm of their admirers we allow them an equal measure of poetic feeling with Henry Kendall.

Even Rolf Boldrewood, who might have been expected to know better, can boom away in the rhapsodical style. In 1892 he delivered an oration to the Australian Association for the Advancement of Science, then meeting in Hobart. He strikes the note from the start: "Australia! birthplace of my soul . . . ! But literature! Mighty word! . . ." The style preserves this level. He declares that Wentworth's poem *Australia*,

> . . . faultless in cadence and rhythm, rolls majestically onward, bearing argosies of thought and classic treasure on its ocean billows, resonant with the rhythm of the southern main, heaving and seething unceasingly through the towering headlands of the great haven of the south.

With Desmond Byrne's *Australian Writers* we seem to enter a new world of criticism, the criticism that we are accustomed to find written today. We no longer find an ecstatic gush of praise written in an exclamatory and poetical style; nor do we find a condemnation utter and complete written, again, in a style just as extreme. Now this does not mean that Byrne is a very important or penetrating critic. He is calm and judicious, that is all. He deals with the usual figures—Clarke, Kendall, Gordon, Boldrewood, and so on. And he produces the effect of unhurried good sense. If his criticisms were to appear now for the first time, we should not think them at all startling; we should merely consider that they expressed what most competent critics feel. A. G. Stephens, not very fond of other critics, says that Byrne is "laborious and heavy". This is too severe: it would be fairer if more ambiguous to substitute the words *thorough* and *academic*.

The Development of Australian Literature (1898), by H. G. Turner and Alexander Sutherland, is the first survey of the field. The book is in two parts, the first being a cursory account of the fiction, poetry, and general literature of the century, and the second a group of three essays on Gordon, Kendall, and Clarke. The attitude of the critics is moralistic and healthy:

> Australia has most assuredly produced no genius of the great calm healthful type. Her writers have, as a class, been ill-balanced in mind, and therefore have had more or less unhappy careers, or else they have bewailed at heart the woes of exile . . .

And again:

> And it is greatly to the credit of Australian fiction that, so far, it has generally been healthy, clean, and optimistic.

The criticism is very much of its age, but it is balanced and reasonable. We may query some of the praise and even some of the condemnation, but as a contemporary expression of how things must have appeared it still remains valuable.

Our first important critic was A. G. Stephens, and he still remains our most important one, at least among critics who have written on Australian writers. He was a Queenslander, and was born in Toowoomba in 1865. He died in 1933.

Australian literature of the period owed a considerable debt to Stephens. He was personally acquainted with most of the writers, he wrote on most of them, and he encouraged many of them; Daley and Furphy and Shaw Neilson, for example, are among those in whom he took a sort of paternal interest. As editor of the Red Page of *The Bulletin* he practically determined what sort of poetry should be written. Some may think that his influence here was not completely for the best. But at all events he made Australian writing conscious of itself. His interest in our literature was not mercenary: he spent a lot of time on things for which he could expect no possible return. For example, the Mitchell Library contains his collection of notes and literary biographies. Stephens did these investigations almost offhand, as it were, and was quite prepared to chase through old church registers to settle a disputed date. The birth of Henry Kendall, for instance, was long thought to be 1841 or 1842. Kendall himself in a letter gave this information. But Stephens showed that the correct date was 1839.

With all this interest he was nevertheless not apt to overestimate Australian writing. He said of Kendall—to take but one case—". . . he has but a small place in the rank of English Poets". He was, of course, far from infallible. He overestimated Daley, for one. He wrote that Daley's poetry was ". . . the most sub-

stantial poetic performance yet completed in this country".
Despite the qualifications that he adds, one cannot help feeling
that this rather smacks of the fond father.

Stephens had travelled, and seen men and places and met
literary lions; he had an acquaintance with the literature of France
and Germany; he had a considerable self-confidence; and his
method of expression was, like his point of view, direct and often
original. If his conclusions conflicted with the traditional view,
then so much the worse for the traditional view. To show he was
not overawed, he then wrote in a cheerful cocky colloquial style.

He had the keen eye of the parodist for mannerism. The best
example is found in his esssay *The Crown of Gum Leaves*, which is
reprinted in *The Red Pagan* (1904). It is an amusing skit on some
of the poets of the nineties.

Here is his version of Christopher Brennan introducing his
poetry:

> I write poems that are to all appearances intelligent, if not intel-
> ligible, and I spread an obvious significance in decorative language,
> much as a peacock spreads his tail. But behind this exoteric mean-
> ing I shall conceal an esoteric meaning which adepts will discover
> . . . my first section represents apparently the attitude and emotions
> of a man who stands under a shower-bath and soaps himself all over
> before he discovers that the water has been turned off . . . This
> symbolises to me the dream of an idealist who has swathed his life
> in aspirations . . .
>
> My next verse is more difficult: it is unwise to make the Symbolic
> path too easy, for the egotism of disciples who have overcome all
> obstacles is apt to lead them to fancy themselves as great as the
> Master—a contingency carefully to be avoided.
>
> > from labyrinthine chrysalis the cluE
> > spars alabaster writhing in reversE
> > of cold lustration: saponaceous gluE
> > adheres that choral heaven can abstersE.
>
> The more you study it, the more you will see in it: it will take you
> many years to understand it fully, and then you will not be certain
> that you understand it at all.

The capitals at the end of the lines of verse are doubtless
Stephens' comment on Brennan's omission of capitals at the start
of lines.

In his booklet on Victor Daley (1905) Stephens demonstrates
his remarkable memory for phrases and his eye for resemblances
and comparisons. Daley was to some extent derivative. Stephens

picks the influences with unerring skill, and he proceeds to quote the passage in the former writer that Daley imitated.

The study of an Australian poet by Stephens that has aroused most discussion is the one he wrote not long before his death. Its subject is Christopher Brennan. Stephens had known Brennan well; he had even persuaded Brennan to contribute some articles to his periodical *The Bookfellow*. With Brennan's poetical affiliations, however, it is doubtful whether Stephens had much sympathy. The parody quoted before may suggest this. The fact is that Stephens considered that Brennan simply was not a real lyric poet. Of one poem he wrote:

> . . . most of the words are "wrong" in English poetry—in themselves and in collocation; they lack harmonious flow. Brennan wrote by eye more than by ear, and (for reasons too many to explain here) the best poetry in all languages is written by ear for an ear.

This essay on Brennan has been blamed for a tone of patronage; Stephens calls Brennan a *lad*, for example. But for all-over competence it holds its own with the other essays on Brennan.

All his criticism, in book form or in booklets or in periodicals, is now out of print. We ought to read Stephens, but we cannot buy his works. The next best thing to a collection is the selective anthology, *A. G. Stephens* (1941), edited by Vance Palmer. It contains a biography of Stephens, and is something of a model of its kind.

CHAPTER VIII

The New Century: First Harvest of Poetry

THERE is a temptation to regard the end of a century as the end of an age. G. K. Chesterton has pointed out the absurdity of this delusion; but from the point of view of the critic of Australian poetry there is something in the conception. Over the Australian poetry of last century, with the exception of a few minors, there hangs the smell of the parochial: the visitors commenting, the native born being very native, the wits aping, the rustics being nationalistic. This gross exaggeration is an exaggeration of the truth.

In the new century the poetry seems different. Seven poets serve to show this. In order of birth they are Mary Gilmore, O'Dowd, Brennan, Neilson, McCrae, Maurice, Baylebridge. They are certainly all of greater stature than their predecessors. There is no particular significance in the fact that their births fall within a period of two decades—about 1865–85. But it is convenient to find this, since the critic may group them in time even if he cannot find other specific linkages. Then comes a gap of about fifteen years, when the new century sees the birth of the poets of today.

The seven members of the group were not precocious: their best works fall within a period extending roughly from 1900 to the early thirties. After this we have the start in Australia of modern or modernistic writing. It is risky to delimit periods, for they cannot be said to start and end at definite times. But if a critic were commanded on pain of death to date the start of the modern period in, say, England, then he might choose 1922, if only because of Joyce and Eliot and Virginia Woolf. If we add some ten or fifteen years to that, which is not long as things go in such matters, then the thirties is about the time when the modern period starts in Australia.

The greatest of the group has been the creator, subject, and victim of a legend. Once a personal legend has been established, the subject of it often does not have to do very much more to support it: the legend then supports him. Something like this has occurred with Christopher Brennan (1870–1932)—the Christian name shortened to Chris by those who knew him and by many who did not.

Brennan attended the University of Sydney, where he took a First in Philosophy and a Second in Classics. From 1892 to 1894 he studied in Berlin, and became acquainted with French Symbolist poetry, especially that of Mallarmé. Returning to Australia, he worked in the Public Library, was appointed to the University staff as lecturer, and in 1920 became Associate Professor in German and Comparative Literature. His home life with wife and mother-in-law (both from Germany) was unhappy. In 1925 his wife sued for a judicial separation. Brennan was dismissed from the University, and ended his days in rather melancholy dissipation.

His characteristics invited legend—a large man, large beaked, with a mane of black hair, black-cloaked, smoking a large pipe, drinking large quantities of liquor, enormously talking. A reader of the writings on Brennan feels uneasily that all this has been thought to have some concern with his poetry: the man's striking traits and the impression of largeness conveyed by physical things and by talk confirmed the conclusion that he was endlessly erudite. (Only a few dissenting voices, for example Dr. Margaret Clarke, have not accepted this conclusion, which is founded on the opinions of his friends and on two footnotes by scholars outside Australia.) If he was large in personality and learning, then it was tempting to suppose that his poetry would correspond in stature.

Much writing on Brennan has dealt mainly with the things previously mentioned—his life, his personal characteristics, the literary influences on him, his learning, and the content of his poetry. All this is valuable—we cannot know too much about a poet. But it seems a little beside the point: the poetry is left to itself. Tom Inglis Moore's essay on Brennan in *Six Australian Poets* is the best discussion of the poetry as poetry, and some may think that the essay is too much concerned with the techniques employed. But Moore's method is the most justified if we ask why Brennan is a good poet; for in the last issue we are confronted with the inescapable fact that a poem as we experience it derives from the words we read. To go further than Moore is really very difficult, and probably it can be done only in short passages. The best is found in Wilkes (*New Perspectives*,

p. 54). Part of that page is the high-water mark of writing on Brennan, for it is almost at one with the poetry it criticises and illuminates.

Some of Brennan's earlier poems were issued in manuscript. Even his major collection, *Poems* (1914), appeared in a limited edition. Others appeared in periodicals or remain unpublished. The 1914 volume contains the work that is important for an estimate of him. *Poems* is the history of a spiritual pilgrimage. The theme has been analysed by G. A. Wilkes in his *New Perspectives on Brennan's Poetry* (1952–3). *Poems*, in five sections, deals with what is called by Wilkes the search for Eden, where Eden is self-fulfilment, the reconciliation of self with the Absolute, in short, the ineffable consummation. Brennan seeks it in human love. But his spiritual aspirations remain unsatisfied, and the poet enters into a sort of night of the soul. This experience is symbolised by the Forest, Night, Lilith, and its understanding depends upon a knowledge of Brennan's philosophy of aesthetics and his theories of myth. The third section, linked to the second by a recognition that philosophy has no validity beyond its human exponents and that man does not know his own self, contains a sort of resignation, an acceptance of the time-process of becoming: man, like the All, moves to self-realisation. The last two sections are recapitulations. (It should be stressed that this summary does scant justice to Wilkes' subtle and persuasive analysis.)

Such a work, with its complex inter-relations, has a right to be considered as a whole. On the other hand, it is not possible to do so without considering the parts. When we are told that "we must give up estimating Brennan's poetry from isolated lyrics, and begin to evaluate it as a whole", then we may agree with the last part of the assertion, but at the same time insist that discussion of the isolated lyrics is still legitimate. Otherwise we shall find Brennan evaluated as the greatest master of the *livre composé* in Australian literature—perhaps in any literature. Which may be true, but it is judging poetry in terms that are largely arbitrary. The estimation of Brennan by his lyrics is simply inescapable. He wrote them individually and at different times, published many of them individually, and fitted them to his pattern in a sequence not that of their composition. And a critic finds individual lyrics capable of discussion and satisfying as units.

His peculiar powers and defects individual lyrics serve to illustrate:[1]

> Sweet silence after bells!
> deep in the enamour'd ear
> soft incantation dwells.
>
> Filling the rapt still sphere
> a liquid crystal swims,
> precarious yet clear.
>
> Those metal quiring hymns
> shaped ether so succinct:
> a while, or it dislimns,
>
> the silence, wanly prinkt
> with forms of lingering notes,
> inhabits, close, distinct;
>
> and night, the angel, floats
> on wings of blessing spread
> o'er all the gather'd cotes
>
> where meditation, wed
> with love, in gold-lit cells,
> absorbs the heaven that shed
>
> sweet silence after bells.

This is probably the nearest Brennan got to poetry that is free from a sense of strain; indeed it is in parts felicitous, while *precarious* and *succinct* are almost flashes of genius. The etymological overtones throughout illustrate the subtle advantage that the scholar-poet occasionally has over the poet. And yet the poem is a queer alternation of the almost poetical cliché and the inspired choice. The second is continually redeeming the first. That the poem is successful, though, is beyond doubt. It is in its sphere as palpable as the opening lines of Hopkins' *Windhover* (where, it has been said, one may press the lines with one's hand). In Brennan's poem the ear tingles after the dying undulations. We pay a considerable compliment, in this empathetic reaction, to his skill in aural imagery. The philosophical background has been stressed by some: the paradox of perfection in music (as expounded by Schopenhauer). For there to be music

[1] From *Poems* (published by George Philip).

there must be sound; but this, determined by space and time, is therefore imperfect. To be an absolute expression of the Cosmic Will it must escape the limitations. So that absolute music consists in silence. The assimilation of the theory by Brennan has left this implicit, to the gain, of course, of the poem. The reader's gain, the enrichment of experience from knowledge of the theory, is debatable. At all events the poem has its own unsupported value.

Imagery of this kind is in individual lyrics Brennan's most successful device. His scope, though, extends further: [1]

> Fire in the heavens, and fire along the hills,
> and fire made solid in the flinty stone,
> thick-mass'd or scatter'd pebble, fire that fills
> the breathless hour that lives in fire alone.
>
> This valley, long ago the patient bed
> of floods that carv'd its antient amplitude,
> in stillness of the Egyptian crypt outspread,
> endures to drown in noon-day's tyrant mood.
>
> Behind the veil of burning silence bound,
> vast life's innumerous busy littleness
> is hush'd in vague-conjectured blur of sound
> that dulls the brain with slumbrous weight, unless
>
> some dazzling puncture let the stridence throng
> in the cicada's torture-point of song.

This poem is found in the section of *Poems* entitled *The Quest of Silence*. It is one of the most competent that Brennan produced, free of his obvious weaknesses, focused in its devices, consistently moving forward to its effective reversal at the end, where the intrusion serves to heighten the feeling. A technician might point dubiously at *drown*, which carries associations that are not quite subdued to the context; might ask if *mood* is not paying too great a debt to rime; might challenge *antient amplitude* as Wardour Street; and might raise an eyebrow at the third-last line as a poetical cliché. The strictures may be granted, but the general surface effect of heat and silence, so adumbrated—as all silence—by sound or contrast with sound, is one of the poet's triumphs. Of its place in the volume and its expression of Brennan's philosophy nothing need be said.

[1] From *Poems* (published by George Philip).

Sometimes, however, awareness of the philosophic background does strongly flavour the reader's experience:[1]

> Lightning: and, momently, the silhouette,
> flat on the far horizon, comes and goes
> of that night-haunting city; minaret,
> dome, spire, all sharp while yet the levin glows.
>
> Day knows it not; whether fierce noon-tide fuse
> earth's rim with sky in throbbing haze, or clear
> gray softness tinge afresh the enamell'd hues
> of mead and stream, it shows no tipping spear.
>
> Night builds it: now upon the marbled plain
> a blur, discern'd lurking, ever more nigh;
> now close against the walls that hem my reign
> a leaguer-town, threatening my scope of sky.
>
> So late I saw it; in a misty moon
> it bulk'd, all dusky and transparent, dumb
> as ever, fast in some prodigious swoon:
> its battlements deserted—who might come?
>
> —ay, one! his eyes, 'neath the high turban's plume,
> watch'd mine, intent, behind the breast-high stone:
> his face drew mine across the milky gloom:
> a sudden moonbeam show'd it me, my own!

The other poems of Brennan quoted before do not depend much for their effect on the inherent philosophy or the symbols employed. This poem does. It may, of course, be read at surface level, and even then it possesses a considerable pictorial value. It was written that way to get its effect, and a successful one, where the impact of the image is felt before it is analysed—a state of affairs frequently reversed in Brennan's poems. Despite its bits of clumsiness and forced phrases it builds up its latent menace to a climax that solves a problem only in turn to present another.

It is interesting from its affiliations. The Doppelgänger theme has been widespread, it was fruitful last century, and it still remains far from exhausted. Brennan is writing in the stream of a European Gothic-Romantic tradition. Here a debt seems owed to Heine, whose *Die Heimkehr* (XX) contains the lines:

> Da steht auch ein Mensch und starrt in die Höhe,
> Und ringt die Hände, vor Schmerzensgewalt;
> Mir graust es, wenn ich sein Antlitz sehe—

[1] From *Poems* (published by George Philip).

> Der Mond zeigt mir meine eigne Gestalt.
> Du Doppelgänger . . . !

Essentially, of course, the poem represents Brennan's interest in man's unconscious self, an interest of his that is indeed surprisingly early. This submerged part of man's self is the city—

> a leaguer-town, threatening my scope of sky—

that part of one's self never known or conquered. And so man is denied self-knowledge and in turn knowledge of what lies beyond the self. The clues in the poem are obvious enough, and the development and references are astonishingly consistent. That such consistency can result in the ludicrous (as in Poe's *Haunted Palace*) is true; but it is a danger that this poem evades.

These three poems may or may not be Brennan's best, but at least they afford examples of his varied effectiveness—the felicity of *Sweet silence*, the imagic power of *Fire in the heavens*; the metaphoric tension of *Lightning*. Now there are at least twenty such poems or sections in *Poems* that are comparable. Despite the insistence that is laid on *Poems* as an architectonic work, it is in some such way as this that Brennan will survive. If a stranger were to ask us for some of the best Australian poetry, we could with confidence point to this score of poems. It does not mean that his best is better than the occasional best of a few other poets, but the bulk and the average level give Brennan his claim to be regarded as the greatest of our poets.

Apart from relations of structure, of "symphonic character", as Brennan put it, a certain note is perceptible through his work. This quality, which pervades his poems, is force, a power of personality. Even when he is writing badly, when his elevated, consciously assumed diction becomes inflated; even when his clumsiness is elephantine; even when the image is not focused or fused, when the reader must approach it through analysis, weary of the analysis—even then his badness is the defect of his qualities. He falls, for example, into bombast, not into bathos; and this is the preferable fault. He is like an enmeshed lion.

His struggles are symptomatic of his quality as a dealer in words. For indeed there is one quality he mostly lacks—the power to give us the "inevitable" word, the magical line such as we find even in minor poets, like Carew's

> For in thy beauty's orient deep
> These flowers as in their causes sleep.

I

There is not much spontaneity in Brennan, where by the word we mean of course not the capacity to write without effort, but the appearance of doing so. His poetry is the work of the scholar, varied in theme, varied in stanza form and metre and rhythm, a poetry wrought out with groans, writhen, almost at times contorted. The word he used for a few poems we may apply to almost all—*epigraphs*—but in its literal and pristine signification. Brennan is cutting with mallet and chisel his characters, sometimes his hieroglyphs, into a wall of stone.

After Brennan it probably does not much matter in what order the remaining six are dealt with. Any reader of independence feels a reluctance to make concessions to the large claims issued on Brennan's behalf: the pressure of the Brennan cult awakens a resentful unwillingness to admire. But despite that handicap he quite certainly occupies his premier position. Any reader who is doubtful is recommended to undertake the physical and emotional task of reading the seven in succession. He will then be struck by Brennan's obvious superiority in weight and massiveness and even in delicacy of technique. We may well ask how many other Australian poets, even in a few poems, can stand at all near Brennan.

Hugh McCrae (1876–1958), more famous than his father, was the son of the poet George Gordon McCrae. Circumstances allowed him to follow his inclinations, whether as poet or artist or actor or free-lance. This vivid enjoyment of life found its musical utterance in his verse. But the life pictured in the verse is not life as we know it but as McCrae feels it: mundane reality has suffered a sea-change.

McCrae is unique in Australian poetry. Other poets, especially those of the earliest period, are strangers in a new and even alien land. The poetry of McCrae makes him seem more than that— a stranger in any land of this century. He writes of the Middle Ages, of hunting and witches and fighting; he writes of a mythical world, of Pan and nymphs and centaurs and satyrs. Though he writes lyrics that are not of one age alone but have their pertinence in all, and though he can be a robustious Georgian, but more facile, dreaming rather than walking, with forest glades for pubs and Bacchantes for barmaids, yet he is in general a revenant, a traveller from a distant time.

If one were to play at word-association and ask a young student to give the name of a person corresponding to "poetry", then most probably the answer would be Keats or Tennyson. These are, for so many readers, "poetical". Now something of this quality belongs to McCrae. It is a matter of nouns and adjectives:

> The smooth slim-sliding castle-tower,
>   Between two olden hazel-kings,
> Rose, like a folded lily-flower.

But when he is in this mood, and he not infrequently is, then it is a little difficult to take him quite seriously. When he writes of his pagan world of sunlight and moonlight and satyrs he is more himself. The poems then have a vitality and vividness that is not quite like anything else written by any other Australian. *Ambuscade*, for example, ends:

> A roar of hooves, a lightning view of eyes
>   Redder than fire, of long straight whistling manes,
> Stiff crests, and tails drawn out against the skies,
>   Of angry nostrils, webbed with leaping veins,
> The stallions come!

The imagery in this passage is extremely vivid. It produces an effect that is both visual and kinesthetic: eye and viscera and muscle respond. This power of appealing to the senses is one of McCrae's most striking characteristics. In aural imagery, however, which is generally the second most frequent type in poetry, McCrae is oddly lacking. There are some lines:

> The thin far calling of a trumpet blown
>   To dead men hunting in the afternoon.

And one of his best-known passages depends on this quality:

> Those days are gone . . . Now he must make
> His bed both long and deep,
> Until the pouring trumpets shake
> His spirit from its sleep,
> When he, all dust from head to thighs,
> Across the stones and mire,
> Shall rattle through the opened skies
> Upon a jade of fire.

But the kinesthetic is more frequent. Here his pictures of action or repose, of sunlight or moonlight, probably predispose him to this type. The theme imposes the image pattern.

McCrae has received high praise from several critics, and one is left with the impression that he is reckoned a considerable poet. The verdict appears rather too favourable. He is, for one matter, a trifle thin. There is not much substance or fibre—sometimes indeed not much emotional content. An object in McCrae mostly remains that object, whatever the freshness of feeling—sometimes because of the freshness. There are few overtones in him, few levels of presentation.

His verse reads very easily; a reader senses a professional competence about it, and seldom indeed detects the fumblings and gaucheries of the amateur. It has been said that he does not waste an adjective. Admittedly his use of adjectives, over all, does not run to excess, and most of them are telling. But he can descend to phrases like *dewy petals, boundless sky, little buds, sweet abandon, fairest flowers, dewy eyes, solemn shades.* Related lapses occur in one of his best poems, *Colombine:*

> Exit the ribald clown—
>   Enter like bubbling wine,
> Lighter than thistle-down,
>   Sweet little Colombine.
>
> Whisht! and behold the game,
>   Long eyes and pointed chin,
> Paler than candle-flame,
>   At her feet Harlequin.
>
> Look how their shadows run,
>   Swift as she flies from him!—
> Moths in the morning sun,
>   Out of a garden dim.
>
> Faint through the fluttering
>   Fall of a flute divine,
> Softly the 'cellos sing:
>   "*Colombine, Colombine.*"

This is as light as a feather, as airy as a whistle. It captures evanescence. But its effect is gained in the despite of some epithets. Those in the second and fourth lines are stereotyped, while those in the twelfth and fourteenth answer merely to the demands of rime. They show up poorly against the deft brevity of line six.

His world of myth, of nymphs and satyrs, fauns and centaurs, is susceptible of various comments. It may be the re-creation of an attitude; it may be the transference of his health and vitality from sick world to pagan world; it may be the escape of a mind unable or unwilling to cope in poetry with the present; or it may be the exploitation of an art material. One may of course dismiss summarily any objection that would impose the theme; the poet writes on what he wants to, and we should be grateful for what he gives us. But a difficulty comes when the theme is several degrees removed from normal experience. Even perfection in the expression of fantasy—and one can hardly maintain that McCrae invariably attains this—is not enough. If the poet does have a job, then perhaps one may say that it lies in a re-ordering of experience. To link fantasy with experience, or rather to use fantasy for a co-ordinating of experience—this would seem to demand a very considerable talent.

The fantasy at its best is seen in *The Mimshi Maiden*. She is on her way to the temple. Enter the tiger:

> Through the thickets strolled a yellow
> Onyx-taloned, whisker-curling,
> Evil-omened tiger-fellow.
> Ribs and muscles! Tail up-twirling!
> Starved and thirsty, hardly pleasant,
> Crouching on his twenty pincers,
> Grinned he down on lord and peasant,
> Baring top and bottom mincers.

He runs off with Mimshi, who "felt she must adore him". Now this is quite possibly McCrae's best poem. Stylised, formalised, orientalised, it is like something by Hokusai. The place for some of McCrae's verse is on a silk screen. With its peculiar charm, the poem is a soufflé, an airy delicacy.

McCrae is a poet of vital artifice: which means that with him the art and the theme have not been quite assimilated. The technique is there—he marks a great advance over the poets of last century—but one feels that the poems are written with a sort of conscious pretence, as though not all of himself went into it, as though only the surface of his experience and emotions were engaged; and that he knows this all the time. The cellophane appearance keeps him from being a considerable poet. Only a necessity of the spirit could make him different.

The most puzzling of these poets at first sight is one who should on the face of it not have been a poet at all. John Shaw Neilson (1872–1942) had as hard a life as any poet—at school for only a few years in all, working on a farm doomed to failure, following odd jobs of every kind from fencing to pick-and-shovel work in a quarry, finally becoming so poor-sighted that he could not see to write.

Out of that came some poems like this:

> Quietly as rosebuds
>   Talk to the thin air,
> Love came so lightly
>   I knew not he was there.
>
> Quietly as lovers
>   Creep at the middle moon,
> Softly as players tremble
>   In the tears of a tune;
>
> Quietly as lilies
>   Their faint vows declare
> Came the shy pilgrim:
>   I knew not he was there.
>
> Quietly as tears fall
>   On a wild sin,
> Softly as griefs call
>   In a violin;
>
> Without hail or tempest,
>   Blue sword or flame,
> Love came so lightly
>   I knew not that he came.

Probably the first effect on a reader produced by such a poem is one of artless charm. This, he feels, is how birds sing: an effortless outpouring. If there is anything in the conception of poetry as native wood-notes wild, then here surely is an example —unconscious, uttered without premeditation. And the knowledge of Neilson's life confirms the impression: it must be a matter of inspiration!

Now such a feeling, however it seems to arise, is certainly mistaken. Neilson's poems are not artless: they are in a high degree artificial. Except in some strained sense (as that everything is natural, since it happens in Nature) no poet writes naturally. Neither metre nor rime, to put it all on the lowest level, is an everyday mode of expression. The simplest thing that Neilson wrote, in the simplest words, is a highly wrought affair, something not natural or normal or everyday.

The feeling that we must resist is the feeling that, because a poem appears simple and spontaneous, therefore it is the product of simplicity and spontaneity. The effect is one of simplicity and spontaneity; but the process of creation is nothing of the sort. The history of poetry and the extant manuscripts of poets go to show that it is constant and unremitting revision that gives the apparently artless result. Simplicity indeed is one culmination of artifice, since in it all the artifice that went to its making has been successfully concealed.

With this in mind, a second look at the poem gives rise to second thoughts. In the third stanza, for instance, the word *faint* is a word obviously chosen. And the inversion in the same line is there for the sake of rime. These are things a poet has to work at.

But Neilson, it may be asserted, was an uneducated man. How could he have learned? The answer, in the first place, is that the learning is not to be confused with learning that is factual. It is a skill that comes (to poets, at any rate) with practice. It is not to be learned from study in the same sense as, say, history. (If Neilson for example had filled his poems with classical allusions, then we should know that he had got these from books.) Again, we know that Neilson's father practised verse. It is reasonable to assume that the son benefited from help given him. The other thing is that Neilson did not write poems without having read poems. He could not have done so. In fact he could not have escaped reading poems, for the simple reason that he did go to school. Even the skimpiest education in Australia would involve some reading of some verse.

We know that he sent his verses to A. G. Stephens for consideration and that that formidable critic made changes—not all of which Neilson accepted. But the process involved revision and rewriting on Neilson's part. When the poems appeared, they were as good as Neilson could make them. But they were no first fine careless rapture tossed off with the ease of normal speech utterance.

All of which may appear so obvious as to be hardly worth labouring. But it seems forgotten by some writers on Neilson. It amounts to saying that Neilson is a careful craftsman, with an ear and a sensibility.

The effect of artless spontaneity derives from the simplicity of the words, the limpidity of the emotion, and often the shortness of the lines. He has, like McCrae, the power to give us the magical line:

> And long-winged swallows unafraid returning

and:

> A glittering bird has danced into a tree

and, from *'Tis the White Plum Tree*:

> It is the white Plum Tree
> Seven days fair
> As a bride goes combing
> Her joy of hair.

His most essential emotion is joy tinctured with the sense of evanescence. It is never strong or deep, but subtilised, a slender thing on the fringes of robust life. It can be suggested and left unexpressed, as in his anthology piece *The Orange Tree*, where the freshness of the child's vision of the world can only be hinted but not explained, its intuition keen but inarticulate. But the outlines of things, as distinct from the emotion, are always defined. His delicacy is clear-cut. His themes contribute to this —springtime, flowers, children, old people, birds, trees. He deals little with landscape, chiefly with things moving in it. The result at Neilson's best sounds like a clear cry of joyous response. He is a charmer—or nothing.

This praise implies his faults. He is in texture, in density, often tenuous. No worse service could be done to Neilson than to read his poems at one sitting; for the lack of substance then becomes evident. After a time the reader feels a suspicion of the childlike, even of the childish—the fairytale element is becoming insistent. This suggestion of the diminutive is emphasised by his favourite words—*little* and *sweet*.

He Sold Himself to the Daisies, for instance, serves as a focusing of these weaknesses, of the tendencies to the trivial and whimsical and infantile:

> He stayed too long in the sunlight,
> He was so thin and shy,
> He sold himself to the daisies
> When no one strove to buy.
>
> .   .   .   .   .   .
>
> But he rose ere the day had broken,
> He rose when the stars hung high,
> And his heart did hope within him
> To die as the daisies die.
>
> .   .   .   .   .   .
>
> The clouds came thick and thicker,
> The blue winds one by one
> Baffled his hopeless body,
> Carried him out of the sun.

> They gave to him small pity
> Of priest or prayer or stone,
> But the daisies climbed together
> And the daisies knew their own.

This is high-class namby-pamby. It is unfair in one way to use it; but on the other hand a poet's characteristics are most apparent when they have run to seed. So that it is always valuable to have some of a poet's poorer verse.

A number of Neilson's poems walk a narrow ledge. The silly and the trivial are always alongside. A poet who is eloquent and sonorous degenerates into rhetoric and bombast when he fails. And this is tolerable to some extent. But the poet of delicacy incurs a graver risk: if he fails he becomes idiotic, which is not tolerable at all. Revulsion results from the former; laughter from the latter. And this is fatal. Even in a poem which starts beautifully, *'Tis the White Plum Tree*, he can let his simplicity and his power of suggesting the indefinable emotion degenerate into something that is nearly sweet nonsense:

> The birds run outward
> The birds are low,
> Whispering in manna
> The sweethearts go.

Such are the dangers that beset the "artless" or "simple" poet, the dangers that occasionally must overwhelm him unless he is a superlative craftsman. It should not disconcert the admirer of Neilson if he sometimes finds Neilson a victim. It is in the nature of the case, for Neilson's background predisposed him to the apparently simple, a type of poetry which in fact makes very great demands on technique. We may justifiably remain astonished that he succeeded as he did in meeting such exacting calls. With or without his weaknesses he still remains inimitable.

The influences of the age appear more in Bernard O'Dowd (1866–1953) than in any of the others. Born into a Catholic household, he early came under the stress of the secular movement of the period, and abandoned his faith before he was out of his teens. As a clerk in the Crown Solicitor's office he delved into land laws and to the end remained interested in agrarian reform. The books he devoured while young, when reading in his University courses and whenever he found time, gave him a storehouse of information. One of the personal forces directing him to his type of poetry was Walt Whitman, with whom he

corresponded. As a poet he was to be a prophet preaching tolerance and aspiration, with a faith in the individual man.

Like Brunton Stephens and Essex Evans he was a public poet
with a message for his generation. Poetry, he considered, had its
function, and part of this function he summed up in *Poetry
Militant* (1909):

> the real poet must be an Answerer, as Whitman calls him, of the
> real questions of his age.

The poet should

> deal with those matters which are in the truest sense interesting, and
> in the noblest sense useful, to the people to whom he speaks.

Before we agreed, most of us would wish to know the limits of
words like *real* and *interesting* and *useful*. The caution is especially
applicable to O'Dowd, for, dealing with matters that are sociological, he has the way open to him to tell readers how to vote.
Luckily, as so often happens with the application of a theory,
the poet steps outside it. The theme becomes more general and
the genesis of it more personal.

He is a poet of wide reading and learning and his knowledge is
seen in his diction. This is crammed with words like *embryonic,
microcosmic, polyandrous, nucleates, palimpsest, glyph, autochthonic,*
while the dictionaries of mythology are dredged for examples and
illustrations. We are familiar with *Olympus* and *Babylon,* and
perhaps *Astarte* and *Cyrus* come within our purview; but after an
avalanche of *Asgard, Brendan, Etzel, Moirai, Niamh, Ragnarsk* and
Broceliande, there must be few of us who do not need to be edified
by the margent. It may be questioned whether the use of the
recondite allusion and the esoteric example is characteristic of
the true scholar using the most illuminating and effective means
at his disposal. Many readers must be left with the impression
that the learning is obtrusive, but thought by the poet to add to
the repute of the scholar as well as to the splendour of the
work.

Another device used by O'Dowd, so frequently used as to
become a mannerism, is personification. Capital letters bespatter
his poems, especially the earlier ones. He was aware of this, for
he defended the use of the figure in *Poetry Militant,* saying that
by means of it "the poet has drawn the majority of ideals from
their wanderings in airy nothing, and given to them a local

habitation and a name". O'Dowd's use of the device is sometimes unfortunate:

> Where Gluttony would to the brutes
> Degrade his loose-lipped gangs;
> Where Tyranny his venom shoots
> From one or million fangs.

Vividness is in general lost by the device. Personification of itself
is not vivid or concrete: it needs details, the particular case.
Personification without them blurs and dilutes the image.

In his hortatory and prophetic verse he is a sort of Cassandra
(one drops into his habit of allusion) with hopeful intervals. He
inveighs against Rent, Mammon, Doubt, Despair, and Fashion,
but has hopes of Young Democracy. He is like an Old Testament
prophet, but without his eye for the sinful deed: O'Dowd attacks
Evil in capital letters.

The form of his early verse was less suited to his theme than
the form he later developed. When Gladstone translated Horace,
he used a stanza with a short final line. The condensation that
resulted caused a critic to remark that these translations were
like a basket of crushed flowers. No-one would call the poems of
O'Dowd flowers—they are potent or acrid or hardy, never sweet.
But the length of line in the early poems is not enough to contain
what O'Dowd is trying to say. In consequence, he often omits
conjunctions such as *and*, and so produces a slightly breathless
spasmodic effect that makes us think of the style of the American
magazine *Time*. Form is tortured to squeeze in the content. The
shortness of line seems, indeed, to render the medium unsuitable
as well as inadequate:

> His whims release the hells of war,
> He gags the consul, judge,
> And helpless peoples hopeless for
> His pander, Commerce, drudge.

Despite the content—perhaps, indeed, from the contrast—the
effect is something of a jingle. It is rather surprising that O'Dowd
should have written so many poems in this form without dis-
covering this fact. One may suspect a certain defectiveness of
ear, a lack of aural sensitivity. This was probably accentuated
by his habit of reciting his verses in a sort of impassioned musical
incantation. The effect, so listeners have recorded, was well-nigh
hypnotic. O'Dowd simply became one of the victims, and any

awareness he had of jingle in the verse was lulled by his own voice.

In his best-known poem, *The Bush*, O'Dowd abandons the short line and uses a stanza form of fairly complex structure in which the lines are pentameters. This poem is his longest and his best. It is a mixture of warning, adjuration, and hopeful prophecy, a blue-print of the Australia that may be. The earlier sections are in O'Dowd's characteristic fashion packed with allusions and unusual words, but the power throughout is manifest. The concluding stanza of the poem may serve to illustrate the qualities and defects peculiar to his oracular utterance:

> Yet she shall be as we, the Potter, mould:
> Altar or tomb, as we aspire, despair:
> What wine we bring shall she, the chalice, hold:
> What word we write shall she, the script, declare:
> Bandage our eyes, she shall be Memphis, Spain:
> Barter our souls, she shall be Tyre again:
> And if we pour on her the red oblation
> O'er all the world shall Asshur's buzzards throng:
> Love-lit, her Chaos shall become Creation:
> And dewed with dream, her silence flower in song.

The other work that will preserve his memory is *Alma Venus!*, a poem in couplets that celebrates the ubiquity of Venus Pandemos. It is a sort of hymn to fertility, ransacking all corners of the universe, from stars to mud, to illustrate the theme. The richness of reference and the climactic effects are sometimes striking:

> Door of existence, beacon of our haze,
> Horn of beatitude, clue to the maze,
> Pole for the Magnet, chalice of the Quest,
> Ark of the wilderness, star of the West,
> Moon of our dream-tide's pallid solitudes,
> Builder of homes and harmonist of feuds,
> Crowned with the stars and throned upon the night,
> Mother of dolour dearer than delight,
> Storm in the lily's virginal repose,
> Flame of the amethyst, breath of the rose,
> First Foam and fairest from the far Deep flung,
> Ancient of Days, perpetually young!

This enumeration glows into life.

Like four or five others, O'Dowd has been acclaimed as our national poet, the seer of the continent. We are not obliged to

accept this appraisal, but we must acknowledge him one of the
most individual of Australian poets. Even a recurrent weakness,
his convulsive and strident eloquence, stamps him unmistakably
—just as he stamps his own utterance:

> Misshapen Muses, interloping, smear
> The painter's vision with salacious leer,
> With tints obscene the sculptured form pollute,
> To a lewd delirium the dance transmute . . .

If only nobility of aspiration, breadth of vision, and wide reading
were enough, then O'Dowd would be a good as well as an
effective poet. He is saved from being something of an oddity by
his manifest force. This is often misdirected, like a hammer
ill-aimed, but no reader can deny the strength with which he
strikes. It is most felt in attack, so that despite his forward-looking
vision he is when at his most powerful as much a satirist as a
poet of fulfilment.

If the volumes of a poet contain reprints of former poems and
if these poems are modified or recast almost completely, then the
task of tracing his development can be heavy. That is the case
with William Baylebridge (1883–1942). This name was taken
in his later poems by William Blocksidge. Born in Brisbane, he
went to England in 1908, served in the first World War, and
returned to Australia in 1919.

A rather mysterious figure, he has been the subject of discussion
and disagreement for some years. He seems to have cultivated
some of this appearance of the enigmatic quite deliberately.
Nearly all his poems he published privately, and constantly
revised or suppressed earlier ones. To trace the changes would
be lengthy; so that it must suffice to look at an early volume,
for example, *Moreton Miles* (1910), note the deficiencies, and
indicate the type of work he was capable of producing later.

This volume contains love poems, in which changes of mood
occur corresponding to the passage of the love affair—awakening
love, appeal, pleading, despair, fruition, grief at the death of the
woman, and resignation in remembrance. They are amateurish
efforts, derivative in form, approach, and diction, and showing
very little control even over the mechanics of verse. The poet
has a pebble in his mouth. A stanza like the following supports
the contention:

> When the winds howl thou shalt not hear them;
> Warm thee my blood shall when thou art cold;

> Sorrow and ills, thou shalt not fear them:
> My bosom is warm and kind and bold.

The inversions for the sake of metre, the staggering gait, the drop into banality and flatness—these are found throughout.

One interesting trait is his use of the image from the outback or the coast. He uses it naturally and with no self-conscious insistence on it as Australian:

> Yet gloze it no unmeaning theft
> That gladly would I gather:
> 'Tis Folly's wool, Beloved, is left
> Stale-waning on the wether.

This may be the earliest use of our landscape as a poetical conceit in serious verse. It may be funny, but it is significant.

The revisions of some of these poems in *Selected Poems* (1919) make for greater smoothness. But no mere revision could make good poems of them: only a complete rewriting of each theme could do that.

The three works that bear witness to the talent of Baylebridge are *Seven Tales* (1916), *Love Redeemed* (1934), and *This Vital Flesh* (1939). The first of these three contains, with one or two minor exceptions, the only tales in verse that he published. They have been unduly neglected. The form varies—a sort of imitation of Anglo-Saxon verse with the alliteration, however, not much insisted on; rhyme royal; couplets of four and mostly five feet; and a type of stylised translator's prose to tell a Norse tale. They are readable and competent stories, none very long (averaging about 300–400 lines), containing excitement and often climax. What must strike any reader is the way Baylebridge has imitated and caught the note of former poets, especially Spenser and Keats and Tennyson. And yet his poems could not really be mistaken for poems by these authors (quite apart from the inferiority to them); for Baylebridge keeps something of himself and is never a mere lifter of lines. He has soaked himself in the older works, and the colour shows.

Love Redeemed, a sequence of 123 sonnets of the English type, is his claim to be considered among the best of Australian love poets. He had dealt with a rather similar theme in *Moreton Miles*, that of love for a married woman, public scandal, and her death. But there is no comparison between the two volumes in value.

This sonnet sequence is his mature work. The influence is

Shakespearean; in a sonnet like the following, for example, this is most marked:

> Who questions if the punctual sun unbars
> Earth's pageant, and flings gold upon the east?
> If the swift intersessions of high stars
> Make beautiful the night, with magic dressed?
> Who asks if grass attires this populous earth?
> If leaves put forth their flourish upon trees?
> If buds on waking sprays have comeliest birth?
> And who, that scans, inquires the why of these?
> Who questions, tell, man's breath or blood, that comes
> We know not whence, yet is, and dates his day?
> These, being, have truth beyond all mortal sums
> Of much and less, and prompt nor yea or nay.
> A certitude sublime they have, above
> Belief and non-belief. So has our love.

The phrases that remind us of phrases we have read but which are not identical, the play on words, the archaic flavour, the series of examples with their application not made until the end —all these points and others incline us to say that Baylebridge has caught conventions. And yet the poem is effective. It is his best sonnet. But to assess the worth of such a poem is difficult. There is a skill in the development, the illustrations are relevant. If Shakespeare had never written, this would be a good poem. But any imitation lacks the new-minted quality that we demand of a poet. These words and phrases are in a way not his, even if he has bought them at great cost of time and patience. He is seeing and feeling things through a language that he has learned specially for the occasion. It is this lack of immediacy that must make any reader pause.

Most sonnets in this sequence deal with human passions. There are, however, some that deal with a background of nature. These latter are comments on or prologues to the former; forces or incidents in the physical world, that is to say, find their echoes in man.

> The fires, like hounds that slip the unloosened yoke,
> Run roaring on the wind; with ravenous tongue
> They lick the earth, and climb, to strip and choke,
> The amazèd trees, with their proud ramage hung.
> Bird, beast, and creeping thing new covert quest;
> Only the pigeon a sad ditty croons,
> As loth to leave her love-encinctured nest;
> Frogs, thick, asylum search in the lagoons.

> All day there, a dun arras washed with rose,
> The smoke has sealed the south; the abated sun,
> Firm-rondured—like a ball of blood it shows—
> Sinks, and the fumid skies to opal run.
>   And now Night falls; and her dark depths proclaim
>   The incursions vast of that audacious flame.

This serves to show how Baylebridge uses the illustration, the following sonnet taking up the figure:

> Our souls, here imaged well, like fire assails.

Baylebridge's attempts at phrase-making, more evident and more pretentious in his prose, give us some typical lines in *Love Redeemed*: the efflorescent—

> her Eden, ploughed and thinned,
> Falls to the naught-exempting rape of June—

the definition, doubled with conceited punning—

> Ambition now, that game of endless goals—

the gnomic—

> The thought that shores creation needs a crutch—

the imagal, unexpected but effective—

> A base defection crouches in his blood—

and last—

> That dark and bright beatitude of brown.

These are his best. The sonnets, though impelled by a powerful emotion, are not as a group comparable. They lack, in general, the competence of Kenneth Mackenzie, the other Australian poet of love.

The third of Baylebridge's chief volumes, *This Vital Flesh*, contains revisions of former poems together with some new ones, a Preface, and some other prose. Not every change is for the better; in the opening poem an example occurs:

> From universal throes, immense
> Past the accompt of reeling sense,
> By primal forces space that cleave
> In their ungripped velocities,
> Through cataclysmic gurge and heave
> Outmatching Chaos, through vast seas

> Of fire, through transformations blind,
> Abysmal, to unjoint the mind,
> The Earth was hurled, its charge begun,
> Into the keeping of the sun.

The earlier version had the last line running:

> Into the harness of the sun.

The revision substitutes a general abstract term for one that is concrete, particular, and much more vivid, and that has in addition associations of curb and guidance that add immeasurably to its significance. Baylebridge was misled by his fondness for the dignified word: the lines before were full of these vocables, and so he found *harness* not so "poetical" or so ostensibly elevated. Hence *keeping*. He failed to recognise that the intensity of a passage can assimilate into its society what at first sight appears alien.

The volume contains most of his utterances on national and international affairs, with comments in a Preface and an Appendix. Students of Baylebridge have spent much time discussing the interpretation—whether Baylebridge was Christian or Fascist or Communist, Vitalist or Determinist, Mystic or Materialist. The critic may allow himself to ask whether the views, whatever they may be, are expressed in a form worthy of a good poet.

He remains an unusual figure. No other Australian poet has devoted himself in just his fashion to mastering his craft. All the poems he read and the poets he studied were means to one end— that he should become their equal. So he continued to practise —and how he must have practised the volume of his work declares—to develop into a second Keats or a second Shakespeare. And through it all he remained Baylebridge. He never became great. That is the pathos of all the striving: the sedulous ape, in Stevensonian phrase, who almost became a man.

What his final position will be in our literature may depend on the contents of the forthcoming complete edition. At the moment he appears as our best teller of stories in verse, one of our most thoughtful sonneteers, one of our most puzzling public poets. His development was so considerable that one is tempted to think that later work would have been better still.

Only one woman belongs to the group. This is Mary Gilmore (b. 1865), created a Dame of the Order of the British Empire in 1936. She had a life unusual in its events, and was one of the party that essayed the ideal commonwealth Cosme in Paraguay,

K

which was headed by William Lane. Returning to Australia after the failure of the attempt, she turned to journalism. Her sympathies have always been with those in need, whether of food or friends or love.

When she writes in her latest volume, *Fourteen Men* (1954):

All things I loved,

we may well believe her. She is indeed the poet of love, not in the sense that Baylebridge or Kenneth Mackenzie is, but in a sense that almost demands a different word. Their passion of love she does not express; in *Marri'd* (1910), for example, it is domestic, a sense of companionship with a husband or protection for a child or sympathy with a woman. In her other volumes aspects of this embracing tenderness or protective passion appear, from *The Passionate Heart* (1918) to *The Disinherited* (1941). In all she has devoted some ten volumes to her response to this demand she has felt.

Now, the world being what it is, one might think that these volumes would not be too many. Unfortunately themes recur; so that a feeling of sameness results. Even the selection of her poems demonstrates this. The repetition extends also to words —*little* is a favourite—from poem to poem; while in the same poem the repetition of words in a line is like a mannerism:

Dead are the young, the splendid young;

and

And whisper, whisper as he goes;

and

Young, young, so young

These are from early volumes, but the habit, though less frequent later, never vanishes.

The figures that occur in her poems very frequently, again the objects of her compassion, are the aborigines. There appears in such poems a note of nostalgia, a pensive lament for a race that has vanished, taking with it ceremonies and myths and even memories. We have, she thinks, lost by our cruelty and neglect something that might have made our heritage the richer. This nostalgic note constantly is felt, not only for these people but for the men and women who made no great mark in their genera-tion but left an unappreciated mark on the country—the convicts, the lonely shepherd, the man and his wife who began what was to grow and flourish. And her childhood, with its vivid recollections of sky and bird and plain, is the recurrent theme of her verse with its retrospective gaze. For the most part her poetry then is quiet, with the intermittent flash of emotional ecstasy. It is the past as she recalls it, versified into a muted harmony.

Since these themes are the most favoured, and since they are ones in which her own emotions were engaged so early and so enduringly, one might expect them to result in her most memorable poems. But they do not. The poems they originate are the honest, heartfelt works of the woman rather than the best works of the poet. In them she lacks the power to express vividly what she no doubt felt keenly. This is noticeable when she attempts the philosophical, the reflective. Needing rather greater originality of insight and subtlety of attack, she candidly exhibits the results of her thoughts on subjects that even great poets cannot always deal with adequately. These efforts display such an artless trust in the response of the reader that the effect can sometimes be disarming.

She is at her most effective when she deals with the external, the concrete object. Her poems on swans are numerous, and many recapture both the mood and the vision. In the following two stanzas silence, broken and settling, not often successfully treated, is held:

> A possum churred, and tree to tree,
> Soft as a snowflake's fall,
> A mopoke flew, careless of me,
> Settled, and made his call.
>
> Lovely the night, lovely the things
> Of night! I stood until
> It seemed the very air had wings,
> And all things winged were still.

The two concluding lines are among those where magic lies in her grasp.

More pictorial than these are the lines from *The Archibald Fountain*:

> The dying Minotaur looks his last look on life,
> As sinks the monstrous tumult of his flesh to naught;
> The dumb ox in his hands and feet no more at strife
> Against the greater beast the Gods within him wrought.

And there sits Pan the shepherd's friend, and keeps among
The eternal hills of youth his flock; while, on the height,
Apollo looks beyond the morning star, low hung,
To where dawn breaks forever on the dark of night.

She often attempts this brooding and dawning insight, and it is in the visual sphere that she achieves it.

Of her poems on people a few are penetrating. In others she admires and praises. We applaud the intention; but the poems hardly capture the essential quality of the person; there is too little evisceration. Once, in a poem that appears uncharacteristic of her, she gives us a living person, the naked soul:

JANE—WHO IS *NOT* DOREEN

I'm no Doreen
My name's Jane;
Chucked in the gutter,
Savage with pain.

Home—on the kerb;
Comfort—the bottle;
Life (and the pipe)
Down to the dottle.

Watch *me* "Doreen"—
"Oh, ain't it a sweet!"—
Shovin' a pram
Down the street.

Porridge for breakfast;
Bye-bye at nine;
Monday (at seven!)
Clo'es on the line.

Tuesday—the ironin';
Wednesday—the dust;
Week after week . . .
Lord, but I'd bust!

No masterpiece, admittedly; and some may think it not poetry, though it is hard to see what else one can call it. But at all events it is something quite itself, bared without shame under the sardonic and pitying flash of Dame Mary's rare intuition.

When the other poets of this group have written social or public verse, they have mostly looked to the future. Dame Mary has looked to the past. It is her attempt to enrich us.

One poet offered up a prayer that was answered—that God would let him do his best things last. This was Frank Wilmot (1881–1942), who wrote and is likely to be remembered as Furnley Maurice. Maurice issued more than a dozen books of verse, certainly too many for his talent. The best of the poems are found in Serle's selection, *Poems by Furnley Maurice* (1944).

A reader who goes through this volume has a surprising and pleasurable experience. It is like watching an apprentice who is working in a certain manner. The manner seems outmoded, and the apprentice does not get very much better as he practises. And then quite suddenly near the end the apprentice ceases every now and then to be an apprentice and becomes an experienced and skilful workman. More than that, he discards the old method of working and adopts one that suits his talent. To put it plainly, most of the verse that Maurice wrote before his *Melbourne Odes* (1934) is so inferior to some of the poems in that volume and so different that it almost seems to have been written by somebody else.

The early poems have little to commend them, when compared with those of his maturity, except a fluency, a shallow clarity, and an occasional felicity of phrase. Mostly lyrical, with some descriptive examples, they exhibit an average mediocrity. Even as lyrics they seem like comment: the emotion is not acutely felt, the image not directly perceived. They are poems *about* these things, they do not have them as their being. This impression derives from certain weaknesses. There are in the first place devices that appear artificial where they are used, such as repetition and inversion. Both seem like echoes of a former mode of writing, as though Maurice were a member of a school of poets. Again, these poems are spattered with clichés—*dark despond, radiant light, ghastly hell, high faith, calm thought* and so on through the catalogue of worn phrases. Allied to these occur adjectives that are general, vague, and presumably "poetic", the armoury of a writer who hopes the reader will respond suitably, will in fact half write his poems for him.

Even *To God: From the Warring Nations*, one of his best-known poems, is deficient in impact and finish. It is a cry for forgiveness, a prayer from humanity pleading its human weakness, but the nobility of its theme does not make it a good poem. Only rarely do the lines rise to the subject:

> God, let us forget
> That we accused of barbarous intent
> The foe that lies in death magnificent.
> How can we hate forever, having proved
> All men are bright and brave and somewhere loved?

Lines worthy of their theme, yes—only to be followed by flat and inept lines. The poem as a whole has its effect, but mainly because of its length and repetitiveness, on somewhat the principle of the Bellman in *The Hunting of the Snark*:

> What I tell you three times is true.

The Gully, descriptive and more direct in vision, has a few passages that are quotable:

> Tall ghostly gums in glacial silence dressed
> Towered in eternal rest;
> A mass of silver fog, a floating shroud,
> Rolled slowly up the hillside to the crest
> Like Silence going home into its cloud.

But even here the amorphous *eternal* indicates the prevailing weakness of the earlier poems. With its noun it forms one of those literary clichés that hope to be mistaken for poetry. Only once, perhaps, do we find a presage of the naked vision that really sees the object:

> The softness of a kookaburra's crown
> The breeze puts softly up and softly down;
> His eyes of love that almost humanly speak
> Peering in softness o'er that murderous beak!

These rare brief passages put aside, the earlier poems are ineffective. Taken by and large they have a lesson for us. Like the early Maurice we are all embryo poets; we feel, we almost see —like Maurice, all we need is the words.

With *Melbourne Odes* Maurice's claim to be remembered begins and ends. Before this he used a diluted and worn phrasing, a Victorian poetic diction, evocative in a literary secondhand manner. Now instead of the deliquescent soft spate of adjectives, the vague prettified phrase, he uses a taut real language. Sometimes, and in three or four poems almost continuously, the eye sees, the heart feels, no longer merely responding as the poet thinks they ought to but as they must if something is really to be said instead of being echoed.

These poems are urban poems of contrast—city, beauty; city, country; dirt, beauty; trade, aspiration . . . It needed some such theme to take the skin off Maurice's nerves, to temper and point his phrases. It extends even beyond his city limits:

> The roaring bees
> Worry and tear at the throats of the swaying poppies.

One of the poems of this acutely felt contrast is *The Agricultural Show*, where the city dweller senses with a sort of earthy nostalgia the background that made the show possible, a nostalgia deepened by the urban experiences of everyday. The device used, of putting, often mutely, two aspects side by side may owe something to Eliot, but the voice is Maurice's own. The ending is representative of the poem:

> We all turn homeward dusty and overcast
> By a sense of cattle-hills without a name;
> Carrying bags of samples of the vast
> Uncomprehended regions whence they came.
> Drenched with the colour of unexperienced days
> We go our different ways;
> Stallions loose on the plains; apples of Hesperides;
> Quiet lakes and milking sheds; "Fares please, fares please."

His best poem is *The Towers at Evening*, and his new note is struck in the first two lines:

> The juggernauting trams and the prolonged
> Crash of the Caféterias at noon
> Are silenced, and the ghostly clouds are thronged
> With towers floating past a cloudy moon.

The antithesis is preserved—here the beauty that springs partly as comment on, partly as result of, the huckstering:

> Out of the years of chaffering, out of greed;
> From crude material, in deep desire;
> Out of some nameless, searching human need
> Arose these towers for traders on the mire.

And the ending, which extends further afield, extends also in significance:

> Maybe the coral of the Barrier Reef,
> In spite of time and thrashing storms and the filth of shags,
> Could raise in blind compulsion, without knowledge or belief,
> A pearly lighthouse over its own hull-tearing crags.

Maurice wrote a Preface to his *Melbourne Odes,* which is both revealing and misleading. "In these verses [he wrote] I have followed a natural tendency to draw imaginative significance from everyday things." The reader may wonder why this "natural tendency" did not manifest itself earlier in his work. The explanation appears in the rest of the preface, which is a defence of modern poetry (expressing certain themes in "unpoetic" words) and an attack on the widespread conception of the "poetic" in poetry. The amusing and ironic thing is that his attack applies very particularly to his own early work. Incredible as it may seem, he apparently was unaware of this. He came upon modern poetry, appreciated its choice of themes and devices, and began to write in that fashion. To his own good fortune and ours, his talent was in accord. So that his successful poems were written by taking thought; they did not arise as the flowering or climax of a development tending in that direction. In brief, he did not develop: he simply found himself.

CHAPTER IX

The New Century: First Harvest of Fiction

AS with the poets, so it is convenient to group some novelists as belonging to about the first third of the century. And as the poets are superior to their predecessors, so a few of these novelists are greater than any of the former century except Clarke. They give the impression, also, of writing for more adult readers, readers who are more sophisticated, less easily satisfied with externals. It does not mean that they are essentially psychological novelists, but it does mean that their interest lies at least as much in characters as in the things that characters do. Of the members of this group one wrote a very odd book; one wrote a very good novel or, as some may think, two very good novels; one wrote a novel notable in its Australian kind.

The most unusual book in Australian literature, one indeed that practically defies classification, is *Such Is Life* (1903) by Tom Collins. This is the pen-name taken by Joseph Furphy (1843–1912). If it is to be regarded as a novel, then it is unlike any other novel we have. The manuscript that Furphy originally submitted was so bulky that A. G. Stephens, the editor of the Red Page of *The Bulletin*, suggested that it should be condensed or pruned. Furphy accordingly cut out two sections. The smaller, a sort of skit on the tall stories told by bushmen, remained unpublished till 1948, when it appeared as *The Buln-Buln and the Brolga*; the larger, modified and expanded, came out in a newspaper, then as a volume—*Rigby's Romance* (1921 in part, 1946 in full).

Such Is Life contains almost every kind of writing—story, reflection, description, essay, satire; a range of emotions from humour to pathos; and even boredom. And a reader need not expect an easily recognisable structure. Figures appear, disappear, reappear; a long reflective or informative passage intervenes; an incident is told, is left without its conclusion until fifty or a few hundred pages have been read. The book purports to be extracts from the diary of Tom Collins, a Government official with the rank of Deputy-Assistant-Sub-Inspector. Some admirers of Furphy find the narrator a sufficient thread of unity; others the general area and background; others the interwoven narratives. It is hard to see in what other form Furphy could have put his material together. The alternative was a sort of guidebook to Riverina life.

One very obvious quality of *Such Is Life* is its humour. Furphy is a master of the dead-pan hoax. Sometimes it is the polysyllabic kind, as when Collins reassures Jemima on the origin of the fire in the haystack:

> ". . . we may assume spontaneous ignition, produced by chemical combination. Nor are we confined to this supposition. Silex is an element which enters largely into the composition of wheaten straw; and it is worthy of remark that, in most cases where fire is purposely generated by the agency of thermo-dynamics, some form of silex is enlisted—flint, for instance, or the siliceous coverings of endogenous plants . . ."

Pulling the reader's leg and letting the reader know at the same time is another device. The best examples are the lecturettes that he ruminatively produces on anything under the sun—the English greenhorn in Australia, religious faction, choice of action, poverty, dirt and vigour, sound vibrations, the man o'war hawk and the penguin, qualities of the expert rider. The farcical accounts are probably the most successful. In some Furphy preaches a sermon, and then he is dull. Occasionally he is scientific: he knows facts, and we are not to be spared them. He is then like the small boy holding forth to adults after acquiring a one-volume encyclopedia.

Closely allied to all this are Furphy's quotations. Sometimes these are given in formal fashion: there is the quotation, naked and unashamed. But mostly they are in the body of the text, literal or varied or garbled. This is not to say that Furphy has plagiarised or misquoted. On the contrary, it is all quite deliberate. The appeal here is to the reader who knows the original. We recognise the quotation, we appreciate the ingenuity, and perhaps even more our skill in recognising it.

Most of what he uses comes from the better-known plays of Shakespeare—*Hamlet, Macbeth, The Merchant of Venice, As You Like It*. Dick L—

> had been run out of every billet for utter incompetency; often having to content himself with a poor halfpennyworth of bread to this intolerable deal of sack.

However the judicious may grieve, the ingenuity of the pun in the last five words is considerable, and commends itself to the unrepentant.

One last example may be taken, the rigmarole. Furphy is talking of Sollicker and a butterfly:

> . . . with a powerful facial exertion, he wrenched his mouth and nose to one side, inhaling vigorously through the lee nostril, then cleared his throat with the sound of a strongly-driven wood-rasp catching on an old nail, and sent the result whirling from his mouth at a butterfly on a stem of lignum—sent it with such accurate calculation of the distance of his object, the trajectory of his missile, and the pace of his horse, that the mucous disc smote the ornamental insect fair on the back, laying it out, never to rise again.

H. J. Oliver, who first commented on this passage, pointed out that no simple paraphrase could take its place: "Sollicker spat" would not serve, for so much would be lost.

Although we tend to look on Furphy as a humorist, one of the best parts of *Such Is Life* is a story of great pathos. The theme is well-worn—the child lost in the bush. Furphy here completely surpasses two predecessors, Kingsley and Clarke. Kingsley's account of the lost child in *Geoffry Hamlyn* is like a fairy tale, and like a fairy tale it cannot be taken seriously by adults. Clarke's story, *Pretty Dick*, is incredibly and lushly sentimental, so that in parts it is like a parody. The story as told by Furphy is far and away the best of the three. The most obvious difference is the change of emphasis. Both Kingsley and Clarke write of the child and its fears, and neither is successful in making us feel as the child felt.

Furphy tells the story from the point of view of one of the men who are searching. We feel impatience with the slow progress, hope when the old black woman picks up the trail, despair as the hours pass, and desolation as the sun sinks. If we were accompanying the lost child we should find one day much like another, one scene repeating another. But with the men, we have all the alternations of mood and the sense of moving to a goal. And over all hangs the question whether we shall be in time.

There is one thing we should notice. The story is told by Thompson. We are warned that "Thompson told a story well". And it is well told. But the language is not always that of a man telling a story by the fire: it is the language of the author, of Collins-Furphy. The impression left is that Furphy wants to have his cake and eat it too. Pathos demands a sporting risk, a willing-ness to run the risk of failure, a bigger failure than with humour. So Thompson is made to tell the story, not Collins-Furphy. And if there should be some lapse, some failure to move pity, then Thompson is to blame. This is literary sleight of hand, which transfers responsibility from the writer to the creatures of the writer.

The background of the book is of the highest significance. Furphy, for one thing, is original in his characters. He uses them often as mouthpieces: almost every one tells a story or an anecdote. These express the deep-seated antagonism between the teamster on the one hand and the squatter on the other. Furphy is the champion—within limits—of the teamster. *Such Is Life* is the first treatment of the teamster at any length in Australian literature. Furphy, who was one for seven or eight years, knows what he is talking about.

Furphy's attitude to men and things is seen most fully in *Such Is Life*. One particular aspect of it, however, is more strongly stressed in *Rigby's Romance*. This book has its own importance. The tone of *Such Is Life*, Furphy wrote, is "offensively Australian". Perhaps it may sound cynical—or conceited—to say that no intelligent man can be truly representative of any country. At all events we may hesitate to say that Furphy is representatively Australian; but he has an outlook that people from other countries say is widely found among us. He is an essentially democratic writer. This attitude finds expression in *Rigby's Romance* in a discussion of political theory. It is, in brief, a defence of socialism: a general statement of its aim, case histories to prove points, arguments commonly adduced against socialism, and answers to these.

Rigby's Romance is in part the explicit statement of a vague ideal, just as the novels of Dickens are an implicit statement: a change of heart would solve all problems. In more than one passage in *Rigby's Romance* there is something very close to that:

> . . . What the expletive can you do?—you ask. Why, simply be a Christian. Let your whole life be a protest against the system which . . .

and again:

> . . . State Socialism must be built on a foundation of religion, rightly so-called. There is no other foundation possible.

Furphy had a fondness for *Rigby's Romance*, and spent much time on expansion and arrangement. Unfortunately, many parts read like a sort of lesson couched in a style that is involved and pretentious. We are left with the impression that Furphy takes it all very seriously. He gives it the form of a sort of Socratic dialogue. Tom Collins serves as a sort of Aunt Sally: he sets up objections, and Rigby knocks them down. And sometimes to save Rigby the trouble, Collins even sees the flaws in his own arguments.

Furphy's importance, however, rests on *Such Is Life*, a book unique in our literature. It is important for the picture it gives of a type of life in a certain period, the fullest picture we have. It is important for its humour and pathos. It is important for its outlook: even today, over fifty years later, an outsider would probably get a better insight into Australians from it than from any other single book. It is important for its sympathy and humanity. And lastly it is important for its gusto, for its vitality and vigour. But whether these large claims entitle it to be regarded as a great work is not so certain.

In the first place the book produces a general effect of oddity, almost of eccentricity. It is a sort of grotesque, an Easter Island carving. This may even add to the interest, but many readers do find it antipathetic. A great literary work of art seldom would seem so strange.

And its appeal is limited. Australians are certainly those for whom the book has significance, and non-Australians would have difficulty with it. It may seem merely silly to say this, since the book is Australian. But if we look at great works from other places, then we shall find that they generally transcend the boundaries of nationality.

Last there are the style and the all too frequent passages of odd and not so odd information and thought that Furphy gives. The effect is to limit the book's appeal not only for outsiders but even for Australians. The question has exercised critics to no small extent. A. G. Stephens, for example, says that Furphy "laboured at language for the dignity of literature". Miles Franklin considers that "Furphy's love of words ran away with him . . . Words intoxicated him", and again, that "He roved the world for allusions to demonstrate his fellowship with other people of knowledge and culture."

We may hazard the guess that much was due to the fact that

Furphy's early education was not elaborate. In his adolescence he already gave signs of literary talent. To develop it he needed facts and a vocabulary. His constant reading supplied him. His parents valued education, and Furphy developed a craving for information and learning, for details and exactness. His letters, especially to his friend Cathels, reveal this.

The danger is that such a student may come to value his learning as an exhibition, as an end, not as a means. That he himself should have acquired such a fund of exact information— though Furphy always modestly deprecated any such claim— must have afforded him a sort of surprised satisfaction. The temptation, not so much to "share his hoard" (the suggestion of Miles Franklin) as to show it, must have proved considerable. And the importance of this stock of information demanded a suitable style.

The exhibition was perhaps a shield. Furphy is admittedly so robustious, so apparently full of confidence, that it may seem sheer perversity to suggest that we can detect any diffidence in him. And yet a case can be made out. His willingness to tell (as Collins) the comic incidents where the possibility of failure is slight; his unwillingness to risk failure with pathos; a confiding in the reader that asks for a collaboration; the self-depreciation that could be a "blind"; the ambiguous aim of his polysyllables —these can indicate an underlying lack of confidence. The erudition and the reflections and the style can be a façade, with underneath a wavering unease. In Furphy may reside the pathos of the self-educated man.

The works of the next writer are very different from the highly individual concoction that Furphy produced. By common critical consent our greatest novelist is Henry Handel Richardson (1870–1946), and she is a novelist in the long European tradition. She was born Ethel Florence Richardson, daughter of a doctor, in Melbourne, where she was a boarder at the Presbyterian Ladies' College. At the age of seventeen she was taken to Leipzig to study music, a career which she was soon to abandon. Except for a few months in 1912, when she returned to Australia to check certain points for her major novel, she lived the rest of her life abroad.

She matured slowly. Her first novel to be published, *Maurice Guest*, appeared in 1908 after nearly a dozen years of writing. The second, *The Getting of Wisdom*, probably finished before this, appeared in 1910. One may say that the process was a long incubation of memories, the sequence of her novels, except for the last, *The Young Cosima* (1934), having the superficial appearance of an autobiography. *The Getting of Wisdom*, for example, tells the story of Laura Rambotham as a boarder at The Ladies' College in Melbourne. It is a picture of the young female barbarian, vivid enough, with patches of a humour that was to show itself in only one more novel. As a novel of school life it chronicles small beer. As a work giving us a clue to her method of writing it has a considerable importance. The point is that it is based on her own schooldays.

Maurice Guest is the next phase. Set in the musical world of Leipzig, it is the history of a young Englishman who becomes infatuated with Louise Dufrayer, a Queensland girl studying in the same city. She is, however, in love with an unscrupulous genius Schilsky, and Maurice is merely an episode and a temporary consolation for her. Eventually, after the faithless Schilsky returns, Louise leaves Maurice who, burdened with an overpowering frustration and sense of futility, buys a gun and shoots himself. This very long and powerful novel may be read from various points of view. It has, for example, humour—the drunk scene is one of the funniest in our literature. It is a novel in which music plays a very large part in plot and background and characterisation. It is a novel also of love, and this aspect will remain for most readers its essential motif. Maurice is possessed by his infatuation. He recognises it as inexplicable, but he can do nothing about it:

> For this face it was—the pale oval, in the dark setting, the exotic colouring, the heavy-lidded eyes—which held him; it was this face which drew him surely back with a vital nostalgia—a homesickness for the sight of her and the touch of her—if he were too long absent . . . And just as his feelings for her had nothing to do with reason, or with the practical conduct of his life, so they had outlasted tenderness, faithfulness, respect. Whatever it was that held him, it lay deeper than these conventional ideas of virtue. The power her face had over him was undiminished, though he now found it neither beautiful nor good; though he knew the true meaning of each deeply graven line.—This then was love?—this morbid possession by a woman's face.

It is also a novel about a city under changing moods and seasons, from baking summer to freezing winter, from streets to gardens to river. And it may be a reflection of her reading; that is, she may be portraying characters that personify the theories of Nietzsche and the claims of the Superman—Schilsky in music, Louise in love—not bound by the orthodox conventions of morality or behaviour.

This rich and rewarding and disturbing novel remains for many readers Richardson's triumph as an artist. Certainly no other Australian novelist has portrayed sexual jealousy with such poignancy. In her development it is important as showing her use of a background that she has known. The theme was suggested by a story told of two young lovers in Leipzig. And but for her own experience in that city it is very doubtful if she would have attempted such a novel—at least at that time.

What is generally considered her masterpiece is a trilogy, the first volume, *Australia Felix*, appearing in 1917 under the title *The Fortunes of Richard Mahony* (later the title of the trilogy itself), the second, *The Way Home*, in 1925, and the concluding volume, *Ultima Thule*, in 1929. The first volume is partly historical, with pictures of Ballarat in the fifties and sixties. But it is mainly an account of Richard Townshend-Mahony, a doctor who has come out to the diggings, and his wife Mary. He resumes his former occupation, becomes successful and then, driven by restlessness and a dislike for Australia, returns to England. It is valuable chiefly for its place in the trilogy, since it gives us the foundations as it were of Mahony's character—sensitiveness, resentfulness, quick affection, impatience with crudity, and nostalgic yearning.

In the second volume Mahony's characteristics develop almost into eccentricities. He abandons one practice after another, returns to Australia, gains wealth, and goes back to England. While there he receives news that he has been defrauded of his investments. So he returns to Australia with the prospect of ruin ahead.

At the start of the last volume Mahony is forty-nine, at an age open to certain physical and mental disorders. These, as though they had been accumulating in a thundercloud, descend upon him with increasing weight and with increasing frequency. His descent is a zigzag, with recoveries that are but temporary and illusive. Oddities of behaviour, of emotional excess, and of speech become manifest; paralysis partial and local begins; a stroke supervenes. He is confined in an asylum, then is entrusted to Mary and nursed by her, and dies in her care. His muttered words, "Dear wife," in the momentary flash of recognition at the last, are the sole return he can offer for her long devotion.

The trilogy is extremely long, and yet analysis would show only a few irrelevancies. Details that appear to have no bearing on the story take their place later in the pattern. As it progresses the characters grow fewer after about the middle of the novel, and at the end the background is pruned to a small village, then a house, then a room with a bed. Man in contact with his fellows is whittled down to man and his body. The details have an accumulative force. Richardson adds them almost, one may feel, remorselessly. Mahony breaks down at last into a mere breathing organism; and the reader's pity endures demand after demand to a degree that is harrowing.

From the point of view of the development of her art and her methods of work it is important to note that the novel is the story of her father. Like Mahony he had come out hoping to make his fortune, had taken up medical practice again, had suffered vicissitudes, had become insane and died in like manner in 1879, when his daughter was aged nine. Upon her experiences in those childhood years and her memories of the concluding months of her father's life she drew heavily for *Ultima Thule*.

There was no more water in the well for her last novel, *The Young Cosima*, the story of Cosima Liszt and Wagner. She could of course have no personal experience of the background; but in any case she had by now transmuted her experiences and memories into art. So she turned to books, and the bibliography appended to the novel is a formidable one. It is a rather bare novel, cold despite the infatuation and the egotism depicted. If footnotes and an index had been added a reader would hardly feel them out of place.

The author stands aloof in this novel. There is very little description of physical background. Dialogue and impersonal accounts of action serve to reveal temperament and character. Some of her awkward and clumsy traits of style here develop almost into oddities: her too frequent commas, the overuse of the nominative absolute, the omission of conjunctions, and the tendency to a stiff formal diction. The book is almost angularly mechanical—as though not she but some machine were engaged in analysing these living human beings.

These comments link up. Leonie Gibson (in *Henry Handel Richardson and Some of Her Sources*) detects in *The Getting of Wisdom* the skeleton of a theory of fiction which Richardson was to apply. Laura discovers that her own stories are successful when she uses probable or real circumstances and background and puts imaginary incidents into this milieu. Since Laura is for the most part Richardson herself, it is reasonable to believe that all this applies to Richardson's own writing. In fact when we look at her novels in this light we do find that she relies very heavily on her own memories and on diaries and books of reference. She uses her schooldays for both background and incident in *The Getting of Wisdom*. She uses her experience in music and German life as background for *Maurice Guest*. She uses histories and topical accounts of Victoria for the early volumes of *Richard Mahony*, and her father's diaries and her memories of him for the last volume. After comparing some sources with the fiction that results, Leonie Gibson concludes that Richardson lacks invention. We may go further. We may say that she is deficient in imagination.

Now to anyone acquainted with *Maurice Guest* this must at first sight appear a perverse and astonishing judgment; for surely this is a work of the imagination, if that quality is the capacity to penetrate and portray the emotional stresses and strains of a character, the capacity if not to create at least to project oneself into the personality of another. But Richardson draws upon herself in this novel, and in her account of her earlier years, *Myself When Young* (1948), she tells of her own infatuation in her early teens for Jack Stretch, Vicar of Maldon. It was, she writes, "an emotional experience, so strange and so shattering, that it compelled me to seek help and comfort from a power outside myself. For now I fell in love, desperately, hopelessly in love, with a man fifteen years my senior." On this the picture of Maurice was later to be founded: ". . . I had written *Maurice* quite unaware of what I was drawing on. Later events had naturally had a certain share in his story. But his most flagrant emotions—his dreams, hopes and fears, his jealousy and despair, his sufferings under rejection and desertion—could all be traced back to my own unhappy experience. No wonder the book had come easy to write. I had just to magnify and re-dress the old pangs . . . gradually the conviction deepened that, to a writer, experience was the only thing that really mattered."

It seems then that the power of *Maurice Guest* to move a reader derives in part from the material that lay to hand—a background she knew and an emotional experience that she had endured. It does not, it is true, show that she lacked imagination, but that she had not much need to exercise it.

In *Richard Mahony* the case is different. The early background came from reference books. But Mahony as a character in the first two books came from everything that she could gather about her father. Here, if anywhere, she had to use what imagination she possessed; for written material will not wholly suffice for a novelist engaged in portraying a person. The third volume is notable for Mahony's gathering insanity. The insanity of her father, there is good reason to believe, was due to the progress of arteriosclerosis, a disease of the arteries that is found mostly in men of about fifty onwards. This also is the disease that afflicts Mahony. The proof of this may be found in the diagnosis made by Dr. H. G. Wilson for an article by the present writer in *The Australian Quarterly* (No. 2, 1955). The clinical details given by Richardson can have come only from a medical textbook. The important thing is that the disease is physical and incurable, and results in personality transformation and deterioration that the patient can do nothing about. He is doomed to pass through certain physical and mental changes, and these form a pattern imposed by an illness. A consequence, from the literary point of view, is that tragedy can hardly be the outcome; for in tragedy we have at the least a victim or hero able to struggle. But the portrayal of a character degenerating into insanity and idiocy, paralysis and death, and all as the result of the decay of physical tissues—this has on many readers of literary sensitivity an effect merely depressing. That is the reason why *Richard Mahony*, powerful as it is, is a work of pathos, not a work of tragic force that leaves the reader, however chastened, yet with a sense of man's capacities and possibilities.

In *The Young Cosima* she lacked all personal experience that might have served her turn. She had not had the emotional experiences to be portrayed, nor could she rely on a textbook to give symptoms. So she abandoned background for the most part and confined herself to depicting character by methods in which she had no real expertness. It remains in consequence, compared with the two great novels, a chill failure.

We have then two major novels, one of them a love story in which she drew on herself for both background and depiction of emotion and character. And *Maurice Guest* is her artistic triumph. In *Richard Mahony* she drew, with not the same success, on books for the background, on her memories for some incidents, on medical textbooks for an illness. And *Richard Mahony*, despite its affecting quality, is not likely to be classed among the greatest English novels. And *The Young Cosima*, as we have seen, fails because she used books for facts, and methods unsuited to her for characters. All this is an over-simplification, but the broad outline seems to fit the case. It lends support to her own conclusion quoted previously: ". . . to a writer, experience was the only thing that really mattered." But had she possessed a more fertile and penetrating imagination, then she would not have felt, or in her last work have shown, how fatal the lack of experience could be. It does not mean that *Maurice Guest*, drawn from herself, must be a greater novel than *Richard Mahony*. It is a more perfect one, that is all. The other is always likely to be preferred to it, and in general terms it may be thought greater. Maurice endures an infatuation, an experience of a kind so intense that it is hardly normal. But poverty and family responsibilities and the ills that attend on age can be our common lot. So that *Richard Mahony* gives the impression of universality, a very potent factor in the consideration of any novel. When we are confronted with a novel that is artistically satisfying but remote from normal life, and another novel that is more imperfect but belongs to our life as we live it, then most of us are human enough to choose the second.

In 1911 an Australian novelist took for a setting Australian city life. Louis Stone (1871–1934) turned to the less savoury suburbs of Sydney, the haunt of the old "pushes" or street gangs. His novel *Jonah* is the story of the reformation and rise to wealth of the leader of such a group—Jonah, the hunchback chief of the Cardigan Street "push".

Stone is writing of what he knew from careful observation. The smells and sights and sounds of the ramshackle area, garish at nights with the glare from the pub, raucous with the cries of the inhabitants, grimy with dirt, but vital and vivid—some of this comes alive in this unusual book.

Its characters live with a sort of galvanic verve: Jonah, the larrikin; Mrs. Yabsley, the Falstaffian good-natured homely philosopher; Pinkey, Chook's girl; Mrs. Partridge, the voluble and malicious slattern. Except for Dyson, these were unusual in Australian fiction, and remained so for about a generation until the city and its types began once more to enter the novelist's range of raw material.

It is something of a period piece now. The story itself—the rise of the ambitious larrikin, with his aptitude for arithmetic and sharp business dealings, his unhappiness in marriage, his love for the cultured Clara—this is of no great originality. But the pictures of a period—the nineties and early 1900s—remain. Indeed, perhaps Stone rather overdoes this. It reads often as if he had collected a store of impressions and were determined to present them. In consequence the reader feels a little like a tourist being shown the markets, the "pushes", the two-up school, Circular Quay, the ferry, and all the other sights of the area. Though things happen in these places that are germane to the story, this impression persists. And the method of presentation strains for effect. The glaring or the sordid appears in a diction that can approach that of the thriller—*carnivora seeking their prey*; or again, *as if an army of locusts had marched through with ravenous tooth*. This over-writing has its obverse in the hackneyed phrase or adjective, *grizzled beard, scowling face, threatening eyes.* . . . When Stone deals with a highly coloured incident or character, then his style roars into melodrama, a sort of raw-meat prose; when he has more ordinary things to tell of, then he loses distinction and fades into cliché.

It is, then, a vivid but not a great novel. It is defective in plot but strong in bizarre characters. Of these the women are more striking than the men. Here the chief merit of the book resides. Mrs. Yabsley is one of the few characters in Australian fiction that stick in the memory. She sticks by her talk, rough and earthy and instinct with a tough good sense.

Stone is a one-novel writer. His other novel, *Betty Wayside* (1915), hardly seems the product of the author of *Jonah*. The setting is the middle-class suburb of Paddington, the main characters are middle-class musicians, and their speech is grammatical. The consequence is unfortunate. Stone's incapacity to write with professional expertness at once becomes visible; for the book is composed in a sort of bright novelettish prose, for the most part intolerably chirpy, tinctured at intervals with discreet sentimentality. Even the mild eccentrics do not save it. Part of the explanation is that in this novel Stone no longer has the unusual settings, the grotesque characters, the salty dialogue and often violent action to distract attention from his clichés and clumsiness. Without these oddities of people and place and incident to serve as distraction, the deficiencies appear manifest.

With its backward glance this second novel makes *Jonah* suspect. This is very natural, but unlucky for Stone. Had he written only the first novel, it would appear even more effective than it does.

A very different period, with its very different characters, appears in the next novels. A novelist may choose an historical period for various reasons—to give a portrait of a figure that lived then, to set a plot that would not be possible in another period, to plug an economic or social theory, to give a picture of the men and manners of an age. This last is among the most dangerous of reasons; and it is one, unfortunately, that has actuated many Australian novelists who have worked in this field. The result of the stress laid on historical settings and details has been that the novels, as novels, are sometimes almost unreadable. They are careful presentations of a bygone age, of well- or lesser-known figures, and they are often faithful and patient pieces of research. But they read like social history.

In the novels of William Gosse Hay (1875–1945) characters and their actions are of prime importance: background is reduced to a means, not elevated into an end in itself.

Hay's six historical novels stretch over many years, from *Stifled Laughter* (1901) to *The Mystery of Alfred Doubt* (1937). All are concerned, directly or indirectly, with the convict system in the 1830s and 1840s. *Stifled Laughter* has its first setting on the transport *Briadene*, though Hay does not use the opportunity to describe the life of the convicts or of the soldiers on it. The novel, a youthful production, is spoken of as containing in embryo Hay's later work. Some of his characteristics do appear, but no reader would guess that its author was later to write *Sir William Heans*. Only the style, with its adjectives and its indirectness, with its oddity like that of a bad translation, gives promise of what is to come. It is the mannerism of Hay before it has developed into manner. Occasionally a sentence or paragraph is predicative of later descriptions:

> Already the room was grumbling and groaning to a shifting jumble of giant soldiers and soft-glinting weapons.

Hay's second novel, *Herridge of Reality Swamp* (1905), deals mainly with a settlement north of Sydney, where Herridge redeems his name and his soul. Coming to Australia because of a scandal about a woman whom he loved, scorned, betrayed, and regretted, he tries to ameliorate some of the conditions of convictism. Sentenced later himself by a miscarriage of the law, he leads back to safety, in a forced march, a handful of convicts abandoned to death. Herridge is a stock example of Hay's heroes, most of whom have a family resemblance—tall, gaunt, with deepset eyes and embittered souls. When they marry, they choose women much younger than themselves.

In this early novel is also to be found a member of Hay's large gallery of eccentrics. This is Mulholland, the "flogging Parson", tough, brusque, but devoted to his wife and with some recognition of duty and pity.

In *Captain Quadring* (1911) we have a grim story of fraternal hatred near "God's Post" in Tasmania. Harsh and unbending rectitude strives with youthful dissipation and charm, and at last is softened into reconciliation and forgiveness by the death of the younger brother. The story begins in mystery and violence, develops by means of the "flashback" technique, and ends with tension and rescue. It would make an admirably exciting film.

The device of a character unrecognised but later revealed helps in this novel to keep the reader guessing. It is a favourite device with Hay. Disguise or an assumed name or the changes brought about by the years deceive even relations and close friends, until at the right moment the identity is exposed.

Hay's masterpiece, *The Escape of the Notorious Sir William Heans (And the Mystery of Mr. Daunt)—A Romance of Tasmania*, appeared in 1919. It is long, about twice the length of the average novel, and has its *longueurs*: some passages for some readers are almost impassable. It is set in Tasmania around the Hobart and Port Arthur areas, and covers the late thirties and early forties of last century.

Heans, type of the Regency buck, has run off with a married woman. They quarrel, and she salvages her reputation by charging abduction. Heans is transported. The story recounts his attempts at escape, the third of which is successful. Interwoven are various subplots, among them the theme of a deeply seated hostility between Heans and Daunt, a police official.

This carefully elaborated work is one of the best examples of an Australian historical novel with the historical material satisfactorily handled. Hay's success in this novel has led to a revival of interest in his works, and he has now come into his own—some may think into more than his own. For Hay is a highly individual writer, and *Sir William Heans* contains in itself most of his virtues and vices in perhaps their respective heights and depths. It must, in the first place, be read with very close attention. Clues are embedded in passages that are not intrinsically of interest. (The revelation that Daunt, the police officer, was himself a former convict can be missed by the unwary.) And the difficulties are made greater by an idiosyncratic style that for many readers becomes repellent. Meredith is the chief influence on this style, with its obliquity, its over-literary note, its allusiveness, its ellipsis. It is easy to quote barbarous locutions and even apparently unimaginative repetitions, and to conclude that Hay simply does not know how to write—to ask, indeed, as one critic has done, how bad writing can make good literature. One reply may run that this "bad writing" produces the effects that Hay seemingly desires. It is useless to set up a standard of style *per se*, for there are no rules in literature—"anything goes" provided certain effects result. It is a matter of weighing these effects against the discomfort of reading, of deciding whether we get value for our exasperation. Hay here differs from many Australian novelists in being aware of what he is doing: he manages his objectionable medium, it is his, he is not floundering in a morass. Change this style and we no longer have Hay.

When he is about to relate an incident that is exciting or tense, especially when the outcome is uncertain, then Hay, like de Quincey, deliberately slows down the action and elaborates details of movement or milieu or relationship with a pertinacity that can bring a passage to the verge of rigmarole. The most quoted example is the fight in the stables between Heans and Spafield. Every move and counter-move, every possibility and feint and manœuvre, is given at length, so that it may be possible, as has been claimed, to trace the course of the conflict inch by inch. But the danger in such writing is that the reader may see only the pieces but not the pattern, the separate movements but not the whole action.

There is perhaps a certain cold-bloodedness in this deliberate squeezing dry of all the possibilities of excitement in a situation. On the other hand we certainly savour suspense drop by drop. The delay heightens tension, and the contrast of pause and immobility with sudden and stabbing action whets the attention to a razor sharpness. It is eighteenth-century *sensibility*—but for a different purpose, a different emotion. Hay is the Sterne of the novel of suspense.

One of Hay's characteristics in this novel is repetition. It is seen, for example, in the narrative. There are three attempts at escape. In the first Daunt overhears Heans in conversation with Matilda Hyde-Saxton, who agrees to help by delivering his smuggled money to a sailor. Daunt in consequence recaptures Heans a mile from the ship. In the second attempt one trick of Heans is frustrated by a mounted police officer. Heans abandons the other method when he sees a ruffianly soldier attack the daughter of his master. The third attempt, across the mountains separating Port Arthur from the east coast of the peninsula, is at last successful. Hay is adept, as indeed he would need to be, in avoiding literal repetition. He does it by stressing different aspects of the attempts. In the first he elaborates the preparations; in the second, the frustrations and the fight with the soldier; in the third, the passage across the mountains. Escapes, it may be noted, occur in most of Hay's novels—up cliffs, over mountains, by ship, by running, by hiding, by disguise. They are all parts of his stock in trade, and he uses them with considerable skill.

But the most noticeable repetition is in words and phrases. R. G. Howarth has pointed out that the essence of narration in this novel is the insistence on external symptoms. We are on-lookers, the fly on the wall. We are not taken into the minds of the characters: we see what they do, we hear what they say, we observe the change in facial expression and hue. From these we draw our own conclusions, as any onlooker physically present would have to do. Hay gives unusually frequent accounts of faces. Daunt's face is frequently *yellow*; Heans' is *grey*. And Heans' face and gesture and look are all too often *fine*. These words occur again and again like a persistent hiccough. To almost the same extent Matilda's eyes *stare* or she *looks wildly*. Repeat a word a few dozen times, said H. G. Wells, and it ceases to have any significance for you. And yet in Hay it is not so. The effect of this verbal iteration is to produce a sort of strained intensity, of deliberately insisted-on melodrama. People hiss in Hay's novels. Commonplace events and trivial movements take on a portentous and ominous quality like clouds charged with lightning. A character can hardly drink a glass of wine without seeming to be engaged in an intrigue. So there glooms through the book a sinister conspiratorial air, often alarmingly akin to a Victorian drama of the black-cloaked mustachio'd kind. And this appears even when we can see no need for the muttered aside or the dark reverie.

This element of melodrama in Hay is undeniable, and any attempt to deny it or cloak it as symbolism is futile. Hay is a romantic: his favourite themes and types of persons and settings and situations are unusual or bizarre or even sometimes almost incredible. His elaboration and his tortuous and oblique narration conceal it to a great extent. And for this reason he is best in a long novel.

Related to the repetition of words is the string of adjectives. It is often arresting and vivifying and illuminating:

> His landlady, a little old pinched woman with long grey ringlets and large, passionate black eyes. . . . To Heans she was a funny, passionate, asperse, tragic, kindly, uncordial, evasive, cheerful, smiling, grim old woman.

The sketch of a faithful servant, determined to protect his master from visitors, yet anxious not to offend, is well done:

> Sir William was superb at this moment. He put up his glass, and hiding his trembling lips with his hand, stared the man wanly in his large, bland, conciliating, brisk, yet bothered face.

The qualities that make *Sir William Heans* something of a masterpiece of its kind are its structure, its intensity, and its emotional maturity. Few long Australian novels have such articulation as this. It is closely knit, with characters and incidents all woven into the pattern and all needed. The highly mannered style and the events it relates, on the stretch from start to finish; the hesitations and delays; the elaborated cessations of action during which the reader is on tenterhooks—all make this one of the most unusual Australian novels written. And the characters—though Hay is no great creator of living characters —the characters are adult. It is a sophisticated portrayal, not a mere physical narration. The reader is following no plain story of adventure with all the significance on the surface. These things put *Sir William Heans* worlds apart from most novels of convictism and bushranging and pioneering that characterize our literature of last century.

The next novel of Hay was *Strabane of the Mulberry Hills* (1929). It may be summed up in the words from the book—"this Goneril and Regan of a southern Lear"—though it has little tragic intensity. Old Heylin Talmash, fearing the intrigues of his nieces, brings into his home young Newton Caillmont, who serves to protect his benefactor from these vixens. In the end, despite all their efforts, Caillmont comes into possession of Strabane and marries the beautiful and brilliant Fannia. Apart from the Reverend Royal Dubson, a maniacal clergyman and one of the author's fascinating eccentrics, the characters are nebulous. The hero, though, for once is of ordinary stature and appearance.

Hay's last novel, *The Mystery of Alfred Doubt* (1937), tells the story of a self-exiled Irish patriot, who goes to Tasmania to do what he can for seven of his compatriots transported for complicity in a plot in which he himself has had no share. He falls in love with Rose Levening, whose fierce brothers, however, fear the recurrence in her of an hereditary deformity. Doubt comes under suspicion of helping his former friends and flees with them. But the ending is rendered happy by the discovery that the deformity is not after all inherited. The novel has Hay's usual ingredients—conventional devices like revealed identity—but is partly redeemed by the excitement and suspense of the flight.

If Hay had not written *The Escape of Sir William Heans*, it is doubtful whether his other novels would win him great recognition. They have demanded consideration because they were written by the author of that considerable work. Hay is one of the craftsmen, creators, and stylists in Australian fiction. He appears as an adult writing for adults, and despite his melodrama, his sometimes incredible plots, his use of coincidence, and his overuse of some other tricks, he remains one of our greatest practitioners in the difficult field of the historical novel.

In 1901 appeared what A. G. Stephens termed "the very first Australian novel to be published", by which he meant that it caught an Australian outlook in Australian idiom. This was *My Brilliant Career*, written by Miles Franklin (1879–1954). This is the autobiography of Sybylla Penelope Melvyn, a young Australian girl living in north-western Victoria, a Cinderella without a prince. The book is perfectly Australian—in setting, in circumstances, in vocabulary. Occasionally, to clarify things for the English reader, a footnote appears: *shouting*—i.e. *treating*. The flavour is best seen in the comparisons:

> . . . comparing the mind of a philanthropist to the Murrumbidgee in breadth, his, in comparison, might be likened to the flow of a bucket of water in a dray-rut.

This total and willing if unconscious acceptance of milieu and language as source and means indicates that the writer feels at home. It is a remarkable first book for a young woman. But it is foolish to praise it for what it is not. It is unlikely, for instance, that she should possess mastery. The book contains the artless outpourings of a youthful spirit dissatisfied with its material and spiritual lot. She wants companionship of kindred souls, the experience of art, and the love of her ideal man—though she cannot explain what this is to consist in. Odd, contrary, perverse, she seems doomed to find herself a misfit, and at the end of the book no solution is in sight. The youthful *cri du cœur* has been compared to the diary of Marie Bashkirtseff; but it is of slighter material. Inevitably it lacks depth. And it lacks sophistication of manner. The expression is immature, the devices of language not fully assimilated. She will use, for example, *loggerheads* in the following way:

In four or five years he had again reached loggerheads.

The meaning intended is that he had reached bedrock, was down to his last shilling.

There is the queerest mixture of the spontaneous and the affected in this book. Its liveliness, its verve, and its oddness of theme will preserve it. It is likely to be read for many years as a picture of an unusual Australian girl, with something of the pathetic priggishness of intellectual aspiration. But its literary value is not equal to its human interest. In a way it has the same claims as Daisy Ashford's *The Young Visiters*.

A pendant to *My Brilliant Career*, written soon after that youthful success, was not published until 1946. In this, *My Career Goes Bung*, Sybylla becomes famous or notorious in the district as the author of an unorthodox book, and then goes to Sydney on exhibit as a sort of infant prodigy.

The style, lively in the former novel, now becomes more colloquial, and develops in the process a chirpiness, a cockiness, that is not an improvement. The satiric note is more acid, possibly because the objects of it, "Society" and "birth" and the like, are more open to attack. They invite attack, true, but they allow the author to grow corners, to start to carry a chip on the shoulder. She underlines her dislike by the use of capital letters—SOCIETY —a device that relies on printing instead of on skill.

Once again we can say the novel is remarkable for a young

woman. It is sincere, but the personality that grimaces through the pages begins to take on the quality of oddness. It becomes after a time a trifle wearing. The literary champion of women's rights has begun to displace the literary woman.

Old Blastus of Bandicoot (1932) is a novel that lives up to its *outré* title. It reads like a travesty of the novels dealing with life on "selections", but unlike Steele Rudd's *On Our Selection* it is not funny. It has the same oddness of style as before, and suffers in addition from the burden of a plot that is stereotyped to a degree —a family feud, the love of the daughter of one family for the son of the other, the bushfire, the sinking of differences.

In 1936 *All That Swagger* won the S. H. Prior Memorial Prize. A long novel, it covers a century from 1833, the date when Danny Delacy left Ireland with his bride and came to N.S.W. to settle and prosper near the Murrumbidgee. A saga novel like this, tracing the fortunes of a family and district over such a period of time, perhaps inevitably overloads itself with historical detail. Some of the earlier pages read like potted colonial history. We learn about land laws, land grants, emigration, the price of horses, of furniture, and of food, the manner of living, cattle duffing, and the background activities that can often read like the product of research. A few sentences are more or less typical:

> Gentle furry things fell into any simple traps or to Rover and his colleagues. Their flesh fed the poultry and pigs, and their skins were pegged out to dry in scores. Those of kangaroos and wallaroos were marketable. Kangaroos were also eaten. Cattle were too precious to be made into beef at the beginning.

An enormous amount is packed into the short sentences and short paragraphs at the start of the novel. Incidents crowd thick —exploration, settlement, aborigines, horses—each incident tersely related; and then we are hurried on. As the tale continues the family bulks larger—their internal and outside relations, their traits and speech, marriages, hates and loves. The novel has been frequently claimed—and acclaimed—as Miles Franklin's best work. But many will prefer her first fresh and breathless effusion.

The middle section of the novel is best: here she deals with persons. The last section is sociological and economic, as the first was historical. The danger in dealing with large conceptions, with visions of a national future, with idealistic panoramas, is the collapse into the bathetic on the one side or an inflation into the pretentious on the other:

> The son of this soil and sunlight thrilled with his destiny as guardian of a habitat for a new race of men—a race, by developments in communication and transport to be liberated from the primitive and panic trade necessity of gregariousness and proliferousness. Why not a people selected from the world's best?—people worthy to occupy a sensitive land protected by phantom qualities, a land that would return to desert to cleanse herself of too dense a population, a delicate elusive land whose suns and floods could cleanse her from the stupid greed of wrong-headed commercialism . . .

Her work has been overpraised. One may dismiss comments declaring "Miles Franklin shares the supreme place with Katharine Susannah Prichard", or affirming that she is "one of the greatest of Australian novelists", as benevolent farewells: in writing obituaries, said Dr. Johnson, a man is not upon oath. She is not a major novelist; she survives as a personality and will be remembered for her first gauche and artless and vital book.

If, as seems probable, Miles Franklin also wrote, or helped to write, or revised the books of Brent of Bin Bin, then she was prolific enough. There are six books under this author's name: *Up the Country* (1928), *Ten Creeks Run* (1930), *Back to Bool Bool* (1931), *Prelude to Waking* (1950), *Cockatoos* (1954), and *Gentlemen of Gyang Gyang* (1956). The first three and the fifth belong to a group. The first covers a period in the relations of certain families from the forties to the sixties of last century, the second continues to the nineties, the third deals with the twenties of this century, and the fifth partly fills in the gap between the last two. *Prelude to Waking* is set in England.

The best of the volumes is *Up the Country*, the first and the freshest. It is prefaced by a rather defensive Author's Note: "I don't care what folks who are artists in literature rather than in life, or who substitute sophistication for wisdom, think or don't think about it." It is a wholesome and in the main a cheerful book, smelling of the open air, a little like Henry Kingsley without his snobbishness.

It is, as its subtitle says, a novel of the squattocracy. It is not about pioneers in the usual sense, for when we meet the families in it—Mazeres, Pooles, Stantons, Labosseers, and the rest—they are already occupants of considerable holdings. The book deals with their inter-relations, mostly by marriage. So that it is partly a social picture. It draws on the customary material, and the list is exhaustive—floods and rivers in flood and crossings and even a death by drowning, gold fields, cattle duffing, herding, over-landing, bush races, bushrangers on a local limited scale—so that a reader wonders what is going to be left for the volumes that are to follow. The picture is thus a full one. The note is one of plenty:

> There was intermingled opulently a fervid smell of open-air sweat from bullocks and men, and of spices and foul tobacco, and of bread that was in the cavernous oven, and of the delicious quince jam boiling in the witches' cauldron, and of hops brewing for the yeast bottle above the fireplace, companions of the smoothing irons, the tea caddy, and other canisters.

The horses and the houses are well kept, hospitality is generous in spirit and quantity, the families are established and form a self-contained community. It is not much affected by things out-side its borders: the Crimean War and the American Civil War are distant murmurs, as of course they were for most Australians.

The novel looks back rather regretfully:

> Men never thought of saying or even thinking they were tired in those days. Theirs was all the adventure, all the hardship, all the reward, all the loneliness of virile path-cutting in a noble continent unspoiled of man.

It is a little idealised and heroicised. An adult reader reaching the middle of the book does not put it down; indeed he reads with a surface interest; but he finds it difficult to feel emotion that engages him very deeply in the lives and adventures of the characters.

The novels that follow are in general inferior to *Up the Country*. The interest is less; a sentence for example from the next novel is indicative:

> Life from Bool Bool to Monaro to Ten Creeks run and there-abouts had pottered along with numerous small changes.

This fairly sums up the novels as well. The setting becomes more urbanised and ends up in Sydney suburbs, so that the interest shifts from outdoor incidents to characters often indoors. Dia-logue becomes chit-chat. Sometimes this is illuminating, a light thrown on the fondness for scandalmongering so characteristic of small Australian communities; and mostly it falls into a pattern —people do something, others talk about it and them.

The heroic note in the early novels becomes a sermon or a satire in the later ones. But a really effective and virulent satire is still to come in our fiction. There is some in our verse, but the nearest approach in our novels is found in Tennant and Herbert. Other novelists prefer the indirect approach through dialogue. Two characters generally play this game, one or both of whom give vent to the author's opinions on current national failings. In Brent's novels these are things like Australian parochialism, cutting down trees unnecessarily, cruelty to sheep, and over-large families inflicted by a heartless husband upon a resigned wife. Each character has his turn, holding the floor or platform until the author recognises that it is time to change the speaker. The other method Brent uses is the reported thought of a character:

> In such conditions Dick became reconciled to the inland suburbs. The common man, he mused, was incapable of appraising unfamiliar indigenous loveliness. The impressions possible to his limited mental equipment resulted in a desire for the possessions of his financial superiors.

One point of interest in a later work, *Cockatoos*, is the figure of Ignez, a young girl of considerable gifts, pianist, singer, and author of a novel that portrays the life and characters of Oswald's Ridges near Goulburn, the country community where she lives. The figure is markedly like that of Sybylla in Miles Franklin's *My Brilliant Career*.

Some of the interest aroused by the Brent novels is almost certainly due to the mystery of their authorship. The reputation they have enjoyed in some circles seems higher than is warranted by their qualities of style and characterisation. Their setting gives them greater claims to permanence. It is possible that they suffer under the disadvantage of being so many and so long. Had only the first appeared it would hold a greater interest.

INTERCHAPTER II

THIS second period, from the 1880s to the 1930s, contains two over-lapping sub-periods. The first of these ends around the outbreak of World War I; the second begins at the start of the century.

A few dates may help to clarify this. The bush ballads began as a more or less continuous spate about the middle eighties and ended about 1914. After that a bush ballad would seem artificial. The public poets, Evans and Brunton Stephens, finished earlier. But even Stephens, writing some of his poetry in the seventies and eighties, was writing for a year into the new century; while Evans began after 1890 and continued to his death in 1909. In fiction Ada Cambridge began her novels with Australian settings in the seventies. She continued to write into this century. Rosa Praed's Australian novels began in 1880, and the last of them was published in 1916. The more notable form of fiction, the short story, flourished in the nineties and the first decade and a half of this century. The major figure, Lawson, for example, published his first volume in 1894 and his last in 1913.

Of the poets of the second sub-period, Brennan began before the century was out, O'Dowd and Maurice both in 1903. Of the novelists, both Miles Franklin and Hay published first in 1901, Furphy followed in 1903.

This suggests that the years of overlapping, approximately 1900–14, are very rich, containing as they do the end of the first sub-period and the start of the second.

It also suggests that the nineties, often thought of as prolific in valuable and representative works, are really rather thin. Only two volumes of Lawson's tales and one of his verse and only one volume of Paterson's verse, for instance, appeared before 1900.

The first sub-period is important for its Australianism. The bush ballad gave to welcoming readers pictures of some Australian types, however heroicised they might appear in the nostalgic verse of Paterson. That is why Paterson is a more important poet than Lawson. Lawson was truer to the facts of the day: the cameraderie of the West as seen in Paterson may have a certain unreality when viewed against the bitterness of the strikes in the Queensland West in the early nineties, for instance. But

Paterson's stamping of types, based on the earlier pastoral age, was to prove more enduring. The ideal of mateship also found its expression in these poems, certainly in Paterson and even to some extent in Lawson's disillusioned verse.

The note of aspiration, of a confidence in the future of a united land, is not heard in these two poets very loudly. When it does, it is in Paterson a positive cry. In Lawson the future holds hope only when inequalities are first removed. He is revolutionary: the present must be mended. It is, however, to Stephens and Evans and the less known public poets that we must turn for a hope of Australia unlimited.

The prose of this first sub-period, however, is more important than its verse. The ballads, after all, were to end when World War I began, and nobody after that could seriously pursue the tradition. But the short story, containing like the ballads some national figures and stressing more effectively the conception of mateship, has a literary value and a persisting quality that makes it much more valuable. Australian short stories to this day are in the tradition of the best of those written then.

In purely literary value this first sub-period is greatly inferior to the second. Only Lawson, and then as a writer of short stories, can stand comparison with the figures that occupy the sub-period to follow.

This second sub-period, beginning about 1900, affords some contrasts. Australian poetry came of age. (The ballads, still being written, seem to us now—though it was different then—survivals, verses written for the young, when compared with the new poetry.) Another contrast is that the best of the new poets were not at all distinctively Australian. O'Dowd is the striking exception, the poet of national consciousness looking to the Australian future.

In prose Furphy, humorous, sardonic, sceptical, pro-Australian and anti-English (in some respects at least) stands as a major figure rather by himself. Miles Franklin, idiosyncratic in her own brand of Australianism, has her own personal chips on her shoulder. But Richardson is more concerned with a man and his fate than with any essentially Australian motif; Hay uses the Australian background, but one feels it as chiefly an accessory; and even Stone, though portraying an Australian type, the larrikin, rather distils a certain section of Sydney than expresses Australianism.

The whole period—from the eighties to the 1930s—containing as it does our greatest poet (Brennan), our greatest novelist (Richardson), and our greatest short-story writer (Lawson), is the richest and most varied period in our literature to date.

PERIOD III
from the 1930s

CHAPTER X

Modern Poetry

§1

THE poets in this chapter were with few exceptions born in this century and most are still living. Those covering the first third of this century numbered seven. The present group is more than three times as large. There are then, so it might seem, many more good poets today in Australia than there were in any comparable former period. But then, of course, there always are. That is the penalty and handicap of any criticism that deals with contemporary writing. Contemporaries may or may not seem as important individually as their predecessors individually, but collectively they are formidable; for they have not finished writing. But it may be admitted that at present only three of this group, Slessor, FitzGerald, and Judith Wright, appear to have claims to a permanence at all resembling Brennan's.

Some Australian poets had a long apprenticeship. One was Baylebridge, another was Furnley Maurice. A third, of lesser stature, is Frederick Macartney (b. 1887). He has written poems of love, of nature, of philosophical and emotional attitude. The list includes satires; but these, though many mark an advance on earlier poems, are not his best work. He is put in this first group, that of the writers of narrative or of verse drama, despite the fact that some of his most competent poems are poems of mood, of a sort of wry or tough acceptance. In these he looks smilingly and laconically on his own attitude, as though he himself like other things were the object of his own sceptical regard.

His early poems of natural description and his love sonnets bear the imprint of the "poetical"—in the popular sense. His landscapes contain *happy skylarks, great peaks, dewy places*; or in less happy moments, *scanty foliage, stricken foliage, lowering skies*. Such phrases are blank in poems of description: a vague general aura is conveyed, but there is nothing defined; for the language of poetry must be exact as well as evocative. The same phrasing occurs even in the sonnets, where limited space would normally result in phrases more telling because more specific. The language is either "romantic" or flat: *a very rose of flame, love's first ecstasy, wistful eyes Upraised like violets* on the one hand, and *avert our eyes, In effect Her elegance is almost intellect, though this is hardly clear* on the other.

The satires are more effective because in them Macartney has less indulged a taste for adjectives and phrases like the examples quoted. *Metropolis* has some bitter and bare force:

> These buildings of the town,
> Street upon street,
> Seem cliffs where troglodytes come scrambling down
> To meet:
> Barter is in their eyes,
> And cunning to preclude surprise.
> Here life is as a ring-barked gum,
> Withering to a skeleton in the blue scorn of the skies,
> Suckling no leafage and giving no shade,
> Dumb
> To the fondling of darkness at night,
> Bone-white,
> Moon-dismayed,
> Perch for such fowl
> As vulture and owl.

The lines are stripped of excrescences.

The satires in a later volume, *Gaily the Troubadour* (1946), are more ingenious. They are couched in various traditional forms —villanelle, ballade, rondel, roundel, rondeau, and so on—and provide acid comments on contemporary events.

One volume demands fuller treatment and praise. This is the oddly but satisfyingly named *Tripod for Homeward Incense* (1947). It is a monologue by the Australian captain of a lugger who, going to China, meets by stealth the girl Chiao. The tripod is dedicated to her ancestor Yi, and as the smoke rises from its incense the thoughts of the Australian turn to his own land. Prepared to fall in love, he is distracted by the urn and the contrast it suggests between the traditional and ordered culture of China—

> . . . a land that lacquers its care,
> carves its sceptical acquiescence in ivory,
> and moulds its ancient filial respect in imperishable metal—

and the withdrawn unwelcoming nature of his own country—

> . . . the last sanctuary of the defeated gods,
> accepting the ministration

of stealthy primal rites,
punishing all other tenure
with arid contempt.

The contrast is underlined by the verse form: when he thinks of the girl and her background, the formalised couplet is used; when his reveries move to his own land, then we have a sort of free verse, occasionally rimed, with long lunging lines perhaps symbolising the sweep of unpeopled space. Of the two, the couplets are the more polished and also the more competent:

I take the tripod where it stands,
Exalting it with both my hands,
And turn it slowly with the awe
Of lovely things that have no flaw.

At last, feeling himself alien, he leaves Chiao asleep and goes to his vessel to sail for home, driven by

a yearning for those bright Austral seas,
guarded by the long sword of the reef.

It is all done, as it were, with the eyes open. It is a sort of half-humorous resignation, of yielding to what he half rejects. And the terse ending preserves the tone:

My country's idioms dismiss
the deeper hurt,
hid in our curt
similitude of your singsong:
So long!

More varied and of greater stature is the next poet. Possessed of the most diverse literary talent in Australia, Douglas Stewart (b. 1913), New Zealander by birth, came to Australia in 1938. He is poet, novelist, critic, dramatist, and has been editor of the Red Page of *The Bulletin* since 1941. He began with poetry, and has never abandoned it, but most readers think of him first as our greatest radio verse dramatist.

His earlier volumes of poetry, for example *Green Lions* (1936), have the voice of youth, with the coloured adjective and the surprising image:

In a cold cube of silence and great rage,

and, a little more strident:

. . . black abysses fanged with jagged doom.

It is all very sought out and chosen, but it does not escape the

stock phrases like *wild desire* and *music rare*, the youthful equivalents of poetry. The result is a certain confusion, a piling up of
unfocused effects, like a tousle of jewels in a window. Quite
different is *The Dosser in Springtime* (1946). Stewart has either felt
that having mastered the craft he can afford to be playful, or else
he has simply outgrown early manner and mannerisms. He has
grown one or two others in their place, though these obtrude
themselves only occasionally. In this volume the whimsical and
the fanciful are his notes; most of the poems are then rather like
jeux d'esprit, ingenious with double rimes and anapests. Now and
then this has its own special delight:

> And the bullfrogs groaning like trombones.

On the whole, though, we read them as they were probably
intended—the light effusions of a man really engaged on more
serious business. They are perhaps disclaimers.

Another book of verse, *The Birdsville Track* (1955), is the outcome of a trip to the Lake Eyre Basin. The poems are in two
groups, the first dealing with the coastal and mountain and river
areas before the semi-desert region is reached. These are competent, but they lack vividness. If one may hazard a guess, this
is due to their subjects, which are aspects of the country he went
through. This kept changing, and the things he saw were part of
a panorama. In the second section, *The Birdsville Track* sequence,
the changes of scene were not so various: the places changed their
names—

> Dulkaninna, Koperamanna,
> Ooroowilanie, Kilalpaninna—
> Only the names
> In the land remain
> Like a dark well
> Like the chime of a bell—

but everpresent were sand and stone, cloudless sky and blazing
sun, the essential makers of the landscape and the things in it.
The changes were only varying faces of the same object. So that
they left a far deeper imprint on the mind and memory of the
observer. But whether this is the explanation or not, these poems
are more vivid than those in the first group. They afford sudden
insights into the spirit of that area. We have no other desert
poems as good as these. Probably the best are the shortest,
almost like epigrams (in the classical sense), with that touch of

fantasy and whimsy that Stewart indulged in quite early.
Grasshopper runs:

> And then the red stone hopped
> Where all the stones were red
> And it had legs like a frog
> And a big strange insect's head.
> Oh where's the green world gone
> When even the grasshopper turns
> To a kind of dragon of the sun
> In a land of hopping stones?

The essence of the landscape is caught in *The Branding Fire*,
where the sun like man leaves its imprint and marks things for
its own:

> The dust, the smoke and the yellow fire on
> The red plain heating the branding-iron,
> As though the sun's long white-hot blast
> Had struck the stones to flame at last
>
> .   .   .   .
>
> Like man's own will I see that fire,
> Who stamps the stones with his desire,
> Who herds his beasts and burns his brand
> Like red-hot iron on this red land.

Of his verse-plays the most famous is *The Fire On the Snow*
(1944), based on Scott's Polar expedition. It is in its construction
and its material as simple and stripped as bare as the reality it
recounts. The voices of five men talking as they struggle or rest,
and the commentary of the announcer like an onlooker pitying
but unable to help; a small group that diminishes as the story
moves on; no startling effects, for even background of sound can
be done without; no events that suddenly flare up, for even death
in the South is quiet—these are the things Stewart has worked
with. The verse, partly unrimed, partly rimed, with its speech
rhythms for the characters, is in parts almost casual. Poetry, in
the sense of a deliberately chosen effect sought and captured, the
poetry of comment, is when employed put into the mouth of the
announcer—

> . . . marching and halting, marching,
> And the sledge's long snowy sigh
> In the stream of their movement, lurching—

or recounting the sacrifice of Oates, who went out to die in the
blizzard so that he would not delay the others—

> They let him go.
> In grief and shame
> They let him go
> Out to the flame
> Of wind and snow
> Where he burns for them.

However good some of these passages may be, the talk of the
men, never so heightened as to produce the feeling of conscious
speeches rising to an occasion, is more moving still.

We may wonder, perhaps, whether the play might not have
been tightened by shortening the period dealt with, whether the
return alone from the Pole might not have made for a greater
unity and focusing of effect. But it would have been different,
and those who have listened to it and read it remain content with
its grave and stern music.

The Golden Lover, published in the same volume as *Fire on the
Snow*, dramatises a Maori legend, the belief in the faery people of
the mountains, red-haired and fair of skin, who kidnap Maori
girls into their fastnesses. Tawhai is captured by Whana, her
golden lover, falls in love with him, but returns to her village by
day. It is an allegory of the dream hero in every woman's
heart:

> He is the golden hawk
> Who hangs in the sky of my dreams.

Ultimately, a realist like every woman, Tawhai faces the mundane truth and returns to Kuarangi, her fat lazy husband, and
her own people to whom she is bound by all material ties. It is a
delightful satire on women. It has a glinting humour, a delicious
raillery, and we can only wonder why it has not gained the
popularity of *The Fire on the Snow*.

Ned Kelly (1943) and *Shipwreck* (1947) and the ballad collection of *Glencoe* (1947) may be taken together. The first two were
intended for the stage. But radio has claimed these pieces, and
they fit that medium better than any other. As plays they are
undramatic: they lack the tense situation, the clearly outlined
character, the movement and structure of good stage plays, and
the significant dialogue. A single example, a few words from
Lawler's *Summer of the Seventeenth Doll*, brings out one aspect. The

daughter in the next room objects to doing something, and her mother shouts: "All right, don't be told." There is more sense of the theatre, more understanding of what drama is for, in those five words than in all the dialogue of these plays: the phrase is idiomatic and colloquial, it tells us about the mother, it tells us about the daughter, and it implies a whole world of past and present and future relations between them. Much of Stewart's dialogue resolves itself into debate, the pros and cons of bush-ranging, the morality of shooting troopers, the right to do this and that, the aspirations of man and the urges unexpressed that simmer below. It is, in short, all too often concerned with things outside the play. This is not to deny the poetry, which has a statuesque sort of effect as of static grouping of characters. It often has that. But these are not the dramatic essentials. In other words, Stewart is one of the most notable writers for radio; but he is not a stage playwright.

Some of the same spread appears in John Manifold (b. 1915), a poet as yet unsure where his talent lies. He has produced a volume, *Selected Verse* (1948), which contains a spare gathering of brief tales, satires, songs, and sonnets. An ex-soldier, a collector of Australian ballads and songs, he is radical in politics, but his satirical verses in this sphere are not his best. One might expect otherwise, for he has an eye for pretence and sham, a colloquial vigour, and some command over the pointed phrase. But the command is not sufficiently dexterous, so that a certain artless-ness obtrudes even where the theme looks promising. His in-genuity is seen in his sonnets, which gather tension as they develop, and explode at the end. Among his best poems in the selection are the short narratives—*The Griesly Wife*, *The Bunyip and the Whistling Kettle*, and *Legend of the Swans*. Here he manages the eerie note with deftness. About as good a lyric as he has written is *To Lucasta, On seeing no immediate hope of returning from the wars*. It has a wry-mouthed humour, a touch of the shrugging cynicism which is his most amiable and prevalent trait. The sub-acid lyric appears to suit his temperament and powers. This brief poem, which will find its way into the anthologies, may be quoted in full:

> The facts may be a bit obscure
>   But all the legends show
> A poet's blood is good manure
>   Where freedom is to grow.

> One dies at Zutphen, one in Greece,
>   Dozens in France and Spain,
> And now it looks, by all one reads,
>   Like Greece's turn again.
>
> The mode is exigent, my sweet;
>   I cannot well refuse
> To stoop and buckle to my feet
>   My pair of dead men's shoes.

But the best still remain the narratives, where the frightening and the humorous provide the standard ingredients for the grotesque. This is a type too easily undervalued. In the words of Arnold's *Scholar Gipsy*,

> But it needs heaven-sent moments for this skill.

Narrative of a different type appears with Francis Webb. Webb's poems are, as it were, commemorations. His earliest volume, *A Drum for Ben Boyd* (1948), deals with a plausible and robust confidence man of the Australian fifties. The man Boyd does not appear: others comment upon him—reporter, boat builder, artist, business man and the like. So that we are given a view, indirect and prismatic, of the man who influenced the speakers. The comments are prefaced by a chatty report, as from an unsuccessful feature writer, and a futuristic Author's Prologue.

The medium is a sort of blank verse, but looser than the normal and verging upon *vers libre*. Webb makes an effort to vary the idiom of each user. Sometimes the humour comes through, but less often the real personality of the speaker: each is typical, not individual, and the result is a sort of mild carica-ture, where the characters parody themselves. But Webb can hit out phrases, as this by the captain holding the presumed skull of the dead Boyd in his hands and ruminating upon its effect:

> Holding it is like splintering a mirror
> And finding a thousand faces round your boots.

Less successful is the picture of the explorer in *Leichhardt in Theatre* (1952). A tendency noticeable in the first volume is more obvious in this, the straining after the adjective that will startle and yet illuminate:

> And from soured plots of earth
> Only the grudged and cringing harvest.

Now take *cringing*, here used with considerable effect, and imagine it made a violent word with a presumed greater force. It is only a short step to adjectives that are sought-out, which tell us how much the poet is trying, and which yet do not illuminate at all. They are there only for their own sake, gate-crashing in fancy dress. The result can be a feeling of laceration, as though the mind had been pushing through prickly pear. *Birthday* (1956) carries things further, and syntax and indirection make the reader's task more difficult. If the reward were a glimpse of a deepened sensibility, then it would not matter. Webb's best poem is probably *Morgan's Country* in his second volume. The ingenuity of approach in the more or less patterned attack that is Webb's characteristic is here seen at its best. We can praise it as a frame for the sharp picture, not merely as an expedient.

The two volumes of Harold Stewart (b. 1916) set him rather apart from the others of the group, indeed from all his Australian contemporaries. His first volume, *Phoenix Wings* (1948), became inaccessible except in libraries, and he rested almost unknown until *Orpheus* appeared in 1956.

He is concerned with art, with myth, with the bearing of legends and psychology on poetic inspiration. This sounds formidable, and we might expect the result of these preoccupations to be a versified body of theories elaborately subtle and complex. On the face of it we get nothing of the sort. The surface of his poetry is polished and brilliant, and many readers will be content to leave it at that. *The Ascension of Feng*, the best poem in his first volume, glitters from the first line:

> The airy aviary of afternoon
> Is vast and vertical. Its light-rings lift
> High in exquisite symmetry, to build
> A cylinder of innumerable strings,
> Whose luminous fragility of frame
> Is limited by towering filaments:
> The fine gilt wires of vibrant heat
> And vivid rods of incandescent air,
> Which circuiting all space, there encage
> Delicate emperies of clear extent
> And realms of a tremulous immensity.

This picture of a tenuous cage of air has made demands on the poet's skill. Stewart conveys the bubble fragility by a mixture of the insubstantial and the concrete. Such an appeal to the senses is constant and varied throughout. Not every attempt is successful:

> The distant silence shattering with a clap,
> Slits and slats of a shutter clatter up—

an example that steps over the verge of the fantastic and the wire-drawn. A contrasting effect, a susurration, lends itself more readily to ingenuity:

> There is an upward gust of beaten wings,
> A wind of pinions with a noiseless push
> Of soft dishevelled feathers.

The shimmering surface of imagery overlays the theme. Feng the Phoenix, the sun bird, represents the creative urge in all the arts, the warmth and power that give rise to vital life. So with other figures in the poem. Behind it lies the theory that the arts are nourished by and spring from the subconscious:

> The glowing germ takes root; and fertilized
> By the primeval filth below the mind,
> Up from its bed of dark obscenity
> Springs as a shoot of flame in brave renewal.

In the second volume the theory is less hidden. The myth of Orpheus, seeking his lost love in the Underworld, becomes a patent allegory. It is a narrative poem in twenty-seven short pieces, each relating a stage of the adventure. Here the clues are given, and their recurrence is like a sort of running key or commentary. They may for some readers render the story a trifle artificial; but on the whole it is easy enough to take them in one's stride and enjoy a tale that in Stewart's verse reads with a sparkling ease. He uses a five-lined stanza, ringing changes on the rime arrangement:

> For poetry and music can
> Lay on barbarous deeds a ban,
> And tame the animal in man;
> And then those bestial powers inspire
> The lucid measures of the lyre.

This stanza, one from the very start of the poem, sets a pattern: the ingenuity and control of the rime, the air of mastery in a stanza form that very easily could become staccato or crude, and the suave air of seriousness as of eighteenth-century mockery. The whole poem is like this, a piece of delightful bric-à-brac. No adult reader is going to take it all quite seriously. To accept all the allegorical undercurrents as profound or as some contribution to our insight into the poetic principle—this is quite impossible: it would render the poem *vieux jeu*. Stewart we must recognise as a master of the ostensible, a solemn jester, and the poem in consequence a little masterpiece in that kind. Humour is doubly welcome in a sophisticated form like this.

The polish so obvious in *Feng*, perhaps so obtrusive, is here toned down; the glittering play of fancy that lay like a veneer over the earlier poem has become absorbed into the narrative. The medium and the story are adeptly suited to each other. Even the introduction of the mother-complex into the development of Orpheus he manages with witty dexterity:

> But as the erotic flames arise,
> Smoke gets in the bridegroom's eyes,
> Which to Eurydice impart
> His mother's image in his heart,
> Transfigured by the dreamer's art.

Stewart has read his Dryden and his Byron to some purpose. It is a matter of the tone that he has caught, of adjustment to the taste and perception of responsive readers. The level of this poem is so constant that almost any stanza would serve as illustration:

> Intoxicated, god-possessed,
> The satyr whom he thought suppressed
> Awakens rampant in his breast.
> With cloven hoof and pointed ear,
> Capricious urges leap and leer.

The use of *capricious*, double and ambiguous in force, is a neatly indelicate instance of verbal innuendo. A poem like this, of a type rare in our literature, is a salted and spiced *bonne-bouche*.

§2

To group the following poets as lyric poets may do violence to terms and probably to the impressions of many readers. Two at least of the last group might well find their place in this, while the first member of this could fit into the last. The classification is largely and fallibly personal. But the best work of these poets shows them as singers first, tellers of tales or poets of reflection second.

N

The eldest of this group is Peter Hopegood (b. 1891). He is the only poet resembling Harold Stewart, and then only in certain beliefs. Much of his life and all his education were carried on outside Australia. He arrived here in 1924. In the last fifteen years he has satisfied himself of a revelation, for an exposition of which a reader is referred to the Introduction to *Circus at World's End* (1947). In brief, he holds that there is a cosmic Self, which is striving for a cosmic self-dominance. It does this by division into parts which interact. This interaction we are aware of as life. As parts or manifestations we ourselves seek union with and awareness of this cosmic Self. To achieve this we must sink through layers of our unconscious or subconscious. Some can achieve this by effort, as for example in states of self-induced trance. Most of us have only dreams at our disposal. From these dreams all our myths are born, which are found represented in literature and beliefs in archetypal patterns. All myths are kin.

This interpretation Hopegood makes use of in his verse. He considers that the traditional ballads contain symbolism that can be understood by his principles. And he has proceeded in his turn to write ballads containing underlying significance. The reader can understand this if he understands Hopegood's introduction. All this may give the impression that his verse is, so to speak, written to order, composed to fit a theory. If so, little of it appears on the surface. To interpret a poem of his no doubt we should need to apply his symbols as he uses them, but in part at least we can enjoy it without too much digging.

The immediate effect is one of great freshness, as of the springtime of our world, mingled with an odd elfish faun-like slyness. It is very difficult to choose lines or stanzas to quote since each poem is so close knit round a core of meaning or mood that any section cut from the rest loses much of its significance. But this extract that ends *The Bargain* may serve. The Green Man has offered the boy a line if, when he catches the strange fish,

> you will let me hold it, too.
> and maybe press its throat a little with my fingers,
> in return for your pretty line?

> .   .   .   .

> Where? Where? Give me the line!
> Ugh—but I see no fish!
> The pool was like a glass but now!

Why, I could see the moon in it,
just above my hand it was, as I reached for the line . . .
just as clear as glass the pool was
but now it is growing dark as night.

Many of the poems are narrative, and frequently they appear in a comic colloquial guise. It is not parody, a debunking, but a sort of modern commentary. Sometimes it is like exuberance let loose. But various as Hopegood is, he is best in the symbolic lyric. The following, a poem entitled *Labrys*, conveys that touch of the medieval eerie, the unreality of moonlight, that he can at his best recapture and transmit:

> Let Wisdom's Core invoke for me
>   a dog,
>   a bird,
>   an elder-tree.
>
> This dog am I,
>   that bird will be,
>   when Time shall roost
>   in the Eildon tree.
>
> This dog, that bird . . .
>   they sponsored me,
> when Love was nailed
>   to the midmost Tree.
>
> Incontinent in rage,
>   This dies,
> but That knew Love,
>   though crucified.
>
> That gained to Paradise,
>   but This
> must guard for aye
>   the gates of Dis.

Love lyrics in Australian poetry are frequent enough, but there are few love poets. Baylebridge is one, and his poems on this theme are emotional and contemplative. The only poet of physical love is Kenneth Mackenzie (1913–54). The first of his two volumes, *Our Earth* (1937), appropriately illustrated by Norman Lindsay with Pans and women, is a long blank-verse poem of over a thousand lines. It is an elaborate pastoral and song of the love of earth and woman. In an Introduction Lindsay writes of it as "a poem driven into being by a passionate disgust for a mechanical universe". As he goes on to say, "Fecundity is the inspiration." The attacks on the sterile world of the machine are used to point the contrast with the natural fruitfulness of earth in its seasons. Interwoven with this pervasive note of fruition is the love of woman, the mother, human counterpart of the earth and its fruits:

> Therefore our summer be a joyful one
> pledged deep with wine beneath the boughs that hang
> heavy and fat with fruit, where fires the light
> its flame in the first peach's bloomy skin.

In a poem of this length on such a theme it is perhaps impossible to avoid a certain monotony of tone. Quite often a passage reads as if it had occurred before, as though things were being said more than once. The poem in fact tends to grow a little garrulous. This works against the effect Mackenzie strives for, that of a bursting and joyous plenitude. And even in the individual description this is hard to convey. These lines are among his richest:

> the leaves their own fruit are; and every star
> quickens and swells, and moonlight rich and thick
> like mountain honey follows on the sun
> in cold nights, from the far fountain's gold
> downsliding.

From the long poem he turned to the lyric in his second book, *The Moonlit Doorway* (1944). Here he writes of love as a lover, of love in its protean aspects—its renewing freshness, its joy-giving, love in memory, love unregretted, infatuation unresented. Many poems are nostalgic and anticipatory, where he looks back on love and forward to its renewal. The transience of love and day and life appears as a motif. As before in the first volume, however, a slight sense of sameness, the reaction to a theme often repeated, is felt. It is rather surprising that, except in one or two of the more completely physical love poems, he is not very vivid, though he can give us lines like

> Beauty's eternal quality, surprise.

He is the odd example of the love poet with too great a facility with words. They come almost unbidden, and he accepts them often without discriminating. If only he had found it all more difficult then he might have made his choice more carefully.

From the technical angle, however, his love poetry is the most competent we have.

The two best poems in the volume are not love poems. One is *The Union*:

> Death at the dreaming candle sips
> and death sits down upon my chair
> and takes the breath between my lips,
> the ebb and swell of midnight air.
>
> And death is in my very thought:
> here in this room we two are one,
> into one timeless being wrought,
> as though my earthly life were done . . .
>
> The moonlight and the candlelight
> burn in death's shadow, sink and die
> across the loneliness of night:
> we are eternal, death and I.

A Fairy Tale is the reaction to the fear of air raids. The child tosses and cries and he consoles it. There are no raids. But one day there may be. The poem has a considerable impact. The murmured repetition that ends the poem is the poignant comment:

> Turn and sleep again.
> The sound you dreamed was just our old friend thunder
> roaring with pain.
> The wet splashing torrents, that showed red
> through eyelids closed on open dreaming eyes,
> were only rain,
> and the footsteps have walked up into the sky,
> away at the street's end. In this bed
> is nothing but a small warm girl who must
> always, always sleep very peacefully
> and not scream in the night—
> (I trust. I trust.)

The most sensitive lyric poet now writing in Australia is Judith Wright (b. 1915) (Mrs. J. McKinney). Her first volume is *The Moving Image* (1946). Of the twenty-three poems in this little volume about a dozen have become widely known and quoted or have found their way into anthologies. This high percentage does not necessarily indicate that they must be very good poems, though it suggests that. But it serves as a measure of quotability.

This is a quality of her early work, the capacity to give us lines that suddenly pierce the reader with a quickened awareness:

> the innumerable chime
> of water

> the gilt clock that leaked the year away

> sea crouches on sand, fawning and mouthing

> the Gothic tree's on fire
> with blown galahs, and fuming with wild wings.

Such lines are more frequent in the first volume than in the later ones. Indeed the movement in her work has been from the objective to the subjective, from outside to inside, a tendency perhaps due to an increasing deafness.

The subjects that in general she deals with are found present or foreshadowed from the start. She is acutely sensitive to time. Its concern with age—decline, and memories of the past, and fears—results in brief imaginative biographies such as *Brother and Sisters*, a short poem reminiscent of Edith Sitwell's longer *Colonel Fantock*, and not unworthy to stand some comparison with it. Time's power to destroy and bury she gives us; birth and rebirth and resurgence are the replies, and here it is not too fanciful to see the woman and the mother. Images of ruin and dust are balanced by images of awakening to new life or fresh consciousness. Even when she conveys the sense of aridity, of sap and freshness withered, of a bareness (the word *bone*, for example, recurs often), again the note of emergence is heard.

On other occasions this is linked with the nexus of time and change. When the linkage is broken, then we have a sense of deep and blank bewilderment—as though nature had abrogated her invariable laws. This appears in *The Cycads* (in the second volume), a poem about these primitive plants that have not changed in a world of change. The compact has been dissolved:

> for time forgets the promise he once made,
> and change forgets that they are left alone.
> Among the complicated birds and flowers
> they seem a generation carved in stone.

And for us this situation is baffling and we are led nowhere:

> Take their cold seed and set it in the mind,
> and its slow root will lengthen deep and deep
> till, following, you cling on the last ledge
> over the unthinkable, unfathomed edge
> beyond which man remembers only sleep.

So we have the conflict—we recognise and accept change, and yet we are hostile to decay. Whether a synthesis is possible she does not say, and indeed we have no right to demand it of a poet. It is enough that with some of her verse she effects a reconciliation of these tensions in the transitory immortality of art.

Her great talent, especially in this first volume, is in the lyric that springs from a scene or a person or a thing. She begins with the concrete. And like other poets of the last twenty years or so she has mastered the medium for it, a language in which Australian words or idioms find their place unselfconsciously. The image, vivid and original, the metaphor assimilating and provocative—here she surpasses most other Australian poets. It is possible that in her later volumes she has become rather conscious of what she achieved: the image has become less fresh, the outline less sharp and coherent, the poem more reflective.

Her second volume, *Woman to Man* (1949), opens with a small group of poems of pregnancy. These are not all of the same level, and one of them for some readers is embarrassing (as though they had eavesdropped and felt ashamed of it afterwards). But the opening poem, which gives its title to the book, demands a different attention. This poem is her zenith. It is a poem tightly economical despite its variation on a theme: the images, precise yet evocative, rising in each stanza like a wave, are subsumed under a mood. And the shattering final line, with its reversal of feeling and its change to particularity, is an example of that kind (*Since there's no help*) in which Drayton (or an unknown) provided the most famous instance. It runs: [1]

> The eyeless labourer in the night,
> the selfless, shapeless seed I hold,
> builds for its resurrection day—
> silent and swift and deep from sight
> foresees the unimagined light.
>
> This is no child with a child's face;
> this has no name to name it by:
> yet you and I have known it well.
> This is our hunter and our chase,
> the third who lay in our embrace.
>
> This is the strength that your arm knows,
> the arc of flesh that is my breast,
> the precise crystals of our eyes.

[1] From *Woman to Man* (published by Angus & Robertson).

This is the blood's wild tree that grows
the intricate and folded rose.

This is the maker and the made;
this is the question and reply;
the blind head butting at the dark,
the blaze of light along the blade.
Oh hold me, for I am afraid.

It is not perhaps a perfect work. Part of the last stanza, for
example, may be thought inferior to what went before; and the
image of the blade is so recurrent in her verse that it may strike
a fastidious reader as a mannerism. But when all is conceded, it
is a poem beautiful in structure and effect. It is so fundamental
as to be humanly universal, and yet only a woman could have
written it. Through it runs a hurrying and triumphant recognition: it is not a woman but Woman speaking—until at the end the
moving and human particular voice breaks in. With its press and
urgency it is in its kind probably the greatest lyric in Australian
poetry.

This device of a concluding reversal of tone needs a tact that
is not always at a poet's command. In *Eli, Eli*, for example, the
end is something of an intrusion: [1]

To see them go by drowning in the river—
soldiers and elders drowning in the river,
the pitiful women drowning in the river,
the children's faces staring from the river—
that was his cross, and not the cross they gave him.

To hold the invisible wand, and not to save them—
to know them turned to death, and yet not save them;
only to cry to them and not to save them,
knowing that no one but themselves could save them—
this was the wound, more than the wound they dealt him . . .

He watched, and they were drowning in the river;
faces like sodden flowers in the river—
faces of children moving in the river;
and all the while, he knew there was no river.

The revelation in the last line is a shock—the conjurer drawing
aside the curtain to show that something has vanished. It provides a pleasure of a kind, but the kind is illegitimate in the lyric.
So it is inferior as a poem, then, despite its grave and pitiful

[1] From *Woman to Man* (published by Angus & Robertson).

music, to *Woman to Man*; for in that poem the reversal comes from and within the emotion. In *Eli, Eli* the reversal comes from knowledge which has been withheld. The first contains the change of mood that is common to all, writer and readers alike; the second contains the piece of information brought from behind the poet's back. The first poem suffuses us; the second startles us.

The other memorable poem in this volume is *The Old Prison*, a tone poem of lament. We think of Judith Wright as a master of visual imagery. Here the imagery is aural as well as visual, a plangent appeal that stirs the reader like a grief:[1]

> The rows of cells are unroofed,
> a flute for the wind's mouth,
> who comes with a breath of ice
> from the blue caves of the south.
>
> O dark and fierce day:
> the wind like an angry bee
> hunts for the black honey
> in the pits of the hollow sea.
>
> Waves of shadow wash
> the empty shell bone-bare,
> and like a bone it sings
> a bitter song of air.
>
> Who built and laboured here?
> The wind and the sea say
> —Their cold nest is broken
> and they are blown away.
>
> They did not breed nor love.
> Each in his cell alone
> cried as the wind now cries
> through this flute of stone.

It is always dangerous and frequently absurd to indicate certain sounds in a poem and claim certain effects for them. The classical example is Tennyson's line—

> And murmuring of innumerable bees—

where it has been cruelly suggested that the substitution of *murdering* and *beeves* would be a salutary corrective to the vowel-hunters. Part of which is true—but not all. Conception and emotion arise first, and then the sounds serve as reinforcement.

[1] From *Woman to Man* (published by Angus & Robertson).

If we keep something like this in mind, then we may say that in *The Old Prison* the sense of desolation is accentuated by the vowels. Predominant are those as in *bees, flute, wind,* and *stone,* vowels termed close or half-close by the phonetician (or with such final elements when diphthongal). There can be little need to say, however, that the initial effects are due to the nouns— *wind, south, sea,* and so on—with the associations that, as used in this poem, they awaken in the reader. It is after this that the vowels, with a noticeably small proportion of open ones, underline the tone of thin despair. The poem, as a pattern, focuses the devices. The brilliant interweaving of the bee motif (*cells, honey, pits*) may be left for the reader to appreciate.

In *The Gateway* (1953) the image grows rarer, though a few examples still hold much of the former magic:

> The snake, the fang of summer, beauty's double meaning,
> shifts his slow coils and feels his springtime hunger,

and

> I saw the eel wither where he curled
> in the last blood-drop of a spent world.

But the verbal felicity we have come to expect occurs only in sparse measure. Image follows theme as an illustration or manifestation. Indeed the book appears, with its use of assonance and half-rimes, rather like a pause after movement. It is tentative. The tendency is to tell the reader about things, to ponder mysteries and convey the results; so that often we hardly seem to have an experience but rather to read about one.

Some of the themes carry over from the second volume— rebirth from death, spring and renewal, the transformations that follow birth and death, memories that reside in natural objects, age and the years destroying, death and youth. Others concern the search for an embracing contemplation, the possessing of one's soul; and here her love poems, those of a woman, contain the notes of aspiration and fulfilment, the fusing of the disparate into unity. That such subjects are important and everpresent is not to be denied; but the depth or importance of a theme is less than its expression. These are poems of comment, with less immediacy than before. A fair enough sample is the following:

> Easier, far easier, to stand with downturned eyes
> and hands hanging, to let age and mourning cover us

with their dark rest, heavy like death, like the ground
from which we issued and towards which we crumble.
Easier to be one with the impotent body of winter,
and let our old leaves rattle on the wind's currents—
to stand like the rung trees whose boughs no longer murmur
their foolish answers to spring; whose blossoms now are
the only lasting flowers, the creeping lichens of death.

The titles of the books are pointers: *The Moving Image* contains indeed the richest collection of her images; *Woman to Man* indicates themes that bulk large even if they do not exhaust the contents; *The Gateway*, not so specifically, suggests the theme of search, and the gateway itself is of many kinds and leads to different forms of self-knowledge. The fourth volume, *The Two Fires* (1955), prefaced by a quotation from Herakleitos, contains poems of these fires—the world that is the manifestation of the one, the vital flame instinct in all, the other the final ruin of all by fire, the fate prophesied of old but never envisaged as one of man's own making:

My father rock, do you forget the kingdom of the fire?
The aeons grind you into bread—
into the soil that feeds the living and transforms the dead;
and have we eaten in the heart of the yellow wheat
the sullen unforgetting seed of fire?

And now, set free by the climate of man's hate,
that seed sets time ablaze.
The leaves of fallen years, the forest of living days,
have caught like matchwood. Look, the whole world burns.
The ancient kingdom of the fire returns.

Some of the themes of the previous volumes are now absent or less frequent. The preoccupation with time and its effects, with the resurgence of things after dearth or death—these are no longer the chief subjects. She turns more to the concerns of the artist, the difficulty of snaring objects in words:

Words are not meanings for a tree.

This inadequacy of the medium is not only felt by the poet, it is even manifest in the poems, for the volume is very uneven: some poems are awkward in movement and imperfect in expression, a condition unusual in her work. Behind this uncertainty that the poet feels lies the foiled searching for truth. She seems to imply

not that "the only joy is calm", but that truth may reside in
calm. In nature even movement may mar the surface:

> A far-off boat moves on the morning sea.
> That broad and equal monotone of light
> is drawn to focus; purpose enters in.
> Its unity becomes duality,
> and action scars perfection like a pin.

To attain the calm is beyond our power as human and self-
conscious beings:

> But life breaks in again, time does not cease.

The aspiration is the pursuit of Wordsworth's "wise passiveness".
We have to detach ourselves from the fret of existence, to become
like a thing growing in its kind, or to attain a state natural and
untroubled that exists in its own right:

> to let the hands fall,
> the mind forget;
> to move like trees in the wind;
> to be the night.

Part of our handicap is our readiness to be distracted—a note
struck last century by Arnold. To be ourselves is so difficult just
because we do think. For the animals no problem exists—

> Whatever the bird does is right for the bird to do—

and similarly, in a rounded vignette, *Black-shouldered Kite*—

> Carved out of strength, the furious kite
> shoulders off the wind's hate.
> The black mark that bars his white
> is the pride and hunger of Cain.
> Perfect, precise, the angry calm
> of his closed body, that snow-storm—
> of his still eye that threatens harm.
> Hunger and force his beauty made
> and turned a bird to a knife-blade.

These later poems then are mostly reflections on these problems. It is doubtful if very many of them give us that sudden
new and fresh vision of our world and our experiences in it which
her earlier volumes provide. It is to those that most of her
readers will still turn; in them we find those sensitive responses
and evocations that give her the pre-eminent position among our
modern lyrists.

A poet who is seeking but has not yet completely mastered the articulation of his search is Roland Robinson (b. 1913). His *Tumult of the Swans* (1953) shows him at his task. The flaws in his craftsmanship, however, are individually small—a repetition of certain adjectives like *red-purple* and other hyphenated epithets with *blood-* the first element, an over-fondness for *hair* in metaphor and simile, an inadequacy in the use of the couplet (where rimes must seem to be inevitable if they are not to seem banal or artificial), and a certain lack of sharpness in the image. He strives to conquer the last deficiency and to gain immediacy by the occasional use of a diction that verges on the violent:

> Orchid, purple-blotched, barbaric
> as this love tormenting me.

This tendency underlines his particular quality: he is the poet of contrasts. His chief backgrounds are scrub and forest and desert, and against them he uses sound and colour. He gives us fire-blackened scrub and the red waratah, the sky and the sharp ridge silhouetted, silence and the sudden cry of birds, the colourless west and black cockatoos, the grey of scrub and the green of budgerigars. These are the physical counterparts often of the searcher and his silence or his poetry:

> Let your cry,
> on this rain-bespattered flood,
> call and tear the wild bird free
> from this my human flesh and blood.

His poems then are a sequence, often linked by movement through the one landscape, of glimpses and scenes and the accompanying moods. In these short pieces he is seldom clumsy or artless, except now and again in his rimes. It is a measure of his competence that the occasional cliché, which in lesser work would pass unnoticed or uncensored, in his verse calls for excision or revisal. Tastes will vary about his best piece, but the following example probably shows him at or near his most fully articulate:

> Over the monotone
> of mulga like mind's despair,
> flights of the budgerigars
> flash, particled, showered in air,
>
> in life that is clothed in fire,
> throated with shrill fierce joy,
> gathered and smoothed into speed
> only to writhe and deploy,

> to stream into earth's grey scrub,
> to swerve there in glittering green
> and soar like a vanishing smoke
> where sudden fire had been.

The relation of scene to mood and reflection is glanced at in the first stanza. A fourth stanza repeats the implication and ties the knot:

> Over the monotone
> of mallee and mulga is lost
> song that was fierce shrill joy,
> fire of its visitant host.

As his technique sharpens to the rejection of near-bathos (l. 12) and his awareness of the cliché adjective (*glittering*) becomes more sensitive, his poems will afford us some unusual and illuminating insights.

§3

Satire in Australian poetry has not bulked large; in the last century it appeared, for example, in the form of occasional verse and generally in newspapers. Other poets have often enough cast an ironic or scornful glance on the contemporary scene, but this has been in the nature of an aside. It is only in the last few years that poets of some standing have devoted much of their time to this type of verse or have possessed a habit of mind that gives this colour to their writing. Since mere diatribe or invective is not in question but rather polished and acid comment, the adept user of the weapon has needed skill. So that we can think of these poets for the most part as technicians. The group is not big, but it is distinguished for competence.

The most notable is A. D. Hope. Probably the first thing that a reader notices in his collection of verses, *The Wandering Islands* (1955), is the preponderance of sexual imagery. A little arithmetic confirms the impression. Of the forty-two poems in the book some twenty-four contain such imagery, fifteen of them having direct images, the other nine indirect references to the relevant anatomy.

Now it must be said at the outset that a poet has a right to use what means he finds necessary to his purpose. If the sexual image illuminates, then he will use it; he will indeed use whatever a publisher will consent to get printed for him or the censor will permit. Or again, if he uses such material for its own sake, because it revolts him or because it is amusing, then he has long had a warrant for doing so. The doubtful joke has an immemorial history. Moralists may deplore it, elders may warn and condemn, but it seems almost instinctive in man, and not only in civilised man, to find certain human functions a subject for laughter. Sex has always seemed funny as well as horrible or wonderful. And many of the greatest writers in all tongues have never hesitated to treat sex as a joke when they saw fit to do so.

So much for theory. In practice, though, we find that the amount of physical sexual imagery in good writers has not been great in the bulk of their work. So when we find proportions such as those mentioned earlier, then we may naturally ask ourselves the reason. Are the verses perhaps merely brilliant pornography, examples of ebullient *jeux d'esprit*? Indeed the academic mind has often enough found relief, if we can put it that way, in subjects rather far removed from normal scholarship. The higher the brow, said Aldous Huxley, the lower the loins. Or is this preponderance due to the theme, to the fact that the poems are on an aspect of sexuality? (And if they are, then why the choice of theme?) Or are the images adventitious, not illustrative or illuminating, but dragged in by an inner compulsion? (And is this compulsion a revelation of the author?)

Probably all these play some part in Hope's choice. Often enough the image is funny, it is there for humour, and the joke warrants it. Sometimes the theme is sexual, and again a warrant is found. But often the reader feels that there is no particular need, that another image just as effective could have been found by a writer as skilful as this. Why, then, was the other image not chosen? It is hardly a case of protracted adolescence, though this has been suggested; for Hope is not in any way an adolescent writer. Nor is it a compensation. When we read some of the more lushly carnal poems of Swinburne, for example, we need seek no further for their reason than a portrait of Swinburne and some parts of a biography of him. The reason with Hope would seem to lie in his early years, a guess borne out by the poem *Ascent into Hell*. An early rigidity of training is not always fortunate in its results, and most of us by experience or from confidences can gain some insight into possible consequences. To the forbidden theme the mind returns with a sort of compulsive fascination, like the tongue to a hollow tooth.

Of all the poems to which this discussion so far applies, the most successful is *Imperial Adam*, tropically luxuriant, as glowingly coloured as a Gauguin, as vividly detailed as a Henri Rousseau. In its particular kind it perhaps goes as far as it artistically can and is as successful as it could well be. Oddly enough, the one point at which a reader may cavil is not sexual in the same popular sense—the conclusion, the birth of Cain. The lines telling of his appearance are effective, and the last line—

And the first murderer lay upon the earth—

comes with the force of a climax, unexpected, contrasted. But it contrasts with nothing, and it is not a climax. The temptation must have been strong to use the idea; but it is not really a part of the poem.

This rather lengthy discussion on this one aspect is warranted by a reader's natural curiosity and by the comment that the poems have aroused. But Hope's chief importance does not lie here. The sexuality in his poems does not spring from love, as it does in the work of, say, Kenneth Mackenzie. There are no poems of Hope on love fulfilled. The temper of his mind has precluded that. Two of his qualities, two qualities that have been notably lacking in Australian poetry, are astringency and wit. And these are the hall-marks of the satirist. Hope's fastidious perception and the values that by occupation and nature he professes render the modern world an inevitable object of his attack—its routine, its artificiality, its mechanical standards, its spectator cults, its apotheosis and degradation of sex. This satire is penetrating and subtle and embittered; at the same time it is allusive and indirect and often hidden. Hope is the sourest and most adept satirist we have.

The allusiveness is part of Hope. A great number of the poems are cast as allegory, or veiled by imagery and symbol. He is as much a metaphysical poet as a satirist. The theme of such poems is mostly dissatisfaction or disillusion—things are not as they once promised to be, the real and the ideal are far apart, the fulfilment is paid for too heavily in the aftermath or in retrospect. The poet forever stands off and observes himself as well as the rest of us. What he desires he tells us by implication, and even then we are never sure if we are right in our surmise. This leaves us with the feeling that he is, as it were, a negative writer; he says No to life, however enthusiastically he may utter that negative.

It is no condemnation of him as a poet in his own sphere, of course, for we have no right to demand an explicit or positive philosophy of any poet. We may wish he had given us different poems, but we must accept what he offers. As it is, he remains the caustic analyst of the sham, the fake, the ersatz.

As a craftsman he must rank as the finest of our conscious, made artists. That is, the sense of apparent spontaneity is seldom present except in his lighter verse. The esoteric, recondite adjective or noun is very frequent; we can almost follow the search for it. This effect of strain is not the characteristic of a great poet but of a poet who knows what poets have done, what poets can do, who is well aware of the pitfalls that beset the way of poetry, who skirts them with wariness, but who very seldom walks as if the pitfalls were not there. He takes us among amusing and fascinating places; but he wears tight shoes, and any reader with responsiveness must often grimace as the shoe pinches.

There are some poets who may be called uncrystallised. These are the foiled searchers; they know that a word or phrase is somewhere; they know what they want it for; but they do not know the word or phrase itself. Their only recourse is the approximation, a verbal locution that hovers on the verge of real poetry. Such a poet is John Thompson (b. 1907), who is always about to find the perfect expression for his mood or the scene he views or the incident he has experienced.

In his *Thirty Poems* (1954) we have this sense of loss. Something has vanished—an opportunity, a pregnant discontent, a freshness of unsophisticated youth—and cannot be recaptured. Others too have lost such treasures, and like him find meagre consolation only thinly and for a moment. And really the consolation is hardly worth finding, for it is recognised as a consolation. This is the note that runs through the poems. The ironic thing is that he has lost also the freshness and point that appeared in his two earlier volumes. In this volume the themes are more weighty, but the expression, attempting to be adequate to importance, lacks sharpness and inevitability. He appears as Arnold, unhappy and disillusioned, but without Arnold's power of enshrining the mood.

It is possible that he has read and remembered too much. Eliot he has assimilated so thoroughly that phrases and moods and attitudes in his verse are constantly and sometimes tantalisingly reminiscent of the older poet. The lack of definition in his verse is perhaps encouraged by the frequent absence of rime. Some

o

sort of discipline, for example a shorter line or a shorter poem or a tauter mood, might prove a corrective. It is significant that the shorter poems are indeed the best, and that satire is his most effective instrument. In such poems the sense of straining is absent. As it is, in his more ambitious poems he writes with the perfect phrase forever on the tip of his tongue.

Certain kinds of satire, chiefly those not attacking a person, depend for much of their effect upon a community of belief between poet and reader. The personal satire, seemingly most limited, is oddly enough most universal. Pope's attacks on his enemies and former friends still prick our response today. And if it is replied that the victims are mere names or shadows, long vanished and often requiring a footnote in explanation, we may answer that this does not matter. A satire that deals with beliefs and institutions, however, is not nearly so sure of our response. If the objects are things we believe in, then indeed the satire for us may miss the mark completely.

James McAuley's satire is of this second kind, and is open to precisely this danger. A convert to Catholicism, McAuley (b. 1917) is the most trenchant poetic defender of some of the tenets of his faith. If we hold the same beliefs; if education, for example, is a thing to be based on certain religious doctrines and inculcated by those holding the beliefs; if secular State education is a danger to the body politic—if we accept this, then much of McAuley's satire strikes home. But if we do not, then some attacks are hardly felt as satire at all.

His satire in *Under Aldebaran* (1946) is best seen in *The True Discovery of Australia*, where Gulliver reports unfavourably on a proposal to float an Antipodean company:

> The Southern Sea, my lord, in time to come
> Will be the Bargain Basement of the earth,
> With nations like demented women snatching
> Remnants without enquiry what they're worth.
>
> Britannia may find herself obliged
> To put a lot of oddments on the docket.
> But you yourself, my lord, I should advise
> To keep your money in your breeches' pocket.

McAuley's obvious quality is a very polished competence. He seldom falters, seldom is clumsy, always knows what he is about. Our confidence in him accompanies us in reading almost every poem, as in watching an expert conjurer or juggler: we are never uneasy lest he drop something. But conscious craftsmanship can make a poem self-conscious. So that it is rare to find in his work, even in the parts that are not satire, much deeper satisfaction. The best poem he has written, *The Incarnation of Sirius*, gets as near as his habit of mind permits to what most of us demand or expect to find in poetry. This starts off with word play:

> In that age, the great anagram of God
> Had bayed the planets from the rounds they trod.

It is a tendency common in other poems:

> O clear day, synecdoche of time,

or:

> Now, by chiasma of its former themes,

or:

> The world's the thing; Mercator its false prophet;
> We scramble on a flat projection of it,

or:

> Five senses build
> A pentagon of pleasure,

or:

> The deuteronomy of daily life.

There is a resemblance in many of the poems to those of the youthful Aldous Huxley. Apart from these half-conceits, half-verbal tricks that stud the poem, *Sirius* is a success in its unusual kind. One stanza has been quoted often:

> The desert lion antiphonally roared;
> The tiger's sinews quivered like a chord;
> Man smelt the blood beneath his brother's skin
> And in a loving hate the sword went in.

This fusion of the "metaphysical" and the esoteric and the hard competence of craftsmanship gives the poetry of McAuley a flavour all its own.

It is not obvious at first sight where one should place Nancy Keesing. But a general tendency in her poems, especially noticeable in her first volume, *Imminent Summer* (1951), warrants her inclusion here. In this volume things are observed, noted, told, and commented on. It seems a trifle deliberate, as if the poet had felt, however unconsciously: I can make something out of that. This slightly calculating approach, as though experience were regarded merely as grist for poetry's mill, is less obvious in the next volume, *Three Men and Sydney* (1955). And there is a clear advance in technical skill from first volume to second.

Though she writes other poems than these, yet she is best when she draws a conclusion from observation or offers a reflection or even on occasion draws a moral. It would be unreasonable to hope for the same level of comment in all. She can be prosaic in reflection; she can wrap up a commonplace in allegory or formality that deceives nobody, as at the conclusion of *A Spell for Speaking*:

> If you do venture, rash, unheedingly,
> No power can bring you back. That step is such
> The land you left will always be in your view
> But, surely, surely, ever beyond your touch.

She may have at her disposal a contrast or an implication that the reader can anticipate and the expression of which he awaits with pleasure—and then she can misuse it or treat it inadequately, as in the ending of *The Play*, where the theme has come too closely home to the audience. But at her best she deals with a situation in characteristically pointed fashion, that of the ironic commentator. Not the best, but quotable by reason of its brevity, is *Morning Politics*:

> An acid sun that burns the mists away
> Reveals the unfleshed skeleton of day,
> And by what miracle might one devise
> To add to bones hands, feet, trunk, hair, and eyes?
>
> We walk along the thin spine of a street,
> On either side grey skinny ribs retreat;
> Must you, must I, apologize for these
> Filched of their dignity of grass and trees?
>
> While windows in gaunt houses, blank and bare,
> Reject all promise in an idiot stare
> Is it any wonder that the impartial sun
> Splits our linked whole to equal one plus one?

She takes her subjects from men and women, the city, a few aspects of nature, things read, and even things believed. This last theme, as in *Evangelist*, she may treat comically. It is a possible

field for her exploration. We may find it in future poems linked
up with her skill in the expression of the symbolic grotesque as
in *Caroline*, a very effective exercise in the use of the couplet, the
introduced anapest, the mixture of the colloquial with the formal.
It is an ironic oddity, a fusing of the intimate and the aloof.

In other poems she has tried different approaches. The pure
lyric mostly collapses in her hands from a failure to avoid the
trite and the flat line. In one example of the mocking short story
she has a nice touch. *Lines to a First Wife* (from the second)
concludes:

> though you may
> Be bitter, have no angry thought
>
> For him or me; for our life's themes
> Contain some music of yours; a growth
> Continuous. And know we share regimes
> For still a name strange to us both
> He mutters when he speaks his dreams.

When she has some inchoate emotion that may be difficult to
articulate, then she expresses it by overt action. We get this in
the poem of the wild cat, killed by a neighbour and shown to the
child, who hopes that a kitten may survive to hunt on its own:

> My grandad spoke gently: "See how its fur is marked."
> But I turned to her image in the blood, feeling wicked and wise,
> And peeped at myself in that mirror for dead eyes.

If her metrical clumsiness is smoothed out, then we may look
forward with some assurance to poems that will exploit areas that
she has in this volume just opened up.

§4

All Australian poets, perhaps all poets, can claim admission
to this group—the descriptive poets. The heritage of nature,
varied and always present, is something that only the blind and
the deaf do not feel. And this is especially the case in Australia.
All our poets have paid tribute to the background. So again it
is a matter of emphasis. Those who are classed in this section
have been predominantly concerned with nature for one reason
or another—for its sake, for the sake of a theory even, for their

own sake, for a message. And they have necessarily varied not only in approach but also in rendering the results of it. The theme is fruitful, and to trace it through our literary history would throw some light on our national history as well.

Though Norma Davis (1905–45) has written some poems of love, and though the religious motif finds a frequent place in her poems, she remains essentially a poet of the Tasmanian bushland. No other Australian poet has so devoted loving attention to minute and accurate accounts of the life around.

Her attitude is a sort of primitivism. She turns to nature occasionally for solace and rest, but her relation with it is really that of a being that draws life from the contact. Sometimes this is physical, of the body:

> And thrusting down my hand I softly felt
> The earth, and found it warm as though scrub cattle
> Had lain in slumber there all through the night.

Elsewhere she gives us detailed descriptions of colour and shape, of movement and the innumerable sounds that accompany it, of insect and animal, flower and leaf:

> . . . white rain spears, that whisper as they fall.

This intimacy of perception is pervasive, but it is harder to convey in longer passages. Sometimes it is sustained:

> old banksia boughs that lie
> Riddled by rot and hollow as a bell
> Under the bracken; fungus-breath of sly
> Small crawling lichens, grey as cattle lice
> Thronging the bovine shoulders of dark rocks;
> The dark leech-scent of ferns that click like dice
> Under the tread.

Such a sequence is among her best, but when the effect as of a catalogue is felt, then she is less successful. There is just a touch of the travelogue. Even these next lines, precise glimpses of minute life stirring or at rest, have a suspicion of the educational film:

> Mailed water-scorpions passing squat and slow;
> Sleek piebald leeches resting closely curled
> Below hot, spicy blossoms of young cress;
> Flat boatmen beetles rowing rhythmically
> With tiny elfin oars; frail loveliness
> Of inch-long golden carp, and bold and free
> The bullfrogs with their wide perpetual smiles.

Children, we feel, are passing through the museum of natural history. This comment suggests her weakness: the freshness of response may sometimes seem unsophisticated. Her feelings, particularly those of protectiveness or maternal love, can descend almost to mawkishness. Then into the background steal the pixies and fairies and elves. Then the reader turns the page. The fondness for the diminutive words like *little* and *tiny* indicates the danger she often enough falls into. The quality that marks her verse at its best is a sensibility of sight and sound that results in the objective vision.

The highly individual response is that of the next poet. The odd, out of the way talent may or may not find a place for itself in a literature. If it fits into no particular pattern of contemporary writing, and if it is not a great talent, it may in its own lonely niche remain unrecognised. This danger threatens the thin sheaf of poems by James Picot (1906–44). Death in a prisoner of war camp in Siam cut short what might have become an unusual if never very substantial gift. *With a Hawk's Quill* (1953) contains a selection of his extant verses.

In many oddly-turned poems of his the influence of Hopkins is patent, and as is usual with those who come under that spell, it is the mannerisms of Hopkins that are imitated—the clustered consonants, the unusual compounds, the tortured syntax, the gravelly rhythm. In such poems Picot is not at his best:

> Lamp, leaf,—the Wished-for-One-O, separate, crimson!

Now and then it comes off:

> Sandal-wood country, and the air that balm—
> One sweet-wood savour, if a leaf should burn.
> Brick earth, and fir-green fronds, and all the night
> Perpetual stars, for it was rainless June.

But here he is rather more himself.

His most sensitive poems are his lyrics. He makes us feel that the sensitivity is his own, that it is keen, even raw, but the poems where this occurs are still uncrystallised. His awareness finds its most competent utterance in his descriptive poems of the Darling Downs. He has an eye for the odd, for the detail that we all remember when we are reminded, but which we do not put down because we have not the recognition of the essential:

> Swift there, neck down, an emu running—look !

He has in addition an ear, not for the sounds in his verse, for he is not a particularly musical poet, but for voices. *Eclogue I: Prickly Pear* and *Eclogue II: Sandal-Wood* catch the stray reminiscence, the tone of the speaker, and transfer and transmute these.

He was far from being an untutored person; he had read and studied, he knew books and poets. But his verse gives the impression of a highly individual sensibility that is untutored, as though he had not yet found the proper vehicle for his often delicate responses.

To call Rex Ingamells (1913–55) a nationalistic poet of nature demands some explanation of the term. He was the founder of the Jindyworobak Club in 1938, a loose association of writers, chiefly poets, who advocated the growth of Australian culture along lines of its own, undeflected or undistorted by English influences. He expressed the general aims of the club in his *Conditional Culture* (1938). With some of these aims many feel disposed to agree. One of his comments in particular is relevant. If a poet writing of an Australian scene used, say, the word *dell*, then this, in the view of Ingamells, would indicate a lack of direct vision. There is much to be said for this criticism. Such a word carries its freight of associations gathered in the centuries of its use. And these associations are foreign to the Australian scene. So that a writer using it here appears to be looking at things not with his own eyes but through a literary medium, and a medium, moreover, that distorts, that gives colours and associations that do not apply. It may be pointed out that the Jindies of course recognise that since we write in English then we simply have got to use the general vocabulary. Their objection refers to such words as carry too obvious a burden of inappropriate associations. Whether it is possible for Australian poets to modify and acclimatise some of these words is another matter. Some words have changed in Australia, one example being the word *creek*. Its meaning in England is not stream or brook or water course; there it means an estuary. But it was not our poets who brought about this change.

One contention of the Jindies has given rise to some discussion and many jibes. The aborigines, they claim, original inhabitants of the land, have been in elemental contact with the earth. They are the sole real inheritors of the Australian spirit of place. Their ceremonies and primitive art and myths and lore have a message for us and for Australian poets. (Many feel disposed to deny this and ask to be shown examples of the heritage these primitive peoples are supposed to offer.) Further, the Jindies have turned to aboriginal words and taken them as symbols of natural pheno- mena. Some aboriginal words we have adopted and made part of our vocabulary, it is true, like *corroboree* and *boomerang*. But there the matter for most of us has rested, and we do not feel disposed to admit more. The Jindy attitude has been fairly con- sistent and they have not feared to risk laughter in their applica- tion of a theory. If we ask how it works, then it is not difficult to find poems where only Jindies think success has been achieved. If we read

> No more the smoke-wisp signal climbs; no more
> The boomerang glints, arching, in the sky,

we accept without demur the native word because it is now our own. It is a matter of custom. But when we encounter extreme examples, here a stanza often quoted—

> Far in moorawathimeering,
> safe from wallan darenderong,
> tallabilla waitjurk, wander
> silently the whole day long—

then the mind revolts. We turn to the glossary at the end of the volume to find the meanings, and then we still are not dis- posed to accept the newcomers. The first formidable polysyllable means *Law of the Lost*. The other native words mean *strong*, *avenger*, and so forth. It would seem that the Jindies have over- looked a fairly simple factor in linguistic change and growth— that a language will coin new words and adopt others when there is a need felt for them. We have taken *boomerang* into our writing and speech simply because the thing exists and we want a word for it. There is no other word at all for the object. But the case is very different with the words in the stanza above. Why should we adopt these words when we have words for the ideas or the objects already? The only answer is that the new words have such associations that it is worth the trouble. But, we may ask, who knows these associations except possibly a few highly-trained anthropologists? And, indeed, do even they *feel* them as well as know them? The only way such words can gather associations is by use. And only the Jindies will use them. If they had produced a great poet or if they had possessed one as their spokesman, then by his sheer poetical authority he might have wrought the miracle and imposed these words upon us. But the poems of Ingamells or of any other Jindy writer have not sufficed for such a task.

One poet has moved in theme from nature to art. This is Rosemary Dobson. In her work there has occurred a considerable sharpening of technique; from *In a Convex Mirror* (1944) to *The Ship of Ice* (1948) to *Child With a Cockatoo* (1955) the polish and the craftsmanship have increased quite remarkably. But the sensitivity apparent in the first volume has not deepened. There has been a hardening of surface, of patina, but the poems are less humanly satisfying. She has, as it were, grown a shell, and into this, the protection afforded by art, she has bit by bit retreated. One may think that human loss has left a scar, and this has been filmed by other interests almost consciously assumed. The total effect is that she has moved from poetry of emotion to poetry of comment. Detachment has become a habit of mind.

Her third volume is in three parts. The first contains her reactions to pictures; the second to books and missals, legends and the theatre, the other arts that are not painting; the third is more directly lyric, pensive, and regretful. A reader has to resist the temptation to think of the first two sections as removed from reality; for our reaction to the arts is as real as our reaction to love or pain or loss or death or indeed any of the other experiences of our mortality. We may feel, though, that the arts are essentially to be reacted to, to be felt, not to be used as departures for further works of art. Rosemary Dobson in effect is writing criticism quite often—only in verse, not prose.

The poems on pictures are brief annotations, partly descriptive, but mostly thoughts suggested by the themes. There is a brief account of the picture, neatly rounded off by an ingenious application. Some are extremely deft, cameo-like in execution, and a reader experiences a corresponding satisfaction. In other poems the first person is used: the artist soliloquises or a character speaks. These form miniature dramatic monologues after the fashion—and the tone and even on some occasions the words—of Browning. Neat, again; though the reaction of the reader is the feeling that Browning did it rather better. The poet is, disarmingly, aware of this, and *The Plagiarist* expresses her consciousness of the debt. The endings of the art poems often have a tartness, a wryness, a miniature malice. Again, she knows this:

> . . . I, who always find
> In anticlimax pleasure and enjoy
> The lifted eyebrow and the humorous shrug.

So that she can be her own best critic. She is the bystander. Her poem with this title deals with one of those figures who have no apparent part in a picture, but it has its secondary application to the poet herself. These poems, all ingenious, sometimes fantastical, mostly successful, are like *vers de société* on art matters, and they are the best examples of her craftsmanship.

It must not be thought, however, that all her poems on the arts treat the arts as excuses, as pegs on which to tag an ingenuity or an invention. It is clear that this is their main use for her as a poet; but sometimes she pays tribute to the eternalising quality of painting, best seen in *The Mirror*, where Jan Vermeer speaks:

> Nothing exists but what we know,
> The mirror gathers in the world,
> Time and the world. And I shall hold
> All summers in a stroke of gold.

Of the poems of immediate experience of emotional and sensory things the best is *Night and the Land*. Here in the two opening stanzas the metaphor has captured the moment and the action:

> Stranger to me, the dark
> Who lies down at my side,
> The horseman from the heights
> Weary of his long ride,
>
> Who hunts the golden sun
> All day from hill to hill
> And with one bound at eve
> Makes his tremendous kill . . .

No twilight, wrote Coleridge, in the courts of the sun. This is the best poem in the volume; for *The Lost*, despite its quality, its tonal consonances and minor key effects, is marred by technical lapses.

The assimilation of the Australian background, its landscape, its weather, the land and the people and incidents that belong to it, has been largely accomplished. And the vocabulary and idiom in terms of which we think of these things after our unsurprised viewing—these too have found their way into Australian poetry: the themes and the language that goes with them are unselfconsciously used. This is the second flowering of Australian poetry. But the maturity is not yet. This applies, for example, to the poetry of David Campbell. In *Speak With the Sun* (1949) the poems are reflective lyrics, drawing their themes from the Australian scene and from incidents of the last war. There is very little straining, very little uncomfortable stress on the Australianism of the background, no half-defensive insistence on the oddity or unusualness of the scene. And this is in keeping with much modern Australian poetry. Campbell's own quality resides mostly in a sort of fresh vitality, some of it due to recurrent motifs—dawn and birds and space. And his competence is considerable in handling the material. One poem, *The Stockman*, which many readers are likely to consider the best in the book, can serve to illustrate these points:

> The sun was in the summer grass,
> The coolibahs were twisted steel:
> The stockman paused beneath their shade
> And sat upon his heel,
> And with the reins looped through his arm
> He rolled tobacco in his palm.
>
> His horse stood still. His cattle dog
> Tongued in the shadow of the tree,
> And for a moment on the plain
> Time waited for the three.
> And then the stockman licked his fag
> And Time took up his solar swag.
>
> I saw the stockman mount and ride
> Across the mirage on the plain;
> And still that timeless moment brought
> Fresh ripples to my brain:
> It seemed in that distorting air
> I saw his grandson sitting there.

One may take this as an example of the unworried acceptance of a setting. There is an easy grasp of a situation that might be called colloquial in the first stanza; there is an adequate capturing of mood and moment in the second; and there is an extension, half inevitable, half unexpected, in the third. But the taste has faltered once or twice. The last line of the second stanza will not satisfy every reader: it may be called strained, a conceit—though perhaps neither the term nor the condemnation matters.

The flaw resides in the forcing into an atmosphere, simply for
the sake of the atmosphere, of an image that has resisted the
treatment. *Swag* is a part of the poem's currency, but it is a
cracked coin here: the Australian poet has tried to do too much
simply because he is Australian. The other line is the fourth in
the last stanza. It has its justification in the poem because of
the setting—the mirage, the heat waves, the distorting air. But
that is not enough to outweigh what must to many seem a
banality of phrase. Both these lines are faults of technique, and
it is in technique that modern Australian poetry reveals many of
its weaknesses.

Another weakness lies in what one may call density or texture
or some such thing. In reading for any length of time a number
of Australian poets a critic finds it very difficult to preserve a
sense of proportion. He can see differences, he can appreciate
competence or delicacy, he may welcome excellence. But if he
does not have recourse to poetry written outside, then he tends
to take what he is reading as what can be done. Perhaps nothing
is so salutary in such a task as to turn periodically to, say, a
volume of Yeats. It is then that the Australian poetry of the last
twenty years or so falls into a truer perspective. We are still
waiting for our complete poet.

Not many of our modern poets are essentially concerned with
the consolations of religion. This theme distinguishes some work
of Nan McDonald, whose poems often end with such an application. Most of the subject matter is landscape or emotion, with
an occasional incident, but often the point made is the solace
afforded by religious beliefs. This turn in the thought can salvage
a poem which might otherwise sink for lack of the essential
adjective. In poems of natural description there must be insight
as well as observation, understanding and penetration as well as
love. Mere description without significance of detail and mood
is a redundancy. The use of the inevitable and illuminating
phrase, if only it could be found, would cut many Australian
poems down to half their length. Some of Nan McDonald's
descriptive poems come under these strictures. They contain too
many of the stock adjectives and phrases to permit her to rank
as a successful nature poet. Her talent seems better fitted to
poems of narration, of which she gives us only a few examples.
The Uncleared Land is an effective and economical piece of writing,
stripped of much of what appears in other poems as distracting

decoration. It is simple and moving, and above all actual. The events of everyday, of fallible human life—these are the themes that fit her best. She is the poet of man who writes as if she aspired to be a poet of the spirit of country.

There are few Australian poets of locality in any strict sense. Poets have sung of the outback, of the mountains, of the coast, of the sea; but there are not many who evoke for us the peculiar genius of an area, or of a township, or of some particular spot that one's finger can point to on a map. One of the few who have attempted to do so is David Rowbotham. He confines himself mostly to the Darling Downs, the fertile plateau not far west of Brisbane. Of this, and of the people and the townships, its weather and its crops, he gives us an affectionate picture. Too-woomba he has made his own—and ours. There is something of Cowper in this pensive fondness for an area known by long familiarity. It is, like all Australia, an old land in nature, but a very young land in history. But Rowbotham has in a way made legends for it: an old inn, an old house, old people—these he uses as symbols. He creates, as it were, local history.

It is, however, not in natural descriptions that he excels, but in interiors. He is really a domestic poet, if effectiveness is any criterion. His volume, *Ploughman and Poet* (1954), for example, contains no better poem than *The Farmer's Wife*:

> I shall never make a poem
> As the farmer's wife made tea,
> With wisdom's slow mill-water
> And a homespun tale at three.
>
> I shall never make an image
> As she, in teapot size,
> Brewed sleep in a steam of sunshine
> Below the lupins of her eyes.
>
> I shall never win the measure
> Her golden apron made
> As it filled the crinkled kitchen
> With pleated light and shade.
>
> I shall never set soft magic
> In my moment, like this wife;
> From the farmland cup she gave me
> I drank all time and life.

His poems of nature can be pedestrian on the one hand, or

importunate for the striking phrase on the other. This mixture
is less successful than the reflective contentment that warm rooms
or old houses arouse in him and in us. The danger that awaits
him, and from which he does not invariably escape—a danger
that shadows even the poem just quoted—is a sort of kindly
garrulity.

§5

This section deals with the poets of reflection. Of all the
groupings used this is the most elusive and the vaguest. Indeed
all poets, whether classed as narrative or lyric or descriptive,
partly belong to this group since they have of necessity selected
their material, and the act of selection has implied some evaluation of experience. The criterion lies in the treatment: the
philosophical poet tells us; the others imply.

The work of one of these poets, Kenneth Slessor (b. 1901),
shows marked changes in theme and treatment. His volume,
One Hundred Poems (1944), is divided into three sections, each
covering about six or seven years.

The first section leaves the impression of experiment. The
themes are past and distant in time and place—legends, the
medieval scene, figures like Marco Polo and Heine and Pan,
thieves' kitchen, robbers, and gods on earth. To compass these
Slessor employs a rich vocabulary, with the pictorial adjective
and the esoteric noun (like *manticore*), the pronoun *thou*, the
apostrophe introduced by *O . . . !* The poems, in short, are
descriptive, and descriptive in the fashion of the nineties. Now
and again echoes of Wilde and Dowson are heard. Some appeared
in the short-lived quarterly *Vision*, in which Norman Lindsay
delineated his women and satyrs and Jack Lindsay wrote with
Dionysian zest. Many of the poems could be illustrated or
summed up in a picture, and a picture that in its turn seems
dated. It is no accident that Slessor has written a poem in praise
of Norman Lindsay. And the artificiality extends to construction,
where the inverted order of verb and object pays tribute to an
older orthodoxy.

These are poems of fantasy and romance, the poetry of the
young apprentice, already feeling that joy is evanescent and
regretting its short-lived tenure. Often lusty, and as often
plaintive, the poems are in the nature of literary exercises. And

since they are prentice work, the poet is not in perfect control of his medium: words and their colours and scents have taken him in hand and imposed themselves. The four lines below are as characteristic as any:

> Now earth is ripe for Pan again,
> Barbaric ways and Paynim rout,
> And revels of old Samian men.
> O Chiron, pipe your centaurs out.

Slessor draws heavily on the names.

The second section abandons most of the former themes for ones more related to sensory experience, for things closer to us in time and circumstance, and for a theme upon which Slessor has written his best-known poems—the sea. The sea poems are *Captain Dobbin, Five Visions of Captain Cook,* and *The Atlas* (a sequence of five pieces). These, together with one in the third section of the book, are not on the sea as such, but on men who have finished with the sea—or whom the sea has finished with. The romance that the poet formerly found in the past is now part of the present. These lines illustrate this point:

> Once Mermaids mocked your ships
> With wet and scarlet lips
> And fish-dark difficult hips, Conquistador;
> Then Ondines danced with Sirens on the shore,
> Then from his cloudy stall, you heard the kraken call,
> And, mad with twisting flame, the Firedrake roar.

These legendary figures are for legendary and contrasting purposes, not merely for themselves. An operative word is *once,* and it seems an essential word now when such themes are employed. Otherwise we might have a convention out of due time. It requires poetic skill of a high order to use legend today; we have none of our own, and yet are unwilling to accept those of dead days and former poetic fashions. A later age may reverse our judgment and wonder at our taste, but it is almost impossible for us now, conditioned as we have been for the last thirty or forty years by a few poets and much science and all our civilisation, to accept myth alone as the whole theme of a poem. Except for the genius poetry must be in great measure contemporary, must have a particular relevance to its period, must, as it were, be born from it and bear its birthmark.

The other point in these lines is the use of adjectives with a certain enigmatic yet essential quality. These are the two adjectives in the third line of the passage. Slessor is the most noted of Australian poets in his use of such adjectives, rivalled only by A. D. Hope. But in the rightness, the marrying of adjective and noun, Slessor at his best is superior to Hope. At such moments we do not feel—this is probably the test—we do not say to ourselves, How clever! We simply accept.

The short third section is notable for Slessor's best-known poem, *Five Bells*, his best poem, *Out of Time*, and his most successful technical experiment, *Sleep*. The poems in this section are poems of impermanence. There are a few on different themes, but the general tenor is sleep, death, and the sea, and time conditioning all and each. *Five Bells* is the brief flash of memory that contains all in the instant, with the title a recurrent phrase marking or minding or recalling the passage of that instant. It has its much quoted lines—

> Deep and dissolving verticals of light
> Ferry the falls of moonshine down—

and the phrases which Slessor in the early poems let us watch in process of becoming but which here are full-blown.

In *Sleep* the musical interweaving and assonance are among Slessor's most skilfully used devices, as in Sleep's assurance to the sleeper, the foetus in the womb of Sleep:

> And you shall cling and clamber there
> And slumber there, in that dark chamber,
> Beat with my blood's beat, hear my heart move
> Blindly in bones that ride above you,
> Delve in my flesh, dissolved and bedded,
> Through viewless valves embodied so—

Tennyson, we may admit, did this sort of thing better, but this experiment is a minor triumph. And the image at the end, which we may if we wish term a conceit, was hardly possible in Tennyson's non-clinical age:

> Till daylight, the expulsion and awakening,
> The riving and the driving forth,
> Life with remorseless forceps beckoning—
> Pangs and betrayal of harsh birth.

It is a poem, with its implicit psychological background, quite thoroughly of today.

The three sonnets that make up *Out of Time* are valuable in

P

themselves and also as examples of assimilated background. The third sonnet, linked to the second (as the second to the first) by an opening line that repeats the concluding line of its predecessor, is the most striking. This may be due to the fact that it rises to its ending. It runs: [1]

> Leaning against the golden undertow,
> Backward, I saw the birds begin to climb
> With bodies hailstone-clear, and shadows flow,
> Fixed in a sweet meniscus, out of Time,
>
> Out of the torrent, like the fainter land
> Lensed in a bubble's ghostly camera,
> The lighted beach, the sharp and china sand,
> Glitters and waters and peninsula—
>
> The moment's world, it was; and I was part,
> Fleshless and ageless, changeless and made free.
> "Fool, would you leave this country?" cried my heart,
> But I was taken by the suck of sea.
>
> The gulls go down, the body dies and rots,
> And time flows past them like a hundred yachts.

The last line is the first line of the first sonnet. The wheel is come full circle; the sequence can be read round; it is cyclic, as it were, and we start it in terms of its ending. And the measure of the temptation to lean against time, to live in a crystal independent moment, and the futility of it are suggested by this device as well as elaborated by each sonnet. The sequence encloses its theme as the moment encloses us. This is probably Slessor's finest poem. And it is worth noting how the Australian background, of Sydney and its beaches, has been assimilated and used without embarrassment. The older insistence on the new background and the self-conscious air when the Australian illustration is used—these notes of former writers have vanished. We read this poem without consciously and deliberately observing the elements in it—Harbour, undertow, the beaches, gulls, the yachts—which taken all together mark the poet an Australian, a Sydney-sider. Probably no poem before this has so successfully digested local experience.

Since this volume Slessor has written little poetry. We can only record and regret the loss. We are tempted to feel that he

[1] From *One Hundred Poems* (published by Angus & Robertson).

practised until he knew he could write each kind he essayed—
and that satisfied him: as though a cricketer had trained, had
been chosen for the Australian team, and then had retired from
the sport altogether. When Slessor felt he was able to write
poetry then he ceased to write. It is probably too much to hope
that Australians should lament this loss more than the defection
of the mythical sportsman.

The only poet of this group who gives an exposition of a philosophy is R. D. FitzGerald (b. 1902). *The Greater Apollo* (1926–7)
is a practice piece, a prelude to his famous *Essay on Memory* both
in style—with its rather obvious epithets—and in theme. The
passage of time marks the contrast between man and nature.
Destruction and change are man's lot. Nature too changes, but
the seasons recur; and this pattern of repetitive phenomena is
continuous.

In *Moonlight Acre*, which gives its title to the volume that appeared in 1938, he stresses the value of effort. His technique is
not yet matured; the imagery for example is startling, as in
Copernicus (another section of this volume):

> Savage great ridges, jarring, test
> strength upon strength, crest reared at crest
> spur jolting spur's flint forehead-bone.

Such illustrations from mountains and other natural aspects
appear in *Essay on Memory*, but in a form that does not struggle
for attention.

In *Essay on Memory* we find the fusion of the themes—man as
transient; effort as virtue or value in whatever form it appears
—as for instance in beauty, the theme of *The Hidden Bole*—

> fresh fronds, fresh berries, score me milestones gained.

To Memory he gives a wide application. It is something
persistent:

> for Memory does not fail though men forget.

It is not

> . . . History babbling from his chimney-corner,

nor the records of geological process nor even the evolutionary
development:

> it is the past itself, the dead time's will.

Even the joy of former men in their present, now forgotten by us, is the loot of Memory. In spite of this, we have a sense of personal identity, a self that persists.

The symbol FitzGerald uses for Memory is the rain—

> Rain in my ears: impatiently there raps
> at a sealed door the fury of chill drops—

just as on earth itself it has its influence in literal fashion. The lighted room serves to symbolise the self, this body being part of an evanescent moment. Change is no mere abstraction, the influences are not intellectualised ideal shape or movement, not mere flux in patterns: they have to manifest themselves in matter, and that is why we have a transitory reality.

We can grasp or discuss these instants because we use verbal argument, and so we hold time momentarily still. But what we grasp is the changes, or the manifestations of the changes, not the reality that lies behind them. Perceiving only the present, we merely guess the future:

> Foresight is but a bargain that we make.

Our faith and our stay is in love, a sort of trust in the future that is forced on us—and yet we do fear for the future of those we beget. Our recourse lies in positive striving:

> Wherefore all good is effort, and all truth
> encounter and overcoming . . .

Only on the firm foundations of unyielding despair, wrote Bertrand Russell, can the soul's habitation henceforth be safely built. FitzGerald's urge to action derives from the same belief, but his presentation of it is a challenge:

> then, launched above that steep,
> venture shall cant bold wings and with their sweep
> splinter such clogging silence as they met
> in older abyss where time slept stirless yet.

In the *Essay* themes and potentialities that were tentative or uncrystallised in his former work appear now in their full shape and development. As one of the most considerable poems in our literature it has its value for what it says and the way it says it. Read for the first time it may seem perplexing, but re-reading for matter alone resolves most of the initial difficulties. It is easy to overpraise it for profundity, a tendency that the expression may foster. It is not after all a work of great penetration, but one of subtlety; for it has to suggest what can hardly be stated. Here the imagery, rich and vivid and often vigorous, illuminates and, as many will think, is a medium for coherent thought. This may seem unexpected, for the images, though at first sight chiefly visual, are in their main effect kinesthetic: they have a sort of physical pressure, of material impact, and this is in keeping with the idea of moulding forces that is the theme of the poem. But the physical and the conceptual are not normally so tied. So that FitzGerald works with resistant devices and yet triumphs. Any brief analysis should bear this out—the number of verbs like *raps*, *scratching*, *pokes*, *jabs*, *choking*, *pushed*, *bar*, for instance, apart from similarly toned adjectives and nouns. There is no other poem in Australian literature of comparable conceptual subtlety that is so packed with such devices so successfully employed.

The poems since the *Essay* are less vivid. *This Night's Orbit* (1953) contains poems published up to ten years before. Only two of these poems are worthy of the author of the *Essay*. The others deal with FitzGerald's usual themes, for example, action as a counter to bewilderment and despair in the face of mystery. The conception, though, is sometimes banal and the expression of this, as if to atone for it, reads as if some profundity were concealed beneath; whereas in the *Essay* there is poetry, a triumph in its kind, and the themes are thoughts that are evanescent, lying on the periphery of the articulate and yet being snared in words and images.

Heemskerck Shoals appeared first in 1944 and is reprinted in the same volume. It is the rumination of Tasman, captain and servant of the Dutch East India Company. Some of the poem's fame derives from the discussion of it, notably the comments of Norman Lindsay and Douglas Stewart, both of whom complain of the lack of imagery. There are some half-dozen lines, which Stewart, more lenient in verdict, has culled and quoted, that momentarily bring the theme to life; but all in all the complaints are justified—if vividness was the aim of the poem. It is after all the sequence of thoughts, the musings of Tasman, that are given. It is significant, however, as marking a tendency in Fitz-Gerald. His verse has become drier, more bare of ornament. It is browner round the edges, as though fresh sap had retreated:

> More could have been done
> but for such tight instructions—

to quote the poem itself. The other poem in this volume worthy of FitzGerald, not unworthy in fact to have found a place in the *Essay* if that poem had been twice its length, is *The Face of the Waters*. It outlines the start of an evolutionary process. Phenomena evolve senses to perceive the phenomena—the growth, as it were, of a cosmic self-consciousness:

> colour, light, life, fearfully
> becoming eyes and understanding; sound becoming ears . . .

And it expresses the tension in the mind, which recognises nothingness and futility as inevitable, and yet recognises the human urge to action as valuable. Here the imagery has not faded:

> Once again the scurry of feet—those myriads
> crossing the black granite; and again
> laughter cruelly in pursuit; and then
> the twang like a harpstring or the spring of a trap,
> and the swerve on the polished surface; the soft little pads
> sidling and skidding and avoiding; but soon caught up
> in the hand of laughter and put back . . .

A long narrative poem, *Between Two Tides*, appeared in 1952, with its main setting in the Tonga Islands. It falls into three main parts. The first tells of the massacre of the crew of a privateer, the only survivor being Will Mariner. The longest section relates the island politics, chiefly the fighting and the treachery of Finau, whose ally and adviser Mariner becomes. At length, after the death of Finau, Mariner returns to England. In the final section we learn of his drowning in the Thames, of Dr. Martin, to whom he has told his story and who edits the material, and of the memories or forgetfulness of those whom Mariner has encountered.

As a narrative the poem is successful, with a sort of stealthy speed that carries the reader almost without his being aware of it. It has more imagery, as should indeed be expected, than *Heemskerck Shoals*:

> On cliffs above
> girls looking down also have flowers about them,
> not a few sprigs for the hair as in Hapai,
> but plaited through scented vines and dripping to their knees
> like the crest of a wave foaming across their shoulders.

The structure has interest. FitzGerald is telling the story of

Dr. Martin's book. Dr. Martin is telling the story that Mariner
has given him. Mariner tells the story of Finau. And Finau often
enough puts his own case. So it is like a series of Chinese boxes,
one inside the other. The point at issue is what FitzGerald is
really aiming at. Dr. Martin maintains:

> That tale was Finau's,

and:

> Mr. Mariner
> was but the eyes of the tale.

But many readers will find the poem really the story of
Mariner, a story with implications—a sort of commentary on
Choice. And it fits its title. The poem starts with talk and ends
with rumination and memories. In between blaze the actions.
The past grows dim for the characters: they are concerned with
the everyday. *Il faut cultiver notre jardin.* Indeed one might regard
the poem as FitzGerald's ironic comment on the little effect that
action of some kind produces—almost indeed the poem might be
considered an unconscious recantation.

The individual point of view, a quirk or even eccentricity of
attitude, is seen in the poetry of John Blight (b. 1913). His
volume, *The Two Suns Met* (1954), reveals this in most of the
poems it contains. An oddity of observation can have its
dangers: it can concentrate so intently on the oddity in the scene
or incident observed that all extension to a wider significance is
precluded. There is no wood, only trees, and strange or weird
or idiosyncratic trees at that. The result is a discreteness. It is
as though one were shown, not the world outside, but little facets
of it reflected in a distorting mirror. Poetry becomes in a way
a method of emotional or spiritual caricature. It is not funny,
it is queer.

To do this and still produce poems of significance requires a
considerable personality, deep and rich enough to subsume all
these grotesque visions, to correlate them into coherence, into a
pattern. The poet is to be the focus, as it were. It is doubtful
if Blight has managed to do this. He has some of Donne's turns
of thought, but not the intensity to fuse. So that there is not a
body of work, but *disjecta membra*, and each *membrum* a quirk.
This is not to deny the force and the touches of originality in
many of the poems. A reader feels that the poet each time makes

his point, neatly and ingeniously sees a contrast or a relationship not before seen or expected. But little illumination results, only a coloured odd-shaped spark. And yet the hope of development is obvious. Originality of viewpoint is so rare that when it appears it seems to promise growth.

Australian literature has never abounded in schools of poetry. There have been a couple of clubs of writers well enough known, but here again mutual influence or influence shared by members was not felt appreciably. Only two schools of poets are or were prevalent—the Jindyworobaks and the Angry Penguins. The latter had a semi-official organ, *Angry Penguins*, a quarterly that ran from 1941 to 1946. The editor and moving spirit was Max Harris (b. 1921). His own verse was marked by "modernistic" devices.

One may loosely say that there are two difficulties in such verse of today. One is the verbal, that of Dylan Thomas. The words used and their functions, often unusual and puzzling, can for the most part be explained by a reader who gains some clues to the principles underlying the recurrent changes that are rung. With some interest in words, and with some awareness of the effects in view he can, after working at an obscure passage, generally make sense. The second difficulty arises from what is more private than words. It is the use of associations that are the poet's own property, that depend on certain experiences and background that the reader may not be aware of at all. It is not the odd words or their odd use but the odd conjunction of ideas and emotions and images that puzzles the reader. If the poet does not give specific clues, then the reader may make no sense of a poem at all. It was this second type of poetry that Harris and the Angry Penguins produced. A passage like the following is likely to remain opaque for most readers not in the know:

> The bird that turns my feathers iron
> my vitals felon, and charismatic violence
> this proud duress my universe,
> is bird and storm, rage that ranges
> the torn edges and rareness of weather.

In 1943 the two poets James McAuley and Harold Stewart laid a mine beneath the unsuspecting Harris. To quote the latter's own words: "I was sent two poems by a Miss Ethel Malley, who wrote saying that they were found among her

brother's possessions after his death on July the 23rd, 1943 . . .
I was immediately impressed that here was a poet of tremendous
power, working through a disciplined and restrained kind of
statement into the deepest wells of human experience." The full
manuscript was later sent to Harris at his request, together with
a fictitious biography of the poet, Ern Malley. Both biography
and poems were printed in the 1944 Autumn Number of *Angry
Penguins*. The title was *The Darkening Ecliptic*, eighteen poems
in all. This is the opening stanza of *Palinode*:

> There are ribald interventions
> Like spurious seals upon
> A chinese landscape-roll
> Or tangents to the rainbow.
> We have known these declensions,
> Have winked when Hyperion
> Was transmuted to a troll.
> We dubbed it a sideshow.

Which is perhaps less difficult to follow than the lines quoted
earlier.

The mine exploded when McAuley and Stewart, approached
by a newspaper, revealed that they had produced the verses as
a hoax, to see if those who wrote and admired modernist poetry
could recognise nonsense masquerading as poetry. "The poems
consisted of free association, confused bits of theme, and passages
in which various methods of ensuring fortuitousness were used,
such as the old game of crambo. The result was a fair imitation
of a fashionable kind of minor poetry." As a result of this
brilliantly conceived and executed joke Harris and others (it is
sometimes forgotten that Harris was not alone deceived) came
in for much ridicule.

A few comments seem relevant. In the first place the poems
are not all lines fortuitously put together. They are grammatically
built and they make sense—silly sense, admittedly—but still
sense of a sort. In brief, the jesters could not have risked putting
lines together haphazard, for no editor however unsophisticated
would be taken in by such a farrago. Some passages in fact are
like parodies or skits. The opinion of Harris and his friends that
the poems were good poems argues a defective sensibility; and
it serves to show the danger of a critical "set" or predisposition
for or against certain kinds of writing. All of us too readily like
or dislike what we are prepared to like or dislike. A reader with

a particular "set" against "modernist" poetry may smile at the
following lines:

> Now we find too late
> That these distractions were clues
> To a transposed version
> Of our too rigid state.
> It is an ancient forgotten ruse
> And a natural diversion.
> —And yet our praise, intent upon one truth,
> Distorts the truth as maps do in projection:
> The centre gives a perfect azimuth
> But other bearings give a false direction.

A reader concerned with the effect of such a "set" may be
interested to know that the last four lines come from McAuley's
own volume of poems, *Under Aldebaran.*

Another point is the suggestion mooted that the authors wrought
better than they knew, and that some of the lines are poetry
despite all efforts to avoid it. Such lines as these on the picture
of Samson—

> Thumbs twisting the great snarl of the beast's mouth,
> Tail thrashing the air of disturbed swallows
> That fly to the castle on the abraded hill—

are really not ridiculous. The theory that art comes from the
subconscious might find an area for discussion here: that despite
all efforts to avoid significance the two authors could not escape all
those patterns of association that made their own poems effective.

The success of the hoax was resounding. Some have wondered
whether it was not all a little too successful. This country has
not been very patient of its poets; and the philistine, ready to find
all art ridiculous, may have found warrant for his opinion when
he saw pretensions to art exploded. Laughter at silly poets may
not spare poets. In the end a reader is left a little uncertain what
he has laughed at—at those critics who grossly erred in praising
nonsense, or at the same persons as poets writing experimentally
in a land never tolerant of the unorthodox.

Some poets, it seems, can be too aware of what others have
done, of methods taken up and laid by, of a habit of mind that
encrusts a period. Such a poet, up to now, is Vincent Buckley.
The World's Flesh (1954) contains the work of a young writer
who is still in search of a phrase, of a technique, even sometimes,
though it may be bold to say it, of a theme. The poetical echoes

and reminiscences in his work are numerous, all probably unconscious; for he has assimilated his moderns and knows how
things should be treated. So allusion and indirection become
de rigueur, even when one feels that something is going to be lost
just because of that.

Admittedly he deals with difficult subjects. He is a religious
poet, and this colours his implications; he is concerned with his
spiritual and emotional and almost (though the time should be
past) his national inheritance. To pin down the intangibles
requires more than a deftness or an allusiveness. What can only
be suggested is best suggested by the concrete. But Buckley leaves
that too quickly; the image, the point of departure, is sometimes
not made significant before the implications, the peripheral
fringes, become his concern. One might almost think he was
afraid to stamp his image. And he is addicted to the change of
image. The original is a Proteus, and the mind is bewildered
as it pursues the evanescent multiform apparitions. The consequence is a lack of impact. The energy of attention diffuses in a
chase. If we are persuaded that a subject is such as to demand
a particular technique, and that the technique employed serves
the purpose better than another, then we have no right to complain that a poem is difficult or obscure. But it is the poet's job
to persuade us.

The following lines from *On an Old Portrait* come from the start
of the poem and are as intent on the one object as Buckley cares
to be:

> Death shadows her. The sallow Georgian face,
> The slight pinpointed beauty in each eye,
> Make no pretence of livingness, but stress
> Death, like the late guest of her family,
>
> Smiling the Dürer smile. And here death sours
> No great seabird on her throne of water,
> But a thin Aesop's child; but a frame of hours;
> But beauty's lonely and distressful daughter.

The alarming thing is the maturity of manner in some of the
poems. Buckley has so much facility and variety in the scope of
his fingering choices, so much acquaintance with techniques, so
much promise, in short, that early crystallisation seems a pity.
The danger is that he may be petrified into a mould before he
has found his own way of writing.

CHAPTER XI

Modern Fiction

§1

IT is convenient if arbitrary to consider the modern Australian novel under three heads—the saga, the psychological novel, and the sociological and social novel. It is especially in this century that we find novels covering a period of time and a large number of people taken as a group. They may be termed sagas.

The first novelist of this group is Katharine Susannah Prichard (b. 1884). Her eleven novels fall into three groups: two of the novels, though different one from the other, are alike in that they hardly seem to have been written by the author of the other nine; a second group comprises six that are occupational and local; the last three express an ideology that was implicit in most of the others but not previously the *raison d'être* of the work.

Few Australian novelists have been so conscientious. She covers periods as far back as early last century and as close as yesterday, and areas as far apart as Victoria and North-Western Australia. And in her novels she has given accounts of the most diverse occupations—pioneering, opal mining, timber felling, pastoral life, circus life, pearl fishing, gold mining. No other Australian novelist has covered such variety in such detail.

Her first published novel was *The Pioneers* (1915), with a setting in Victoria early last century. The background is the pioneering work of the farmer. Treachery and hate and death are described in this novel. But we simply do not believe in them. They are intruders, brought in because excitement and tragedy are thought to be necessary. They seem like ogres in a fairy tale; and that is what *The Pioneers* is. It has in many sections a simplicity and an appealing quality that indicate where Katharine Prichard's real talent lay. Parts of this novel read as if written by some grave, wide-eyed, and articulate child.

Though one of our considerable novelists, she has recurrent faults. If we wish to survey them, then *Black Opal* (1921) serves as a text. One fault is her inability to make a selection from a mass of material:

> Jim Johnson and Charley Heathfield were riding together in the Afghan storekeeper's sulky with his fat white pony before them. Anwah Kaked and Mrs. Kaked had the store cart themselves. Watty and Mrs. Frost were on the coach. Ed. Ventry was driving them and had put up the second seat for George, Mrs. Woods and Maggie Grant. Peter Newton and . . .

Nor is the amorphous normally lightened or clarified by the style. And yet the general statement can be made that her early style, as in parts of *The Pioneers*, is her best. Only in *Coonardoo* does she write better and for longer stretches. Another flaw is her addiction to the mission, to reform, to exhortation. In *Black Opal* we have its explicit beginnings. The story, set in north-western New South Wales on an opal field, is in two parts. The first gives us an account of the miners. In the second part the chief stress falls on the struggle between Brady, spokesman for the miners, and Armitage, a company representative. The heroine, despite her love for another, marries a deserving young miner and remains on the Ridge to work for the ideals that it stands for. She triumphs as a sort of penance. Solidarity on all fronts is thus assured. Women, we may venture to say without cynicism, who abandon love and marry a Cause do not really do so—they simply marry a Cause. The abnegation is their illusion. This is a law of nature; and it would be well if it were also a law of fiction.

In *Working Bullocks* (1926) there is the same note as in *Pioneers*, a loving description of the natural background, this time of the south-west, the karri country in West Australia. It is a novel characteristic of her early period. As *The Pioneers* has its sensational patches, so *Working Bullocks* contains its discordant note, later to become obsessive in her final novels—the insistence on a message.

But the novel has the same simplicity of expression as keeps her early novels fresh, and there are phrases that remain in the memory—"Bone-white and silver . . ."—and a vivid account, in telegraphic prose, of a savage fight between two dogs. The style may still be thought to lack finish. Any one of a dozen modern English novelists writes with greater mechanical competence than Katharine Prichard; and Katharine Prichard has greater potential sources of fiction than a dozen modern English novelists.

The best novel she has written is *Coonardoo* (1929), where the theme has not permitted her to preach her political creed, where the setting and characters have fitted her early simplicity of style, and where formless accretion of detail is absent. Coonardoo is an aboriginal girl, and the story of her life on a north-west cattle station is her tragedy. The earlier novels, uneven yet oddly promising, seem almost preludes to this. Subject and style are in harmony, and we have an integrated work of art. Passages remain in the memory after the book is closed. Warieda is breaking in a wild filly:

> At last, arresting, magnetic, with a greeting, like a brumby boss, head thrown back, eyes challenging the wild bright eyes before him, his own as wild and bright, Warieda went up to the horse, his arm, the dark sinewy arm of a black that was like the branch of a tree, stretched out before him.

Had she always written as well, then we should have an interpreter, subtle and evocative, of much of the Australian background. The book is in its fashion beautiful, a grave pastoral, moving and pathetic, with its gushes of clarity and charm, its level and ardent background, its simplicity and earthy force. It is the sort of novel for which her knowledge and experience and talents fitted her. It is a sort of legend. Coonardoo, the heroine, not really a picture of a person, of a black woman, is simply black woman; and the novel has a power to give atmosphere vaguely defined, indefinitely felt.

Haxby's Circus (1930) is remembered because it gives us an insight into the workings of a circus while on the road: we are taken behind the scenes of an activity dear to our childhood. The most obvious flaw is the style. This has been mentioned frequently enough, so that an example may seem called for:

> When the tents were up and the cages in position in the menagerie, Dan thanked his helpers heartily, and without squandering a single free seat, for their labours of the morning. He invited two of them across to the pub for a spot; and over the drinks was so jovial and chatty about the work and adventures of the circus that everybody was more eager than ever to see the show.

This has something unfinished about it, and even the richest of themes will bog down when treated in this way.

The next novel deals not with systems or occupations but with people. *Intimate Strangers* (1937) concerns the relations of Greg

Blackwood and his wife Elodie; the attempts of Greg, psychologically broken by his war experiences, to orientate and later to rehabilitate himself; and Elodie's estrangement from him, her love for Jerome Hartog, and her final renunciation. It is her most sophisticated novel. It and an early work, *Windlestraws* (1916), stand apart from the rest.

The third group is a goldfields trilogy, a saga of the development of the industry in West Australia. In *The Roaring Nineties* (1946) she traces the alluvial period, the beginning of the companies, the rise of speculation, and the incipient hostility between companies and diggers. And this volume blueprints the pattern for the other two—*Golden Miles* (1948), an account of the growth of mining unions, covering the period of the first World War and the 1920s; and *Winged Seeds* (1950), which carries the history to 1946. The pattern is one imposed by her political sympathies.

In this trilogy the characters are subordinated to the message. Even Sally Gough, the ostensible heroine, can become a mouthpiece for the author's beliefs. So we have histories of a system where human beings seem hardly more than ciphers. These novels are essentially didactic, plugging a party line, drawing a moral, urging a reform, indicating with sincerity the defects of the social order. This attack upon the reader's sympathies and beliefs is for the most part an intellectual one. But we feel with persons, not by logic. Had Katharine Prichard concentrated her effects and created for us real characters as victims, then she might have attained more readily the end she sought. As it is, the reader feels the candid and almost artless direction of the writing.

Dialogue and technical detail are the most vivid parts of the trilogy. She has caught the Australian idiom with great fidelity: the abbreviations, the slang and the locutions, the turn of phrase and slant of attitude. Perhaps a greater selectivity would have made it even more vivid, for fictional dialogue has to be a compromise: art is not a transcript.

One may conclude, then, that her best novels are those of her earlier period. When she is an artist she is by talent a fabulist, a writer of a sort of pastoral, serious and tender. The change in her work has been from idyll to ideology. She has come in her last novels to serve as the sincere, honest, respected champion of the cause of the underdog. There have been other such novelists in Australia in the last thirty years, competent and earnest.

Katharine Prichard is their superior by the early novels that she wrote before the advocate displaced the artist.

The best-known result of a literary collaboration has been a saga covering part of last century from the forties to the eighties. This is *A House is Built* (1929) by Barnard Eldershaw, the pen-name of Flora Eldershaw (1897–1956) and Marjorie Barnard (b. 1897). The title has more than one meaning—the literal dwelling of the Hyde family, who move to larger and larger houses; the business that Hyde builds; the family itself. The story concentrates chiefly on relationships, those of the members of the family to one another and to the business. The growth of Sydney and New South Wales is traced by summaries which have something of the quality of the lecture room:

> Hunter's Hill was a locality fast becoming one of the most fashion-able and select in the neighbourhood of Sydney. Lying on the high, narrow spit of land between the Parramatta and the Lane Cove rivers, its history went back almost to the beginning of Sydney's history. The name Hunter's Hill was first given to a farm bought as early as 1794 by a Mr. Thomas Muir, one of the famous band of convicts known as the Scottish Martyrs. Muir's offence, for which he was transported for fourteen years, was that he had advocated Parliamentary reform and had recommended his hearers to read the works of the notorious infidel Thomas Paine. The French Revolution had so terrified the British Government that in those days even a mild suggestion of reform was regarded as rank sedition, and Muir had to pay dearly for his liberal view.

But the historical section of the novel is for the most part a background.

The real concern is the members of the family, and one device for revealing and contrasting them is marriage. Fanny, the most vivid and vital picture, attempts an elopement, is rejected with a kindly impatience, and is on her guard against men and even women ever after. When she does have a chance to marry later, she rejects it because an incident brings out the human, passionate aspect of her suitor, and this was to have been purely a marriage of convenience. Then Maud provides a contrast—a happy elopement; William, a marriage to which his code has bound him; Esther, a marriage of consolation; Katie the servant, a failure to marry in which the pathos—and she recognises it—lies in her no longer caring. All this provides part of the irony of the book: the capriciousness of life, that offers happiness with no regard to merit.

The note of irony is found in other novels by this pair of writers—*The Glasshouse* (1936), *Plaque with Laurel* (1937), and even in their politically flavoured story of the future, *Tomorrow and Tomorrow* (1947). In *A House Is Built* it is pervasive. The business offers further opportunities of underlining life's ironic dealings. Hyde, the creator of the business, hopes to hand it over to his grandson, James. But James is drowned, and the shock prostrates and kills the tough old man. William, chill and mechanical, efficiently but unenthusiastically runs affairs. And Lionel, the other grandson, for whom the business was not intended, who in fact does not want it, remains its inheritor at last. The tone is emphasised by the reaction of Fanny, who wanted to share in the management. Tight-lipped and self-controlled after her early disappointment, she would have found it a partial fulfilment. And she is denied it.

The stress laid on this—the human intention that results in what is not desired or what is even feared—is no accident in the book. But a danger resides in such a plan. To show life as ironic tempts a writer to force incidents into that pattern; so that unless he is very careful (and even the great, like Hardy, can fall into the trap), there will be found unmotivated action and convenient accident. Coincidence then becomes an ally to prove a point of view. Probably the drowning of James is artificial—James ironically viewed as needing love and destroyed by his faith in it; repenting of a betrayal and seeking relief in action that destroys him; dying before he gets what he seeks, the business, and leaving Lionel to inherit; planting the seeds of a scandal that only Adela, the wife outside the family circle, can preserve the family from.

This novel may not have claims to greatness, but it must be one of the most carefully planned novels we have.

The greatest of this group is Eleanor Dark (b. 1901). Even from the start she has seemed one of our most practised novelists, her first novel, *Slow Dawning* (1932), being an exception only in style. Some of the ingredients of her later novels are to be found in it: a husband and wife problem, introspection, and the ventilation of the author's opinions on certain subjects, especially the folly and horror of war. It was the next novel, however, that opened her career.

This began startlingly with *Prelude to Christopher* (1933). A doctor, Nigel Hendon, marries Linda Hamlin, in whose family runs the dark strain of insanity. Her uncle, a sadistic biologist,

Q

has tortured Linda with predictions of the same fate. She fights a losing battle, revenges herself on her uncle by taunting him into madness, and at last, after attacking Nigel's mother, commits suicide. Christopher, the child not yet conceived, is to be the son of Nigel and Kate, the nurse in love with him. The four days of the novel are the prelude to a future.

This extremely vivid novel is told by mental flash-backs. Nigel has been injured in a motor accident. In his delirium he reviews the past. So does Linda, so does his mother. The device is ingenious, though the reader comes to expect it. The memories are convenient in arrangement, falling into the pattern the novelist wants, divided up neatly for the most part between Nigel and Linda. Such sequences are not the usual results of delirium or brooding. They take on the appearance of a mechanism to give a cursory account of what might otherwise not easily be made credible.

Her style has not yet reached its maturity. Linda in the following passage recalls how she taunted her uncle with the contrast of her self-control:

> . . . All the torments he could inflict, had inflicted on her, were nothing, nothing, her mocking eyes had told him, unwavering in their fixed smile. Yes, you're hurting me, yes, you're shaking me with every passion, every lust and fury and despair on earth—but you can't move my hands! Here I stand—still, quite still, quite passive—not the murderer but the murdered. Come along, homicidal biologist, and fulfil the destiny of your protoplasm! . . .

This exclamatory prose Eleanor Dark was to outgrow. But it is no bad thing to have excess at the beginning: one may then prune; but one cannot make the dead wood flower.

Much more than a thriller, the story has a considerable thriller interest. A reader turns the pages to find out what is to come; so that it may be classed as a suspense novel as much as a psychological one. The structure helps. In the four days the present and the past are interwoven. And the remembered past illuminates and reinforces the events of the present. The novel stretches the reader's interest taut.

Something of the same pattern appears in *Return to Coolami* (1936). On this occasion four persons, in a car travelling west from Sydney, recall the past. The shifting of the attention from one character to another is very frequent, and the reader feels the need of an excuse for these kaleidoscopic changes. An im-

probability is the transformations the men undergo. At the end
one has fallen in love and the other has discovered in himself a
love of the country, and intends to buy a large property. They
are unduly convenient. That such changes can occur within
forty-eight hours in life may be true; but that is no defence of
the implausible in fiction.

The next novel, *Sun Across the Sky* (1937), is much more deft.
It concerns a financier's hostility to a huge ravaged genius closely
resembling Christopher Brennan, and the concern with them of
a vital doctor who has a wife afraid of life, an antiseptic beauty.
The characters are more subtle, their relationships require more
skill in the handling, and the events are, except for a fire at
the last, fewer and more commonplace. The difficulties, then,
appear greater; but though greater, the author overcomes them.
It is an expert, experienced novel. It is so easy to read that it is
not until half-way through that one begins to take note of what
is being done. From the earlier novels to this the tendency has
been for the author to take over, especially in the introspective
musings of characters. Here the assumption is more or less complete. So that we have a series of comments on the importance of
accepting life in its fullness, and on the sterility of fear and of
resistance to experience.

In *Waterway* (1938) the manner of telling has grown into a
mannerism. A tendency observable before is here manifest, a
slightly hortatory note: the author is beginning to preach a little,
not about politics, but about life, which is shown as real and
earnest.

Eleanor Dark was to write one more of this type even after
turning to the historical novel. It is *The Little Company* (1945), the
story of a Sydney family, the Masseys, and their relations to
one another and to the crowding events of 1941-2. The theme
of the story is that we must be prepared to face reality: no relationship is purely personal. Any character who does not recognise this truth is either stupid, or neurotic, or egoistic, and is
punished by the author accordingly.

These novels form a group. Certain situations, already found
in *Slow Dawning*, recur; introspection continues and serves various
functions; and some themes are repeated in the introspections.
The writer has come to occupy more and more of the stage.

The Timeless Land (1940) is the first of the second group, the
historical. It covers the first four or five years of the infant colony

of New South Wales under the governorship of Phillip, its growth under fantastic difficulties, the relation of aborigines to whites, and the change in men under the impact of the new land.

The book has been highly praised and is sometimes regarded as her best. But it contains so many characters that the interest is diffused, and the rapid and very frequent transitions from one character to another sometimes produce the effect of a badly cut film. It is probably true that to trace the fortunes of a few characters vividly and movingly depicted is the best solution. The universal is best adumbrated by the particular.

One function of the aborigines in the novel is to serve as part of the enigmatic hostility the new land presents. The early picture of them is idealised, but the reason is clear enough; for they are used to show that one may live in a strange harmony with a land that the whites find so recalcitrant. Not only do the whites see the land as strange: the land, through the aborigines, sees the whites as alien.

What helps to hold the sections together is the theme—the land itself. Against it actions happen, against it, as a backdrop, the characters move. The aborigines take it for granted. For the whites it is something to be subdued, with deliberation or ferocity or even at last with understanding. Phillip is perceptive here:

> He thought that this was a harsh country, which kept its inner tenderness concealed; a country reticent of its beauty, demanding a wakening of the heart and a new perception in the eyes of the beholder before it spread its treasures for his gaze.

The reaction of the individual white settlers to this problem helps to characterise them. Eleanor Dark makes this almost a test: those whom she depicts favourably for the most part have faith, whole or partial, in the future of the land; the unpleasant characters hate it.

A further novel of the colony in subsequent years has to be different in certain ways. The land, no longer something quite new and alien, can no longer be the essence of the story; the natives in their turn retreat from their position in the book as they do from the coastal area; new characters and former characters now grown more important dominate the scene. These changes indeed are found in *The Storm of Time* (1948), which traverses the governorships of Hunter, King, and Bligh, and takes the story to 1808.

Though there are several threads of narrative dealing with Johnny Prentice, the child who grows up among the aborigines, Finn, the escaped convict, Mannion, the Irish settler and his wife Conor, Macarthur and his intrigues, the three governors, and last the penal and economic systems, nevertheless the predominant and pervasive theme is the feud between the governors on the one hand, representing Imperial authority, and on the other the Corps together with its moving spirit, Macarthur, standing for individual self-aggrandisement.

The advance made on *The Timeless Land* lies in the vividness of characterisation. The picture of Macarthur (its historical validity aside) is a convincing one. And the contrast of the governors is well brought out—Hunter, surrendering to himself as well as to the forces arrayed against him; King, defeated and at last bitter; Bligh, never surrendering but overwhelmed by force. It is from these figures and their struggles that the book draws its strength and its value.

The third novel of this group, *No Barrier* (1953), relates the events of the early years of Macquarie's reign from his arrival at the end of 1809 to the end of 1814. In this novel the style has become an instrument wielded with an easy assurance: the former striving for effect—and the frequent attaining of it—has now gone; and often the reader is hardly aware that he is reading. Words have become a sort of transparent medium.

> It was just dawn of a mid-December day when Mark stood at the gate of his cottage and watched Dr. Redfern out of sight along Elizabeth Street. Late last night Cousin Bertha had died, and this morning, but an hour ago, his son had been born. There would be much to do when the day began, but this was a posed moment in which, released from anxiety and the demands of daily tasks, he could be still, admitting his fatigue, and tasting his joy.
>
> The eastern sky towards the Heads was reddening; the early morning fog which lay over the harbour and dimmed the town with its soft, shifting vapour was already warmed by it, and would soon be dispersed. In the one night both death and birth had come close to him, and the scene—at once sad and luminous—matched his mood. He remained for a moment watching it, and then turned back to the house.

This note of grave formality does not vary greatly through the book.

In *The Timeless Land* the land itself is the main actor; in *Storm of Time*, the governors and their problems; in *No Barrier*, the other characters. This novel has no startling incidents, no clashes of historical temperaments, and so the author makes the most of things like the crossing of the Blue Mountains and the dogged building of the road. The chief character interest has been discovered in Johnny Prentice. In the second half of the novel he grows aware of his partial identity with the whites, puts aside a heritage of revenge, and becomes human under the influence of Emily. It must have been a task of some difficulty to trace these changes. The depiction, though not completely convincing, is one of the author's triumphs.

In this novel the colony breaks through the western bounds set by the mountains. The period of struggle against material obstacles is over. If a fourth volume appears—and it seems inevitable—then clashing personalities will occupy the stage. Despite a suspicion of the chronicle, these novels are the most substantial and successful of their kind that we have.

Of a projected trilogy Brian Penton (1904–51) completed two volumes, *Landtakers* (1934) and *Inheritors* (1936). They are in the saga tradition, a fact that we begin to suspect from the start when Derek Cabell is shown us as a young Englishman in Queensland in 1844. Penton has given this saga a plot. Interwoven into its strands are the stories of McGovern, enormous, brutal, at last seeking a quiet life; Gursey, ridden by his nightmare memories of convict days with McGovern as the source of them; Emma Surface, ex-convict, seeking security but always in the rôle of protectress; Flanagan, vulgar, pushing, rising to political power and harbouring a long grudge against Cabell. Near the end the threads come to a knot. McGovern, blinded by the blinded Cabell, is killed by Emma with an axe and is consumed in the fire that destroys the homestead.

Penton wrote that he had set out to show "What happened to a sensitive but strong personality thrown into conflict with an unpioneered country" and what sort of legacy he would leave his children. But it did not work out in quite that way. It is his striving against men and for a time against his wife that makes Cabell at last what he is. He looks at first with horror at the types surrounding him, dreading that he may come to be like them. In the end he recognises that what he has feared has in truth taken place—but he does not hate it any longer. Destiny has had this in store for him.

This novel is brutally bloody. There is hardly a character in it that is not either cringing or malicious or idiotic or sadistic. Only Cabell and perhaps Emma escape these labels. And they live amid nature that spawns things just as cruel:

> A plague of rats came out of the north . . . Even the ants came in greater force than ever . . . There was a plague of snakes at the same time . . . Dingoes in stronger force. Eagles carrying off his lambs . . . Every mug of water wriggled with the tadpoles of mosquitoes. Venomous black centipedes . . . Flies . . .

And all these within two pages of the novel. If anything can happen it does; all the ingredients are present—convicts, floggings, flooded rivers, unscalable mountains, the monotonous bush, drought, blacks, bogs, bushfires. The pitiless narrative is broken now and then for the sake of reality—since otherwise the land would be completely deserted—by good seasons. All is related in a style to correspond, as though Penton thought that brutality of man and nature, told in a correspondingly brutal style, would result in force and power. Incredibly enough it does. It may be melodramatic often, it may be overpacked, but it is one of the most emphatic of the saga novels we have.

Sequels and second volumes are notoriously failures. *Inheritors* is not. It opens some forty-five years later, with Cabell and his family at Christmas dinner, and then retraces the steps to that uneasy meal, with the patriarch shouting and damning his sons and petting his daughter. The danger in this volume is that now the interest will be spread. Penton avoids this by keeping Cabell still the chief character, his nature changing and expressing itself in his attitude to his children—to Larry, who hates him; to Geoffrey, who cringes to him and robs him; to James, who at last converts him into a Pioneer of the District; to Harriet the beloved, who deserts him.

The triumph of the two books, especially of the second, is the figure of Cabell. The change in him from maturity at the start of *Inheritors* to senility at the end is consistently portrayed. He has become quite detestable—mean, avaricious, deceitful, suspicious, domineering. He is friend to no man. A redeeming trait is his passionate devotion to Harriet, but even this seems perverse and grotesque. In the end he is simply avarice driven by will. But he has courage and power, and these breed an unwilling respect as well as the hatred that is his due. The reader, like any other person who meets him, responds in the same way.

Inheritors has an ingredient rare in these saga novels, and that is humour. The chapter where Mrs. Bowen alternately scolds and mollifies James for his relations with her daughter is as good as anything of its kind. But the superlative comedy appears in the last chapters. Here the dry prig James, a slave to orthodoxy and respectability, gradually takes over the reins from the old man, who is going blind. In the process James gradually builds up, to his own satisfaction and that of the general public, the picture of his father as the heroic pioneer—which he was—and the reputable and public-minded man of business—which he certainly was not. Part of Penton's motive in writing this volume, one suspects, was a sardonic impatience with public reputations, an aspect of life that his work as a newspaper editor gave him full opportunity to survey. It is a sort of debunking of the pioneer legend, as though he had remembered all the foundation stones and obituaries with exasperated persistence and then had said to himself: This will show them.

The last novelist of this group, like Eleanor Dark, turned to the saga after first writing psychological novels. This is Patrick White (b. 1915). His early novels, however, are more experimental than hers, and they set him apart from other Australian writers. They free him from the criticism made overseas that our literature is extremely traditional, that methods and techniques used in England and America take long to percolate to us, and in fact may often not appear in our writing at all.

His first novel, *Happy Valley* (1938), uses the device of the "stream of consciousness" and even extends the application of it. He was anticipated in Australia, at least in the simple use of the method, by Chester Cobb in *Mr. Moffat* (1925) and *Days of Disillusion* (1926). Cobb at first introduces the reverie with *he thought* or *he reflected* or *his thoughts ran* or with three dots (. . .), and he sometimes ends a passage in the same manner. It is as though he were feeling his way, as though he suspected he had a new and unfamiliar instrument, or even as though he considered his readers a little slow of thought. In the jargon of pugilism, he telegraphs his punches. Such passages seem intrusions into the narrative. Nor does the device serve to differentiate characters by their varying use of it, since only one character ruminates like this. Cobb, in short, leaves the impression that he is unaware of the potentialities of the method.

White, though not completely successful, is much more expert in *Happy Valley*, set in a mountain township west of Sydney, where the characters live unhappily. Oliver Halliday, a doctor with a consumptive wife and two young boys, decides to run away with a young woman. Their journey, however, is interrupted at the start when they come upon a man who has been killed. The shock and the delay prove fatal to the mood of both, and Halliday decides to return to his wife and take his family up to Queensland. In one sense this may be the fulfilment of his nature; but the general effect is one of frustration, a note that pervades the whole book. A pattern recurs: many of the characters are offered a chance of love and possibly happiness, and each reacts to the situation in a different way.

In this novel the use of the interior monologue is extremely frequent: as soon as a character is alone, then the rumination begins. This is undoubtedly what occurs in life; but then art is not life inclusively perceived and recorded. To report every interior monologue is no more fitting than to report every sneeze and cough, even though the monologue is much more important. The method, when applied to children, is less convincing. White uses adult language to express the interior monologue of children. He seems in fact to regard them as adults, only half the size.

His extension of the device is the communal interior monologue, where the thoughts of characters at a particular moment are put down in a sort of intermingling. So we have a picture of a little community of minds and their last waking thoughts before sleep descends.

In 1948 *The Aunt's Story* appeared, to mark a different sort of analysis. It is the story of the changes in a personality, Theodora Goodman. Her querulous and demanding mother, whom she has felt constrained to serve, at last dies, and Theodora at last is free. The rest of the story concerns her growing absorption in an inner life. Eventually she is taken away for observation in a mental hospital. The warning to her is quite terrifying in its calm reassurance. It is given by Holstius, a creation of her fantasy, in whom probably her dead father appears:

> "They will come for you soon, with every sign of the greatest kindness," Holstius said. "They will give you warm drinks, simple nourishing food, and encourage you to relax in a white room and tell your life. Of course you will not be taken in by any of this, do you hear? But you will submit. It is part of the deference one pays to those who prescribe the reasonable life."

We are left with the conclusion that Theodora abandons sanity to find happiness. This is a condition known to the alienist; Devine, for example, in his *Advances in Psychiatry* sums up:

> It is not unusual for a patient to say that his whole life had been like a dream and that now he feels awake for the first time. The delusion is, as it were, the inspiration for which he had long been waiting.

White presents all this as a strange reality, quite unlike any other account in our fiction. We identify ourselves with Theodora and share the hallucinations and delusions that crowd upon her.[1] These are not described as figments but as things happening, people talking, places seen. Then we come to recognise them not as what is happening but as what Theodora thinks is happening. Some of the people, so it seems, are patterns. They are people who also withdraw for their own reasons, just as Theodora is withdrawing. It is a picture of a separate community, all deranged, who do not invite you to become deranged like them, but merely show you why they are like that.

These novels render White unique in his kind in our writing.

Eight years after *The Aunt's Story* White published a saga. He left his own specially cultivated area to show that he too could grow a dinosaur. For that in a way is what *The Tree of Man* (1956) is, one of those bulky progeny that the Americans produced in number some years back—*Gone with the Wind, Raintree County*, and the rest. White's novel like these is too long.

Anatole France tells the story of the old king who wished to know the story of mankind. So his wise men after some years brought him many large volumes. Since he had the impatience of advanced age, he sent them away with orders to condense this information. At last the sole survivor of these savants tottered back with only one huge volume. The king, now upon his deathbed, lacked not only patience but time. He commanded the sage to condense impromptu. Whereupon the old scholar reported what we all know—that man was born, he suffered, he died.

Patrick White's method in this novel is the very opposite. Chapter Four starts: ". . . Life continued . . ." and that fairly sums up the theme. Stan Parker and his wife Amy pass through the three stages. They are a simple man and a simple woman. The choice of simple people, it appears, strips non-essentials away and we get humanity. But since the three simple phases so

---

[1] Professor D. W. McElwain's diagnosis : simple schizophrenia.

blankly put do not make a novel, White fills in all the details, especially those that deal with living and suffering.

It is a sort of allegory, man's life in rather Wordsworthian guise but harsher, with misfortunes that he meets, with aspects of life that he does not understand. The style, in parts at least, is stripped down to its elements to correspond with the theme. But the elemental can become monotonous over five hundred pages, so sections contain what may be called the allusive mystical. This is to provide depth and significance.

The chief fault of the book is its inclusiveness. There is such an enormous amount of the little. All art implies selection, the transitory and eternal moment in some short stories, the flowering climax in some tragedies, the action taken from a lifetime, which reveals past or future but does not tell it, in some novels.

Trying to perform so much, White in consequence does less than we have grown to expect of him. Neither Stan nor Amy comes to life. We are told so often (instead of being shown) their human reactions, but not their personal ones. It is like reading a volume of general psychology and trying to find in it the description of a friend that marks him out from other human beings. He is in the volume, of course, but so are we all. White is best in a section of about a hundred pages in the middle of the book, where he moves from outside houses to inside, from Stan and Amy and their relations with earth and life to individual persons like the O'Dowds and their particular relations to particular things. It is in particulars that people reveal themselves, and this revelation with White is most vivid when he is comic. The vividness is found also in some passages where White gives the significant detail and forbears to show its place in Life and Time. It is found in Amy's vision of Madeleine. Perhaps even better is the description of Sam's wandering movements in the burning mansion:

> He went from that room, brushing a tapestry that shivered at his shoulder, and rippled, and regained eternity. All things in the house were eternal on that night, if you could forget the fire. Time was becalmed in the passages, and especially at their ends, in the depths of which brooms stood, and possessive winter coats, and scarred garments in old leather. There was a horse that rocked at a touch, with something rattling in its belly. A woman's scratchy straw hat hung from a hook, still smelling of roses and sun.

Verdicts on the novel given by overseas critics were, some of

them, more than a little exaggerated—"The Hardy of Australia",
"A timeless work of art". That it is a work of importance is true,
but it is futile to make claims like this for it. Its value lies in its
humour, often in its pathos—the death of Gage, for instance, is
powerful and moving—and even in its devious and exasperating
attempts to convey cosmic implications. Despite faults almost as
large as its virtues it adds to the stature of White, who remains
the most significant living Australian novelist.

§2

The novelists in this section may be given the vague label of
the psychological novelists, a term wide enough in all conscience to
include many others as well, but denoting more an emphasis than
a general quality, an interest in character more than in period.

Probably no other Australian novelist subdues his work to
the colours of everyday as does Vance Palmer (b. 1885). Part
of his contribution to our fiction resides in his use of Queensland
scenes in his novels, the acceptance of the local background. It
is some measure of our rawness that we can still feel uncomfortable when we find names of Australian cities and streets in an
Australian novel. Palmer has done something to make us feel
more at our ease. But when it comes to characters and action,
then his pervasive acceptance of the commonplace almost as *de
rigueur* has its disadvantages.

He has been both attacked and defended for avoiding the issue
of action. A kettle that does not come to the boil, it has been
suggested, represents his narrative. The defence is that he is
seeking to portray what life is—its ordinariness, its frequent
fizzling out of what promises to flare up. His novels like *The
Passage* (1930), *The Swayne Family* (1936), and *Golconda* (1948)
offer themselves as subjects for both this attack and defence. We
may say that the attack is beside the point if it condemns Palmer
for failing to do what he does not attempt; and we may say
equally that the defence is correspondingly irrelevant if it thinks
that a work must be great because a writer achieves his aim.
The point is that the aim may not engage the interest of a
willingly attentive reader. The fact that things so often fail to
happen in Palmer's novels is not in dispute: it is the interpretation and evaluation of this that seem to have gone astray.

The tentative note in Palmer is seen in characterisation. One essay on his work refers to "the same respect for the feelings and reticences of his characters as he would feel for those of his friends". The implication in the phrase is that the characters have a life of their own independent of their existence in the novels. In a way, of course, some characters of fiction do seem to exist like this, and have given rise to acrimonious critical discussion of their goodness and badness, their early life before they appear in the novel or play, and their probable future outside the work. That this should be possible is our greatest tribute to the power of the writer who has thus imposed his creatures upon us. But this is not a point at issue here. A man refrains from probing his friend. But the friend exists. A novelist must continue to probe his characters for the obvious reason that they do not exist until he has done so. He only refrains when he has probed enough. Palmer is engaged on portraying ordinary people, a task that is extremely difficult, for the hypothetical and perfect norm would have no traits that stamp him as a person. When we remember ordinary people it is for extraordinary reasons. All characterisation has some element of caricature because art is selective. It is the process of selection itself that is untrue to the reality of life but true to the reality of art.

This tentativeness appears in the dialogue and the descriptions in his later novels. Palmer knows Australian talk, the undertones and the banality. He knows also the physical background of coast and inland. But he can hardly be called vivid. And probably the same cause is operating. To choose the salient and characteristic phrase, to use the essential adjective, this he has found difficult. His earlier novels like *Cronulla* (1924) and *The Man Hamilton* (1928), though containing some repetition of phrase, situation, and character, nevertheless have a greater tautness of structure than the later ones. He writes best under the constraint of a mould predetermined. That is why his short stories are better than his novels. He is always competent in the sense that there is no amateurish note of poor writing, of gritty phrase, of not recognising what a novel is. And he knows his Australian settings and characters. His novels are not real measures of his capacities. One is tempted to think that the paradox of Palmer is that he has too thoroughly assimilated the ordinary in our national existence.

His development in the novel has been from the structural to the characteral to the panoramic. Had he produced a novel with the qualities of each period manifested at the one time then we should have a work greater than any he has yet given us. It is almost as though he had discarded what each stage of his development afforded him.

One novelist seemed blessed early with more talents and brilliance than have been the lot of almost any other Australian novelist. This is Christina Stead (b. 1902). Her early studies, her travels, her various jobs, all were additional aids to the growth of a personality that seemed at one period capable of anything in fiction—except perhaps writing a really great novel; for the ability to create characters she seldom gave signs of possessing.

She is one of the few novelists from this country with a style. Anyone who has read many Australian novels must have been struck by the frequent lack of distinction in the manner of writing. She differs also from most other Australian novelists in being what we may term sophisticated. She does not preach, she is not—or was not—obvious, she deals with people of the world, and with the subtleties of behaviour. The arts, and to a lesser degree the sciences, the more delicate (some would say indelicate) relationships of people, nuances of mood and emotion—these are her themes. There is about most of her work an aura of a civilised culture, almost of worldliness, as though she could find herself at home in the most cosmopolitan society.

A comparison will serve to illustrate her command of prose. The following passage comes from a novel by Djuna Barnes, *Nightwood* (1937), a work praised in a preface to it by T. S. Eliot. A painting is described:

> Against the panels of oak that reared themselves above the long table and up to the curving ceiling hung life-sized portraits of Guido's claim to father and mother. The lady was a sumptuous Florentine with bright sly eyes and overt mouth. Great puffed pearled sleeves rose to the prickeared pointings of the stiff lace about the head, conical and braided. The deep accumulation of dress fell about her in groined shadows; the train, rambling through a vista of primitive trees, was carpet-thick. She seemed to be expecting a bird.

In *The Salzburg Tales* (1934), Stead's first published but second written novel, there is a short passage that is parallel to this. It is a description of a man:

> The Viennese conductor was like a tasselled reed, with shoulders and hands spreading outwards, delicate hips and a soft long feline

stride: he sometimes took shorter steps and sometimes longer as if
to show that in him the passion of rhythm was constant but tidal.
He looked this way and that as he bowed obsequiously over his
companion's conversation, smiling to himself on the side, as if he had
a tiding of joy in his sleeve, and gathering in the ladies' glances: it
might have been harvest time and he a reaping hook.

The resemblance between the two passages is very close. There
are differences, however, and they serve to characterise the
writers. One passage is a description of a painting, the second of
a person; one is static, the second is in motion; Barnes has more
adjectives, Stead has greater suggestiveness; Barnes is visual,
Stead chiefly kinaesthetic. This is a style that one can have too
much of—like spice. But at all events it is a style that is unusual
in Australian fiction.

Her other early novel, *Seven Poor Men of Sydney*, was written
before *The Salzburg Tales* but was published a little later in the
same year. So it is tempting to say that in *Seven Poor Men* she had
not developed the style she was to use in the *Tales*. The explanation, probably, is that she did not need to use it; for the theme
demanded a rather more commonplace or at any rate a less
elaborate style. But whenever she wants to, when she thinks it
necessary, then she draws on her resources. One small example is:

It was low water; a transparent wave two inches high rang its air-
bells along the sand.

The story is one of human oddity and human failure—bank-
ruptcy, paralysis, the fear of insanity, suicide. The list, though,
is rather misleading. The characters are queer, but they have
been selected; the author recognises they are not representative.
The reason for the general air of seediness is the period depicted
—the depression of the early thirties.

A third novel ends the early stage of her development. This
is *The Beauties and Furies* (1936). After this her style is to alter,
the themes are to become longer in the telling, and the characters
are to be more closely connected with one another. Set in Paris,
this novel has no concern with Australia.

Of her other novels one deals in its first part with Australia—
For Love Alone (1944), the story of a young girl's long and
ultimately futile infatuation. Devoted to Johnny Crow, who goes
to England on a scholarship, Teresa Hawkins saves up money to
follow him. It is all useless, for he does not really care for her.
The picture of Teresa's saving and the expedients she is reduced

to—eating little, walking to save fares, doing without new clothes —is painted with a strange intensity. It is too long, like all her novels after the first two, but the iteration and accumulation of detail wear down the reader's resistance until at last he surrenders. *The House of All Nations* (1938), three times the length of most novels, gives an intimate and revealing account of international banking. Formidably technical in many sections, it is a tribute to her assimilation of background during her business experience in London. *The Man Who Loved Children* (1940), *Letty Fox* (1946), and *A Little Tea, A Little Chat* (1948) are all set in America, and tend in one direction, the providing of reading matter demanded by a large public. It seems unlikely that she will ever give us another Australian novel.

As well as writing poetry Kenneth Mackenzie wrote novels under the name Seaforth Mackenzie, and something of his poet's skill transpires into the new medium. In a dedication of *The Young Desire It* (1937) to W. G. C. he writes that "you made it possible for me to give all my mind and all my time to the difficult task of writing prose". A reader can only comment that the effort has not been wasted.

In this novel Mackenzie displays a delicacy of treatment in the handling of a difficult theme. It is on the surface a school story, an account of the experiences of young Charles Fox at a big boarding school in Melbourne. He is a type new to his companions:

> Among the mass of boys there, he was in fact like a person from some remote land that had been civilised without sophistication. He was a visitor from the very real country of childhood, and from that innocent demesne in it which all others of his age had left, long ago. His innocence was only ignorance in that he had never been schooled to guard against and suspect his fellows.

The relations between Charles and the others of his age, however, are less important than those with Penworth, a lonely young master from England with homosexual traits. The innocence of the boy and the tortured feelings of the man provide a situation that is resolved by Charles's entry into adolescence and his awareness at last of the unhealthy nature of the attachment. Probably no good novel is possible that purports to give us what children really think and feel; but this novel of adolescent youth with its uncertainties and slow realisation is the most penetrating and sympathetic picture of early years that we have in our fiction.

It is a very carefully written book. A description like the following serves to show Mackenzie's slightly mannered style:

> When he bent his head and stooped gracefully, looking sideways across his nose, away from the person to whom with exquisite friendliness a small, delicate ear was inclined, and holding the folds of the gown in against his loins, there was revealed a pinkish tonsure of mathematical perfections in the middle of the crown, and from its decisive edge the dark hair was brushed away all round. The impression of his head, and of the face with its carven eyelids and lips, suggested a subtle parody of the head of an Apollo as sculptured by an ancient master.

The descriptions of the languor and heat of summer, of the coolness of water, of the strain mounting towards the examination period, of the passionate awakening between Charles and Margaret—these mark the novel as a mature and sophisticated one. The deliberation of manner is perhaps to become with Mackenzie a trifle obvious, as in *Chosen People* (1938) and *The Refuge* (1954). Here the note of cultivated ease, though not obtrusive, is perceptible, a tone of slightly formalised and even of mincing enunciation. It is rather too perfectly well bred. The reader follows the assured guide, now and then wondering if the façade can possibly crack. But such comment seems captious, like the complaint of the pernickety old Irishwoman, after a good harvest of potatoes, that there was nary a bad one for the pigs.

The two best-known novels of Leonard Mann (b. 1895) are *Flesh in Armour* (1932) and *A Murder in Sydney* (1937). They are better in their kinds than are *Human Drift* (1935), a story of the goldfields last century and the assimilation of newcomers, *Mountain Flat* (1939), a picture of the rivalry of farmers over land, and *The Go-Getter* (1942), a story of intrigue behind political measures in Melbourne and its suburbs.

Flesh in Armour traces the fortunes of an A.I.F. battalion during part of the first World War on leave in London and in action in France. Mann avoids the danger of too many characters and concentrates on a few, Frank Jeffreys, a corporal in love with an English girl, Mary Hatton, and Charl Bentley, who has already seduced her. The discovery of this added to his own feelings of insufficiency as a soldier and his increasing fears is too much for Jeffreys, and he at last kills himself with a grenade. But the story, though it serves as a unifying thread, is subordinate to the pictures of the Australian soldier with his grouses, his sense of

R

democratic independence and solidarity, and his national outlook. Mann's own service in the A.I.F. provides warrant for the accuracy of these pictures.

The novel is Mann's first book and exhibits his narrative yet unmatured. He was later to develop an easy unpretentious style, almost in parts under-writing, with very few oddities to mark it.

The best parts of the novel are the vignettes of the London streets and the dialogue of the soldiers. It is the latter that gives an insight into the Australian quality of the men. The novel has been praised for its power to depict this Australianity, and it is chiefly in the speech that the power resides. Other characteristics of the men, the sense of belonging together, the sardonic humour, and the traits which we find it hard to describe or even enumerate but which we recognise when we see or feel them—some of this Mann tells us. A great novelist shows us. But the book is nevertheless a solid performance, authentic and in parts stirring. It is an experience perhaps felt by the author at too close quarters, a work from which he has not been able to detach himself sufficiently, but it contains his pity for his fellows, for humanity inside uniform:

> . . . the flesh of each soldier enarmoured itself . . . with duty and military necessity, fortitude, endurance and courage.

Mann's variety of theme in fiction is considerable: *A Murder in Sydney* is a far cry from his first novel. The title, it has been pointed out, is rather misleading, for though there is a murder the novel is not a mystery story. We see Barbara Hallam kill Chloe Morton, her father's mistress. The suspense in detection is replaced by suspense of a different kind—the waiting for Barbara's conscience and misery to show themselves in action. She confesses, is sentenced to seven years' imprisonment for manslaughter, and goes to her fate with the assurance that Dyas will be her comfort when at last she comes back into the world.

The novel, then, concerns itself less with action than with people, and contains some convincing characters. The weakness lies in its motivations, chiefly that of Barbara's decision to do something to stop Chloe from filling the place of Barbara's dead mother in the household. The passage where Barbara's musings come to this issue does not convince the reader. It is also the only passage in the novel, significantly enough, where Mann's style gets out of hand. But this apart, it is an unusual novel of its kind, with descriptions careful and studied, avoiding the obvious but not letting the avoidance appear. It is Mann's most competent piece of work, professionally smooth and articulated.

§3

Not so much the motivations and passions of persons as their relations with one another—such a theme serves the third group of novelists. They are the social or the society novelists, who choose areas where urban aspects predominate. An extension or variation appears in the work of the sociological novelists. The stress turns to man and his dealings with society or, perhaps more frequently, to society and its dealings with man. The economic forces that make society and determine a man's fortune in it bulk large.

A brilliant and persuasive essay by Kathleen Fitzpatrick in 1953 commented on the position of Martin Boyd (b. 1893). Boyd's ancestors were settlers in Victoria before the gold rushes, and established themselves as persons of wealth, influence, education and social standing, regarding as distasteful the pretensions of those enriched by gold or by speculation; and so, to use the words of *The Montforts* (1928), "the gentlefolk drew more exclusively into their own gardens and their grey houses" in Toorak or Kew, shutting their doors against the opulent upstart. In this closed circle questions of ancestry bulked large, and England was "home". In such a milieu Boyd grew up, spending his formative years in this country. After service in the first World War he returned to Australia, but "outside this circle I was in a foreign country", as he puts it in his autobiography, *A Single Flame* (1939). So he returned to England, where he remained for about thirty years, writing there all his novels except the last two, *The Cardboard Crown* (1952) and *A Difficult Young Man* (1954). Fitzpatrick's thesis is that Boyd is in the position of Henry James in the last quarter of last century, with physical roots in one country and cultural affiliations in another. And further, by reason of his upbringing and his movements to and from England (a family habit), he became "the man without a country and the writer without a theme".

Boyd has a theme, but there is no doubt that he is extremely repetitive. Any reader of *A Single Flame* is in possession of the essence of his main novels. Some of these are laid in England and have no concern with Australia; but his best known contain Australian characters and settings, and are variations on his family history. The earliest example is *The Montforts, A Family Story*, in three parts. Part I is crowded with characters and incidents and often covers many years in few pages. The book grows more leisurely as it progresses: part II deals with Richard and Aida and their frustrated romance; part III with Raoul, with whom, at least partially, we may identify Boyd himself. *Lucinda Brayford* (1946) is the longest of these novels and has greater unity than *The Montforts*, the thread being Lucinda, her girlhood, her marriage in Victoria to the Governor's A.D.C., the relations with the Brayford connections in England, her love affair with Patrick Lanfranc, the collapse of this, her son Stephen, and his death after ill treatment in a prison for conscientious objectors during the first World War.

The first of these two inevitably invites comparison with other novels of the type, and in the comparison with, say, Galsworthy Boyd suffers. The picture of the background is shallower by contrast, and its potted biographies and character sketches seem a little amateurish when put beside Galsworthy's illuminating and sometimes penetrating pictures. It was, so it happens, written with a different purpose. Boyd writes of it in his autobiography as "a pseudo-Galsworthian account of my mother's family over five generations, full of thinly disguised portraits. It was rather witty and enabled me to pay off grudges against aunts and uncles who had been rude to me as a child." Its concern with Boyd's family is obvious to any reader of his autobiography. *Lucinda Brayford* is a better novel, more coherent, written with much more control over characters. And its dependence on the author's family history is not so marked. He has, in short, relied less on memory and family anecdote, and more on his observation and creative imagination.

The literary cannibalism continues with his two latest novels. *The Cardboard Crown* (1952) tells the story of Alice and Austin. She has a passionate but pure affair with Aubrey. Twenty years later they meet again in an idealised relationship—at least on her side. (Love, wrote D. H. Lawrence, love is for lovers. This is as disconcerting a saying as the motto one used to meet on sundials —It is later than you think.) Austin's liaison is less innocent; he is caught by Hetty, a man-eater, and they have a spate of sons in consequence. The repetition of situations already found in the autobiography and in *The Montforts* is striking. In *A Difficult Young Man* (1955) the field is narrowed down to one main character, Dominic, introspective and difficult and at cross purposes with life from his childhood until his elopement with his youthful love Helena.

In these novels the names are sometimes changed, the incidents are attributed to different people, the places are varied; but all are recognisably similar. There seems no reason why the process should not continue indefinitely, since the chief requirement is ingenuity in shuffling round and fitting together the constituent pieces.

In a way Boyd's novels are as much English as Australian. If you set your scenes in cities, if you choose characters who are well-to-do middle-class folk, if your concern is with social and marriage relations, then a novel of Australia may be almost indistinguishable from a novel of England. What makes the reader believe them the product of an Australian is the frequent concern with English criticism of some Australian thing. The English, we gather, despise the Australian accent, with its "flat-vowelled nasal whine" (as a character puts it). Boyd, we may gather, does not suffer from it, since the heroes or heroines—Raoul, Dominic, Lucinda, and others—are acknowledged as speaking the English of England. What marks Boyd out from many other Australian novelists is his style. It is that of the witty, polished, and malicious contemporary English novelist, though sometimes the flavour of the nineties makes his prose seem dated. It is like remembering Wilde's *Dorian Gray*, especially when one takes into account the epigrammatic and cynical middle-aged connoisseurs and the beautiful young men who inhabit so many of the pages of both authors. One oddity is Boyd's hobby-horses, such as pacifism, which often gallop off with him. Here even children are requisitioned. Stephen, a mere child, is given a mechanical toy, a tank. It is, however, an instrument of war, so that the wretched boy is called upon by the author to respond in the proper fashion:

> . . . behind them was the soft splendour of the lovely room. Their faces were rosy and eager. In the middle of the circle, the focus of all this beauty and attention, the tank whirred and waddled like some huge obscene slug.
> Stephen looked up at Lucinda and wrinkled his nose.

But these are tolerable faults. Boyd is so readable and witty that

we forget them as soon as they are past. Some of the ironical and
mildly profane passages are his best. The narrator in *The Cardboard Crown* comments on the gathering of older members of the
family, some of whom have not met for sixty years:

> I was the only one conscious of the distinction of the party, as to the
> guests themselves it seemed merely like the Resurrection Morning
> with sherry.

This air of sophistication and ease is uncommon in our literature,
and we cannot be too grateful to Boyd for the offering. Had he
not fed so voraciously on his ancestors, had he only a greater
power of invention, then we should have a collection of entertain-
ments varied as well as sparkling. As it is, any of the novels is a
delight, provided we do not read others too soon afterwards.

Helen Simpson (b. 1898) is an example of sheer professional
competence. This particular quality does not ensure the greatness of novels, but it does their readability. (It is interesting to
note, in parenthesis as it were, how often what we call great
novels may seem clumsy in structure or awkward in style.) The
Australian novelists who have this finish, for example Christina
Stead and Martin Boyd, have written of English settings as well
as Australian, and have themselves lived outside Australia.

This applies also to Helen Simpson, who went abroad in her
middle teens and has lived, except for visits, outside this country.
Only three of her novels have much concern with Australia. The
most significant is *Under Capricorn* (1937), a novel set in Sydney
in the early thirties of last century. She has chosen this particular
period for reasons of plot. She needed, among other things, a
society of bond and free and a time when exploration was still
being carried on. Lady Henrietta is saved from a capital charge
by Flusky, who is consequently transported. Married to him, she
takes to the bottle, but is rescued from it by the help of Adare.
Flusky, half grateful, half jealous, encourages the latter to go on
an expedition to find gold with a guide who, it is anticipated,
will see to it that he does not return. Susan, a currency lass, helps
bring about a happy ending and marries Adare.

The happenings are perhaps a little too convenient, and underneath there are skilfully concealed sentimentality and poetic
justice. But it is only on later deliberation that a reader feels
anything like this: as he reads the book he is carried along with
no sense of strain or embarrassment or discomfort. And this is

one perfectly legitimate enjoyment that fiction offers. It is not easy to point to any short passage that demonstrates this capacity in the novelist, but the following gives some idea of what it is. The extract comes from near the start, where Adare has just seen a chained convict gang pass along King Street.

> Mr. Adare, impressionable, but fortunately volatile; wax to receive, but water to retain; Mr. Adare did not care for the mixed feelings this encounter had roused in him. Pity without the means to relieve is emotion wasted; anger with the human race in general on account of the cruelty or folly of particulars is not to be justified. So he told himself as he walked on towards George Street, while the shuffling and clinking took itself off in another direction. Nevertheless, the generosity in him was uneasy at finding no outlet, and he stared offensively at passers-by who took convicts in chains for granted. A quarrel would have quieted him down by allowing him to translate emotion into action; a translation in which, as happens often enough, the original impulse might be lost. But he went unsatisfied. No man took exception to his looks, no woman observed him. In a mood still half-truculent, he found the turning for George Street, and entered the premises of the Bank of New South Wales.

This is not and is not intended to be pathetic or moving. But it is extremely deft. One does not need a very extensive knowledge of other Australian fiction to recognise how the incident would generally be treated: the scene would either be elaborated, the brutality and harshness underlined; or the observer would be portrayed feeling as the novelist wants us to feel—indignant, disgusted, humanly outraged. In other words, there would have been a direct frontal attack on the reader's emotions. But in the passage there is none of this naïvety of technique. We are treated as adults and assumed to have some subtlety of reaction. And in consequence the effect, for the literate reader, is the more considerable.

All this readability is no mere slickness, a stylistic patina as of a glossy magazine story that merely films a vacuum. But there is the danger that it may be so interpreted, that it may suffer by contrast with the gruff half-articulate medium that seems to smack of sincerity. This novel, though not a great one, is thoroughly adequate. It serves as a sort of norm of competence, an indication of what some novelists, greater in stature, have yet to learn.

To say that a novelist is too humorous to produce all the effect he is seeking must seem very odd. But something of the sort

occurs with Xavier Herbert (b. 1911), who has used his knowledge of Northern Australia to do for the Northern Territory
what Furphy did for the Riverina. The book in which he per-
forms the feat is *Capricornia* (1938), a long rich comment on the
area.

The book falls into two almost equal parts. In the first
Herbert gives us the setting, the officials, the settlers, the natives
and the half-castes, and some of the ludicrous events that take
place and the relations that exist between these often discordant
elements. The essential figures are the brothers Oscar and Mark
Shillingsworth, the latter becoming the father of a half-caste,
Norman. It is a fantastic picture of rain, drought, sloth, drink,
lechery, incompetence, corruption, injustice, and racial dis-
crimination. It is not the sort of information found in a guidebook.

The second part of the novel concentrates chiefly on the half-
caste problem, where Norman serves as the example. Educated
in the south, he returns as a young man to Capricornia and finds
his colour a barrier. Misunderstood and often taunted, he passes
through a series of misadventures, and at last stands his trial for
murder. He is acquitted, and the book ends with the promise of
good fortune on his cattle station.

Capricornia is the most readable long novel of importance in
Australian literature. Something is due to the rapid sequence of
exciting incidents that light up page after page; something also
to the vividness of description, seldom found in set pieces but
generally in brilliant vignettes put down in earthy homely comparisons. The picture of Blossom runs:

> Her eyes were as black and lustrous as well used engine oil. . . .
> And her hair was as glossy black as a dry tar-brush.

A snapshot of a lizard flicks past:

> A large admiral lizard leapt up on a rail, stood on hind legs with
> fore legs raised like hands, and watched for a moment that trund-
> ling Thing, then loped down the cess-path with arms swinging and
> iridescent frill flying out like a cape.

Most, however, is due to the pervasive note of ironic zest that
Herbert employs throughout. Accidents, drinking bouts, fights,
broken legs and bloodied heads, deaths by disease and violence
—these are related with a gusto that removes them from the
realm of horror to that of sardonic adult fable. The laconic and

offhand way he disposes of people removes any momentary
queasiness the reader may feel. It is not too much to say that,
with perhaps two or three exceptions, we enjoy every death in
the book.

A gusty humour results from Herbert's power over phrase and
from some rather more mechanical devices such as the use of
capitals—Booze Artists, Getting On—and the names of characters that have a superficial resemblance to those of Dickens.
Dickens relies more on sound and a subtler sense of association—
Guppy, Micawber, Turvey Drop, Mulberry Hawk, Smike,
Gamp, Squeers and so on through that immortal list. Herbert is
cruder—McCrook, O'Theef, Pondrosass, Ramble, Thumscrough.

The two parts that the novel falls into are a little uncomfortable
in contrast. The first part is a roaring burlesque, enjoyable as
probably no other Australian book in that fashion. In the second
half, however, Herbert begins as it were to consider that after
all there is a serious problem to be presented—the social and
economic position of the half-caste in Capricornia. So there are
patches in that section where we encounter comment on the
injustice of discriminating against half-castes, together with some
informative lecturettes on the art and religion and intelligence of
the aborigine. It reads as though Herbert had been enjoying
himself and then had become conscience-smitten. The reader
finds it hard to respond. He has been revelling in the comic and
he almost resents having to compose his features into serious lines.
And Herbert himself cannot keep it up; the Old Adam continues
to break out and give us hilarious accounts of trials with Caesar
Bightit as the defending counsel. It is possible that Herbert was
not quite sure in his own mind what he intended; and then his
great gift for humour took over.

On the whole *Capricornia* provides a pleasure that is unmatched
in its kind by any other of our novels, and with its unfaded
freshness after twenty years it has probably not had its full share
of recognition.

One theme that Australian novelists may be expected to
exploit more and more is inter-racial relations. Assimilation into
the community of a new country, probably easier last century
than today, is the subject of *No Escape* (1932) by Velia Ercole.
The travels of this author and her residence in Brittany have
given her an insight into the mind of others than Australians.

The story deals with the social difficulties experienced by Leo

Gerhardi, an Italian doctor, in the small country town of Banton in the early years of this century. He himself is accepted and respected, and his impetuous demands for the town hospital together with his other foibles are excused as the oddities expected of a foreigner. But his wife Teresa, a singer who has given up her career to accompany him, hates Banton and all it represents. Impatient, cultured, despising the pretensions of the townsfolk, she is exasperated to the verge of insanity and at last commits suicide. Feeling himself in a manner responsible, Leo abandons the long-cherished prospect of return to Italy and decides to stay in Banton. It is his penance. He later marries an Australian woman, goes to the first World War as a doctor and while abroad meets some of his compatriots. Their outlook is not his; he has even lost his facility in his mother tongue; and so, recognising the irreversible changes he has suffered, he accepts, without joy, almost listlessly, his Australian destiny.

This is a very competent novel. Its faults are mainly mechanical. There is a break in structure after the suicide of Teresa, when Leo's bursts of rage, not manifested before, appear in his second, and happy, marriage. In humour and irony, the prime weapons in dealing, as she does, with small-town snobbery, Ercole is not very expert. And she can be doughy in style, where her lack of control in punctuation is apparent. On the other hand she has insight and a power to depict changes in character. The alterations in Leo's outlook are depicted with subtlety. The triumph of the book, however, is Teresa, whose moods of depression, elation, anger, despair, resignation, and neurotic self-pity that lead to her death are as convincing as any other such picture we have. Nor perhaps have we a better picture—though it is too kind—of social life and relations in the small Australian town. The only defect in these pictures is the feeling a reader has that the incidents and crises are a little too conveniently introduced. They are all true in Ercole's way, not in life's way, and the job of the novelist is to make us believe that these ways are one and the same. The illustration that is just too pat is good for the plot but bad for the sense of reality.

This novel is likely to prove more popular with Australian readers than Ercole's other novel that contains Australian interest. In this novel, *Dark Windows* (1934), the position is reversed: instead of a foreigner in an Australian community we have an Australian, Julie Purvis, in a foreign community—Rennes in

Brittany. Assimilation into the Breton household does not take place, and this because of a deep-seated lack of understanding, so thorough that it seems generic rather than racial. It is a dark strange menage, with its odd quarrels, its cross-currents, the sense of intrigue in the veriest trifles, the implication that all things are different underneath. Julie attempts to express her feeling of this in talking to Leon:

> Everybody is polite, and kind. They do all that can be expected of them, but I can't find any point of real contact. Even the furniture, the shape of the houses, the posters on the walls, things in shop-windows, all seem alien. When I come into a room, people make conversation specially for me. I am a stranger. I cannot find anything in my own life that really interests them. They ask questions, but their eyes don't seem to be listening. And it is the same with me. When I listen to them, I seem to be taking part in a play. It is not me. It is some person I am acting for the moment.

This power of producing atmosphere is something not very common. It is this, and the teacher, Jeanne Villeneuve, beautiful, vivid, sexually inverted, that make the novel memorable. It is a better novel than its predecessor, but it is not likely to win as wide popularity, at least in this country.

Complementary to the saga novel, which deals with time, is the sociological novel, which deals with numbers of persons in a place. The most notable writer in this field is Kylie Tennant. Her first three novels are variations on this particular theme—*Tiburon* (1938), where the place is a township in the mid-west of N.S.W., the time the depression years, the persons mostly the unemployed on the dole; *Foveaux* (1939), the study of a suburb and those who inhabit it; *The Battlers* (1941), where the group is small and on the move, or larger and static, and the period still the thirties.

The difficulties confronting the author in these novels are quite considerable and at the same time related. To portray a group of people as a group with common characteristics is to run the risk of painting a drab and boring picture. The same applies to the portrayal of a town or suburb or to the evocation of a period with its colours and moods. And sometimes the aim is not quite clear. These novels are unlucky in that they inevitably invite comparison with some classics of their kind. An impartial reader is forced to the conclusion that the Americans and the English have done it better. *Tiburon* is eclipsed by *Main Street*; *Foveaux* dims beside the galvanic flashes of *Manhattan Transfer*; *The Battlers* lacks the stretch and scope of *The Good Companions*.

Probably Tennant has tried to do too much, has not omitted enough. A novel is not life; dialogue for instance is not a transcript of everyday conversation. If it were, then it would be enough to transcribe the tape from a recording instrument concealed beneath any café table or behind any bar counter. In general, however, Tennant's dialogue is her most vivid instrument. It has variety, it is made of slang, of fussiness, of scandal, of dialect, of characteristic turns of speech. It has some caricature perhaps, but then that accusation can be levelled at practically all fictional dialogue. There is variety amongst her characters, but for the most part we are told of them, not shown. Most freshness blooms in *Tiburon*; from there to *The Battlers* the interest falls off.

The suspicion that this type of novel is not the author's forte is confirmed by the fourth novel, *Ride On Stranger* (1943). The general tendency in criticisms of her work has been to praise the first three, or at least the first two—serious sociological analyses of the Australian scene at a certain period and place. Humour is a different matter, critics seem to think—it is, in short, not serious. This type of criticism is common in Australia, and it is unjustified. It is far better to have written *The Rape of the Lock* than *Creation*, the brilliant mock-epic than the lamentable epic. *Ride On Stranger* is a delightful novel, and certainly her most successful one. The theme of the group of people crops up now and then, but most of the story portrays individual figures. A young woman, Shannon Hicks, comes to Sydney and in a mild way may be said to take the lid off the city. It is a sort of respectable picaresque novel, a set of loosely connected adventures linked by the figure of the heroine.

Some of the figures and incidents, a reader may think, have had their counterparts in the life of Sydney, and they make a rich and fantastic stew—Lucy Rossingale, "The Pride of the Harem", fat, voluble, electric, jealous, malicious; Litchin, the teashop owner, running the scale of emotions from elation to depression, persuasive, unscrupulous; Southwell Vaughan-Quilter, the beautiful shell over anything you wish, who begins as the Abbot in a New Thought movement and ends as a politician used as a front by his Left-wing backers. Characters, movements, conditions, and scenes of Sydney are hit off with satiric gusto. We needed a book like this. It is a mere guess to estimate the percentage of Australian novels of the last twenty to thirty years that have bored their faithful readers; but it must be quite high. This is a shining exception.

A later novel, *Lost Haven* (1946), reverts to the earlier method. It portrays the life and denizens of a coastal township. It has one very interesting point: its characters seem to sum up in themselves most of the vices—and a few virtues—that unfriendly outsiders have detected in Australians—but run to seed: sloth, procrastination, leaving things half-finished, parochialism, souveniring, good humour, hospitality, and scandalmongering. Lost Haven the Village, in short, is an Australia in little with certain traits writ large.

Kylie Tennant holds up a miniature distorting mirror. And as a reforming preacher scolds us for our sins but seldom expatiates on our virtues, so she here uses the novel to warn and reprehend. But the unrepentant will prefer *Ride On Stranger*. Indeed laughter has proved in literature as good a scourge as any.

§4

There are four periods in the history of the short story in Australia. The first period, from the beginning to the nineties, contains few good examples. The stories are objective narratives and even then, apart from occasional exceptions such as John Lang's, they are not told very well. The second period stretches from about 1890 to 1914. The supreme names in it are Henry Lawson and Barbara Baynton. Some storytellers since then have reached the level of these two, but the great bulk of Lawson and the sustained intensity of Baynton put them rather much by themselves. In the two decades after 1914 there is a falling off. The fourth period, that of the last twenty-five years or so, has been very productive, and the names are numerous—Katharine Prichard, Vance Palmer, Harley Matthews, Marjorie Barnard, Hal Porter, Judah Waten, Brian James, Cecil Mann, Myra Morris, Henrietta Drake-Brockman, Alan Marshall, John Morrison, John K. Ewers, Don Edwards, Gavin Casey, Dal Stivens, Douglas Stewart, Peter Cowan, Margaret Trist, Ken Levis, Jon Cleary . . . to take names almost at random. And the list could easily be extended.

The difference between the stories of 1890–1914 and those of the modern period is a greater inwardness. In the earlier ones there are emotion and implication as in all good stories, but the stress on events, especially in the lesser writers, is much greater than today. The link between the two periods is best exemplified in Vance Palmer. It is likely that the moderns have learned from him.

In brief, the stories of the earlier period were really stories, there was a narrative in them. Many short stories of the last twenty or thirty years have almost abandoned narrative; some have turned to description, others to character sketches. In this tendency the short story has resembled many novels.

There are dangers in the change. In the first place it seems certain that a greater skill is needed in the modern type of short story than in fairly straight-forward narration. If this necessary skill is not present, the consequence can be thin pieces of writing, which do their best to appear significant, but often succeed only in being enigmatic; or which attempt to capture a mood, but succeed only in lacking point. Perhaps a consequence has been a wider catching and depicting of the Australian temperament in all its forms and under varying strains and stresses.

There have been probably about thirty very competent short-story writers working in Australia during the modern period. Roughly they may be classed in three groups—those limiting themselves to an area or a class or an occupation, those who are stylists, and those whose narrative gift is unusually strong. Of these only about half are treated here, mainly as the varied representatives of the groups they belong to.

With a foot in both camps of the short story, a sort of link between the older tradition and the modern experiment, stands Vance Palmer. In his earlier stories he tends to concentrate on character, to give sketches of persons under stress. In the later stories he seems to have the best of both worlds: there is a narrative, as there was in the period around 1900, and yet implications and extensions are there as well—a personal development, in fact, almost the opposite of the general tendency. In these stories Palmer writes under the constraint imposed on him by space and structure. In consequence he has a concentration that he often lacks in his novels. Some of these stories are among the best we have. *Dingo*, for instance, is a moving and memorable tale, and it has reverberations that move in the mind long afterwards, like a mood that may accompany us for days though we may not know why.

The earliness of Palmer makes him important for other reasons.

When the Australian short story gave up being the tailored piece
of narrative and decided to be more of the character sketch or the
evocation of a mood or the ruminative comment on the significance of an incident—this date is indeterminate. But Palmer,
writing quite early, must be one of the pioneers.

Now the chief difficulty in much of this type of fiction is the
ending. The writer knows that the incident or the conversation
or the situation has an implication, and at the end he wants to
round it off, so to speak, not to leave it all in the air. Here the
nicest judgment and tact are essential: too overt a comment and
the story becomes a parable, a lesson; too little comment and the
reader may be left puzzled or vaguely dissatisfied, as if, say, there
were no salt on the table. The Australian weaknesses have been
the first fault—crossing the t's and dotting the i's. Even so capable a writer as John Morrison can falter here. In his *Man in the
Night*, where the youngster at last encounters the milkman and
despite his idealisation of him is not disappointed—even in this
good little story the ending has this fault:

> That was the day that I learned for all time that the creatures of
> fable and fantasy are never half as nice as the creatures of real life.

This makes the point, certainly, but is it not perhaps rather too
formal, too portentous, too much the wagging of the finger to
emphasise the issue? But some of the best things in Palmer are
precisely these endings, where so often he offers models to younger
writers.

Two examples may illustrate. In *The Search* the young Spanish
soldier finds weapons in the house—rusty and useless, but still
weapons. He ought to do something about it, but he does not:

> His face broke again into its embarrassed grin. He was trembling,
> either from nervousness or from lack of food and drink.
> No going back now; he had given himself away. Thanks, com-
> rade, my heart said; the same pulse beats in us. You belong, like
> me, to those who shy away from conflict—through softness of heart,
> through laziness, through sheer incapacity for pursuing things to
> their logical end. How good to meet with such innocent corruption
> when caught in a jam!

Palmer had to say this, explicit and analytical as it seems. But it
is too obvious to end there. So he goes on:

> "You up there, Pedro?" snapped the little dark man from below.
> "Coming down now."
> "Nothing to be found?"

"*Nada.* Nothing at all."
He tumbled down the stairs as if from some time-bomb that was nearly due to explode.

Perhaps better is the end of *The Birthday.* The day begins magically for Darrow and the twins, and then is shattered. A shark mauls young Delaney with whom Jessie (Darrow's house-maid) is in love, the twins' puppy is run over by a car and Darrow, returning home, finds his wife distracted by their grief. He looks at their tear-stained faces as they lie asleep, and then goes out into the moonlight to bury the puppy:

> Picking it up, he carried it to the back, stopping suddenly as he saw a figure by the fence in the shadow of the ti-tree. Jessie, leaning on the rail, with her head in her arms and her body as rigid and motionless as if it had been turned to stone. Moving away, Darrow began to feel emotion rise like a warm, expanding bubble in his brain, till it softly burst.
> "Life! . . ." he thought vaguely, feeling for the spade in the darkness of the outhouse.

That is probably as good in its kind as it could well be. Palmer is not invariably so successful, but a large proportion of his stories provide this same satisfaction. If we put Baynton aside as being *sui generis*, then it is no overestimate to say that Palmer, by reason of his considerable production and the general level it preserves, is our best short-story writer next to Lawson.

Occasionally a writer has struck out in more than one direction, and has surprisingly succeeded in both. Dal Stivens, for instance, first gave us stories that were the temporary arresting of a mood, the capture of the evanescent moment. His *Solemn Mass* is his triumph in this kind. The girl has listened, has come away entranced, rapt, bemused. She cannot tell herself what it is all about, nor the man whom she puzzles by her mood. Nor can Stivens. But with a considerable delicacy he has suggested it all for us in a sort of pastel wash of emotional colour. Beside this ability to let us glimpse, in the occasional flash of complete success, the crystalline moment, Stivens also has written some of the better tall stories, the Australian equivalents of the American Paul Bunyan yarns. Whether the time for these has not gone past some generations ago is a question we may ask ourselves dubiously; but Stivens can tell these belated folklore tales with enormous invention and gusto. Reading them is like running before a big wind.

His rival, indeed his superior in some instances, is Gavin Casey. When Casey writes the tall folk-tale he spreads himself more than Stivens and probably is more elaborately funny and inventive: if Stivens then is the wind, Casey is the cyclone. But Casey's favourite setting is West Australian. His pictures of the miner, of the danger and the boredom and the pathos, are among the strongest of their kind. His best story, now a classic, still remains *Short Shift Saturday*, a rather longer story that builds up relentlessly an atmosphere that is unforgettable. For days after reading it one looks at life through smoked spectacles. This accretional triumph in the short-story field is unusual, for concentration is generally held to be of the essence of the kind. When Casey moves from the setting and the characters that he has made his own, then he is not superior to other serious writers. But in his own field he is supreme.

Most of his stories are grim or hopeless or resigned. The preoccupation of the miner is "dusting"—the effect of certain dust on the lungs—which when detected means his exclusion from underground, and when undetected means his death. This lies at the back of some of the stories like a suspended sentence. Another recurrent theme, sometimes linked with the first, is the unhappy marriage, the dissatisfied wife hating or fearing the mine. In his treatment of these subjects Casey is the most powerful of our contemporary writers of the short story.

Many Australian short-story writers possess one ability in common—the power to convey a feeling of time wasted, whether in pubs or in talk or at the track. An almost physical sense of futility results from these details of action and conversation. Allied to this is the description of the unhappy or incompatible marriage, a sort of commentary on the Australian wife, mostly in the outback or in the suburbs or in mining townships. The wife is lined, and pallid or brown of face, jaded by household chores and the demands of children, her hair is streaked with grey, and she has developed a stringiness. The husband is not invariably a drunkard but he uses liquor as a solace or an anodyne. Marriage appears as an unheroic ordeal that mostly leaves its victims drained of enterprise and joyousness. The characters are for the most part ill-educated and belong to the humbler strata of society. They seem to have few inner resources and in consequence they seek escape through the grosser or the more physical alleviations of boredom.

S

The most skilful in such portrayals is Gavin Casey, but in this respect Peter Cowan runs him close. Cowan's short stories have rather more substance than those of some of his contemporaries, and appear more thoughtful. The atmosphere he conveys is depressingly real:

> Saturday afternoon the town lay under the heat as though deserted. There was one truck in the wide hot main street. Over from the station and at the far end of the town the low jam trees closed in, their flat tops stretching away, slightly iridescent in the heat. Jim parked the truck over from the hotel and they got out and went across. There was nobody else in the bar.

His style is often staccato, consisting of short unconnected sentences, blankly independent of one another, and this iteration builds up with accumulative force a sense of dull routine. He uses the same method to give the emotion of intolerable isolation, an effect superbly conveyed in *Living*, where the husband returns to the lonely selection after the death of his wife. Cowan has a sort of stealthy strength in his stories that after a page or two takes the reader in an unshakable grasp.

It has been already mentioned that some of our short-story writers have made certain themes or types or trades or areas their own. Occasionally the result is anonymity or family likeness; bush themes, for instance, are very frequent, but many who deal with them are not individual. Pick up a story of this kind, and you can say it might be by one of half a dozen writers. But you cannot always says which one.

Amongst the best of "area" writers is Frank Dalby Davison, author of two classic short novels—or long short stories—*Man-Shy* (1931) and *Dusty* (1946). His other stories deal with the settlers of the area where *Man-Shy* is laid. Any anonymity, if one dares use the term, derives not from mediocrity but an absence of any mannerism. The stories are the most adult of the type, and their essence is human emotional relationships. The influence of Vance Palmer, to whom Davison has warmly acknowledged a debt, appears in *Lady with a Scar*, a masterful little study with treatment and ending that could come from one of the older writer's best stories.

Some of his stories contain misfits, or people who fail or who cannot for temperamental reasons cope with the demands that the land makes on them. In these sketches of people and places Davison reveals a humanity that is neither sentimental nor patronising. Some writers on such themes do not go much below the surface. Davison has considerable insight, and in *The Woman at the Mill* and *Sojourners* he reveals a capacity to analyse subtleties of reaction and relationship that is mature. On the technical side it is a measure of his skill that in, for example, *The Wasteland* he can persuade us to read pages of natural description (which are the parts we skip in most other writers).

If the choice is an unusual group of people, then a writer has a certain advantage. This has been the case with Judah Waten, who has written racy and penetrating and flavoured stories of a Jewish immigrant group. These stories have a taste all their own. This background of belief and attitude gives Waten perhaps an unfair start, as it were; but certainly his knowledge of and sympathy with his characters give the stories a personality lacking in many others. They bear his trade mark.

Rather like Steele Rudd, but at his best better, is Brian James. He tells stories of a small area, or of a township, or a street, sometimes a group of stories about a family. He writes better than Rudd, he has more insight and a greater command of pathos, but he is not so clownishly funny. That perhaps is why he and his characters will not become the household words that Rudd and his characters have succeeded in becoming. It is something not completely explainable. Another factor probably is the constant reappearance of certain characters in Rudd. Mere repetition imprints these on the mind—like an advertisement.

James' early stories were mostly sketches, vignettes of a setting or an atmosphere or a person. His later stories are longer and richer, and the command of phrase has become more expert. When these phrases are humorous—and the best of them are—then they are complete little things in themselves:

Grandfather was a great believer in hanging as a complete cure.

James' scope extends to pathos also, and *Brosie* is a restrained and successful story in that kind.

The picture of the area that James works in is not idealised. He is a realist, and we get ironic pictures of the local mayor, the drunks, the loafers, the mean father and mother, the sham pioneers who lament the olden days, the famed outback hospitality and kindness (on which schoolteachers posted outback can make some heartfelt comments), the family jealousies, and parochial snobberies. Mostly James treats it all with salty dialogue and earthy good humour. And he is extremely readable. Even when he starts off with description or general statement (a pretty good test) he carries the reader with him. The small township and its surrounding selections have seldom been given us so vividly and in such racy prose.

Also local, though it may be a misnomer to speak of West Australia in these terms, are the short stories of Katharine Prichard. Most of them have the mining and wheat areas as their setting. They have at first sight a certain lack of structure, but to counterbalance this they have a considerable actuality. The explanation lies, so it appears, in their origin. Katharine Prichard writes that the narratives are "authentic fragments of the life of our people—yarns that have been told to me". Indeed quite often a reader feels that an author is not likely to invent such incidents. The stories are then, if not slices of life, at any rate crumbs. The humorous stories, which are as numerous as the serious, are not her most successful. Her best stories are *The Cooboo*, a grim vignette of an aboriginal woman who throws away her child, and *Marlene*, an ironic and bitter story with more than her usual amount of structure.

All writers have found children a most difficult theme to treat adequately. Sentimentality or flatness, misunderstanding or sheer misrepresentation—these are some of the pitfalls that lie in wait. Perhaps the safest as well as the most vivid and least distorting method is to reproduce children's talk. The task of the writer is then narrowed down mostly to selection. It is here that Alan Marshall has scored some of his effects. *Tell Us About the Turkey, Jo* is a very lifelike little picture of a child of nine and one of four or five. There is no attempt to analyse, to *tell* us what the children are or how they think and feel: the story *shows* us how they react, how they talk. It is all we can expect, and as it happens it is perfectly adequate to the situation. The simple fact is that Marshall's ear is acute and his memory is retentive. He uses reported conversation in other stories, which in general turn out to be his most successful ones. When adult characters are concerned, the stories are often his most humorous ones as well.

Another theme is animals—bulls, kangaroos, dogs, brumbies, wild duck. A danger here lies in sentimentalising the subject, and it is a danger that Marshall has not always escaped. Indeed sentimentality is his fault in other stories as well, so that *The Baby*, for instance, can arouse in a reader an incredulous protest against violation of probability, exploitation of the hackneyed, and assault on the unwary reader's sensibility. Marshall, to put it in brief, is a humanitarian, kindly and indignant, hating what hurts the defenceless whether brute or human, and prone to let these sentiments find their way into his art. But life and art, however closely connected, do not happen to be the same. Marshall is at his best, and a very penetrating and subtle best it can be, when he is objective.

The talent of Margaret Trist as a story teller has developed and changed very considerably. The development appears in a much greater vitality, an increased power in managing dialogue, and a more penetrating insight into character. She began by portraying and suggesting the moods of children, generally little girls. Such a task is never an easy one, for the view of the writer is adult; or if it is memory, as here it seems to be—an extraordinary retention of childhood fears and embarrassments—then one cannot be certain how much has been added. Nevertheless the reproduction is satisfyingly lifelike. The main weakness is an obviousness, a tendency to tell the reader. One odd characteristic of these earlier stories is the repetition of a situation involving a little girl and her grandfather.

The later stories, which mark an advance in technique, deal mostly with adults. *Elsie's Third Baby*, for instance, a cynical portrayal of a tough amoral family, would have been inconceivable among her earlier stories. Dialogue, again, has become salty and colloquial, and results in such humorous and dramatic vignettes of life in a small town as *The Village Dictator*. And whereas her early stories portrayed mood, these stories portray change of mood: the characters have a certain unhappy slant on life, and then, almost as it were by accident—as in life— find they can reorientate themselves. So that some of her stories are solutions of life's problems—at least for the characters concerned.

Limited in length, the short story can lend itself to a quasi-poetical treatment that a novel cannot support except in chapters. Marjorie Barnard affords the most notable success here. Her brief study, *The Persimmon-Tree*, already established as a triumph, is a short sustained evocation that she has never before or since equalled. In a period of convalescence, when some responses

seem subtilised and rarefied far beyond the normal, the narrator
puts out antennae that have a tremulous sensibility:

> My mind was transparent and tender as new skin. Everything that
> happened, even the commonest things, seemed to be happening for
> the first time and had a delicate hollow ring like music played in an
> empty auditorium.

Even in the brief space of the story her variations and with-
drawals and extensions are given us as though we were watching
some strange plant growing. There is a sort of inevitability about
it: all moves towards a fulfilment, an ecstasy that is not of joy or
pity or tenderness but almost of pure response, the whole self in
a consummation that cannot be really described but perhaps only
communicated. It is unjust to quote in part, but the well-known
ending may be given, where she looks across the road at another
solitary woman. If it does not convince, torn from its context like
this, then it may perhaps induce a reader to turn to the almost
perfect original:

> One afternoon I looked out instead of in. It was growing late and
> the sun would soon be gone, but it was warm. There was gold dust
> in the air, the sunlight had thickened. The shadows of trees and
> buildings fell, as they sometimes do on a fortunate day, with
> dramatic grace. She was standing there just behind the curtains in
> a long dark wrap, as if she had come from her bath and was going
> to dress early for the evening. She stood so long and so still, staring
> out—I thought at the budding trees—that tension began to
> accumulate in my mind. My blood ticked like a clock. Very
> slowly she raised her arms and the gown fell from her. She stood
> there naked, behind the veil of the curtains, the scarcely distinguish-
> able but unmistakable form of a woman whose face was in shadow.
> I turned away. The shadow of the burgeoning bough was on the
> white wall. I thought my heart would break.

The most surprising stylist is Hal Porter, a half-poetical, half-
realistic writer with a delicacy of response to mood that evokes
a memory or a nostalgia or a regret. He describes the objective
world with a subtle and *recherché* accuracy. This means that he
must be read slowly. And there is a savour in his prose. This
enshrines incident or scene and gives to it suggestions and
implications. Whether all themes lend themselves to this treatment is doubtful, but Porter chooses what he can handle. No
other writer does it in his fashion, and he is if not inimitable at
least unmistakable:

> They threw long shadows in which my flimsy mother hissed like a
> cinder.

This sentence from *Act One, Scene One* is a characteristic example of his descriptive quality. Such sophisticated lighting can, of course, conceal as well as illuminate the object. The following sentence is from a description of the country in summer:

> In its summer pelt of peroxided grasses a lice of grasshoppers perpetually itched, clicked and whirred.

So far his prose has remained mannered. It remains to be seen whether in quantity it will develop mere mannerism.

Cecil Mann is the best of those of our storytellers who have the apparently natural gift of hurrying the reader along. It is of course not really natural, for the skill is something that a writer develops; but when it occurs it has a most welcome freshness. This pressing-on in Mann has great liveliness, especially in his sardonic humorous tales such as *Stiff Luck for the Colonel*. The terse vernacular of the opening, the personal idiom admirably caught, the vivid image, the spate of minor and then more important incident all combine to rush us through to the ironic ending. Compared with, say, *The Reader*, it is rather on the surface of things; for the latter is a masterly cruel little comment on deceived man's willingness to be deceived or to shun the revelation. Just the same, stories like the former, so full of gusto, so urban and in a way urbane, are rare with us and doubly a delight when they appear. These two stories, each very different in theme, are probably Mann's peak, and exhibit a control over matter and manner that is so adult, so easy, that one may forget how much skill went to their telling.

Like Mann, John Morrison has sheer narrative capacity. The beginnings of many Australian short stories, especially those that are setting the scene for a character diagnosis, are sometimes detailed to the verge of dullness. But even here Morrison has the power to hold the reader from the first word. What this consists in it is impossible to define completely. Some of it derives from a very easy, almost colloquial style; some from the concrete, the image, the incident; some from the theme itself.

Morrison, dealing in narrative, can infuse into it humour that is unforced and natural—witness *The Sleeping Doll* or *The Door*. Now and then he shifts ground. *The Battle of Flowers* is told by a gardener, but the chief concern is the two middle-aged sisters, and their growing rivalry. It is a long and elaborated build-up, funny at first, but becoming increasingly more pathetic and grotesque. And it ends with a wryness that is inevitable. Quite a flavour. His characters could class Morrison also with the earlier group. He deals mostly with manual workers, wharfies, swagmen, gardeners, and sailors. His sympathies, arising from his knowledge of the trades, are with them in their struggles.

We may wonder how the modern Australian stories compare with those of the past. There are, necessarily, more of them, and the chances of a superlative one turning up are greater. The average level seems certainly higher. To read conscientiously through much of the early short story crop is a trifle deflating. Put Lawson and Baynton aside and the rest are really not impressive. A modern may not be a great writer, but he gives the effect of sheer competence, of the professional touch. Some of this is due to idiom—the early ones date often because of an old-fashioned flavour that may seem comic or even absurd. Some of it is due to attitude, to a tolerance for melodrama and sentiment that we can no longer share. Uneasily one asks if all this is going to be repeated. Will our present-day short stories seem so out-of-date in another fifty years? We feel sure they will not, but we have no real certainty.

CHAPTER XII

Essays Literary and Critical

L AMB is as famous as Keats and, if it is not ridiculous to compare incomparables, as superlative in his own field. In Australia, however, the essay has never rivalled poetry or fiction, and only one essayist, Walter Murdoch, has won a fame equal to, say, that of Paterson or Richardson. Nor indeed has the pure essay flourished in number. "If we were to list only the essays, published by Australians, which were strictly classifiable under the purely literary form of 'essay', then we would not find many authors." This statement made by Morris Miller in 1940 is still true. If we extend the term a little there are, however, some essayists to be considered: scholars, doctors, novelists, poets, professionals. Only a few representative examples are dealt with here.

Certainly the most learned and probably the most pedestrian of the scholarly group is T. G. Tucker (1859–1946), who in his day as professor of Classical Philology at Melbourne had a worldwide reputation. The criterion of excellence that Tucker almost invariably applied to his reading and criticism was the excellence of classical writers. And since he moved with equal ease in modern languages he was able to apply comparative methods. Perhaps because of this, perhaps because of temperament, Tucker's literary essays are slightly hortatory, there is a flavour of the teacher. The student will read Tucker with benefit; it is not so certain that the non-academic will read with eagerness.

On the other hand, Archibald Strong (1876–1931), onetime professor of English at Adelaide, wears his learning lightly. Even when the essence of the piece is directly classical or is taken from some rare volume or is esoteric in itself, even then the reader does not feel he is being instructed instead of (or besides) being entertained. *Peradventure* (1911) is a collection of pieces, in which we find Strong's ability to use the colloquial with the deliberate effect of debunking, while still remaining scholarly:

> . . . Diomede, that sporting hero of shady antecedents, who, in conjunction with the king of 'spielers', Ulysses, had recently effected one of the biggest horse-steals of all antiquity from the Trojan camp.

Not unlike Murdoch is Frederick Sinclaire (d. 1954), formerly lecturer in English and later professor, writing for newspapers, collecting the essays into volumes. But he is more literary and less matey, more forthright and vigorous and less selfconsciously purveying personality. Occasional sentences like the following read momentarily like Murdoch:

> Admit, my dear fellow-countryman, my composite Croesus, that you haven't a leg to stand on, and I have done with nagging. Let us now lay our heads together and see if we cannot find a way to remove our common shame.

Scholar and poet and walker, J. Le Gay Brereton (1871–1933) occasionally collected his notes. The best known is his *Knocking Round* (1930), with its reminiscences and criticism and descriptions. Brereton has an easy and humorous tone, some of it due to the theme, some to an unassuming personality that does not obtrude itself even when the first person is used and he is telling of his own experiences. For this reason Brereton is probably the most pleasant of the group.

The scholar's danger when writing essays is that he is a scholar before he is an essayist. A little of this appears in the essays of F. J. H. Letters, for instance in *In a Shaft of Sunlight*. They are easy enough reading, but the faintest of films comes between reader and writer. They are not the less interesting (at least to some readers) for all that, but the essential quiddity of the author is not so manifest. That aside, the essays have a turn of thought and phrase that is attractive. The most entertaining bits are the *obiter dicta*, the odd phrase or thought thrown off, as it were, sometimes not an essential part of the essay—

> I have never yet met the polyglot who could tell me the word for "weevil" in six languages—French, German, Spanish, Tamil, Arabic, and Chinese for example—without the help of almost as many dictionaries.

The only Australian essayist to have gained a wide popularity is Walter Murdoch (b. 1874). He possesses, at first sight, most of the qualities we expect to find in an essayist. His essays are short enough; they are on all subjects, from literature to tripe and onions; they are informal and easy to read, and probably nobody ever had to read a sentence in one of his essays more than once to understand it completely. And if we look for what is commonly called personality, then we shall find a plentiful use of the first person. Occasionally an essay is quite serious, but for the most part they are light and frequently humorous, and the humour is produced in various ways. He does not like pretentiousness, putting on airs, pomposity. Indeed most of us do not, and we feel that he is expressing our own views on a subject. He thus engages our sympathy by adopting or having an attitude much the same as that of everyone else.

After a reader decides that Murdoch has all these qualities, it is only a step to thinking that he must be a great essayist. But a closer look at Murdoch reveals certain characteristics that make us revise a first impression. He says little, for instance. That of course is not unusual in modern essays, and perhaps it is not very important; for the aim of an essay is not to provide information. But at all events it would be admitted by most people that he does not give us much to chew on. Another point is that his style is not really individual. It certainly reads easily; it is clear and unambiguous; it is light and in its way attractive. But he does not say anything in a memorable way. He does not suffuse his essays with the flavour of a full and enriching personality.

The most serious charge one can make against him is his feeling and tone. He expresses a point of view that some people think he should not. Murdoch was professor of English in the University of Western Australia, and as a professor he was the interpreter and champion of the best that has been thought and written in prose or verse in the English tongue. His task was, among other things, to defend excellence. (And some may think that excellence needs a lot of defending in this country.) In his essays we find a different state of affairs. It is hard to resist the impression that Murdoch was writing down to his large public. Let us be clear on this. A reader does not feel that Murdoch is patronising, or leaning down from a height, that he is "writing down" in the usual sense of the phrase. No, the reader feels the opposite: that Murdoch is like him, an average sort of fellow, with average tastes, with not much time for this "arty" business or even perhaps for literature, rather despising in fact the odd person like Walter Pater who takes writing and art so seriously. This attitude is felt by most readers, and in the view of most critics it is unfortunate. For Murdoch is not an ordinary person, and his attempt in his essays to make his readers think he is has the unhappy result that they feel fortified in an indifference to art and literature.

It is no accident that an essayist with these particular

characteristics should be accepted and valued by many Australians as the great Australian essayist.

If it is thought that this verdict on Murdoch is too severe—and it may seem ungracious to end on such a note—then it must be conceded that he has persuaded the Australian public to read his essays, to take an interest in a form of literature other than the trivial or sensational.

The literary man, lacking a background of training in law or medicine or science, may seem a trifle thin when put beside, say, the doctor who turns his hand to writing. Charles MacLaurin used his medical knowledge in *Post Mortem* (1923) and *Mere Mortals* (1925). These had a considerable and understandable popularity. They are diagnoses of the maladies that presumably afflicted the great in ages past. Not essays in the strict sense, being so to speak professional rather than amateur comments, they are extremely readable and, though the style rather lacks shading, they are witty and often ironical. Some may think them iconoclastic. The volumes are so fascinating that one wonders how MacLaurin would read if he were dealing with subjects where he could not make use of his medical training.

Only if we give the word *essay* a wide meaning can W. A. Osborne be included. He was at one time Dean of the Faculty of Medicine at Melbourne University, and his popular writings bear the imprint of his profession. His learning is manifest as extremely wide, and this gives his essays a factual interest different from that of the "pure" essayist. He builds on facts—an incident or a person or a phenomenon—and the originality we enjoy is thus an intellectual one; it is not an interest that derives essentially from personality.

Any reader of the fiction of William Gosse Hay, uncertain whether his style is an elaborated medium, should find in Hay's essays some evidence. *An Australian Rip Van Winkle* (1921), though not fluent or pellucid, lacks the indirection of Hay's famous—or notorious—novels. Passages are not unlike Carlyle. The pieces in this collection are mostly historical and local. The opening is a short story. So that the contents are mixed, and probably only one or two can be termed essays in the literary sense. Hay's talent is not suited to the type. He is best when he has room to move in, and short pieces (though these are longer than most others dealt with in this section) seem to cramp his detailed and accumulative methods.

The prose of poets has nearly always possessed distinction. Perhaps Furnley Maurice was a little conscious of this in *Romance* (1922), a brief collection of essays on themes mostly literary. To write on subjects like *Courage* requires considerable tact in an essayist if he is not to make the reader feel embarrassed. The literary themes in the volume might place it in the section on criticism, and in such essays Maurice is at his best. He can then be laconic and at the same time judicious:

> Let us be Australian. I do not know what that is—excepting that it is not the Australian verse of to-day.

That was a true enough comment in 1922. The volume also contains what is probably Maurice's most discussed and controversial judgment:

> Genius can afford to have nothing to do with art. Shakespeare unconsciously breathes poetry and knowledge of men to the air about him, while Mr. W. B. Yeats, as in his "Deirdre", holds down the warm body of humanity with a marble, beautiful hand.

The professional leaves some sort of a trade mark on what he writes, a touch of competence, a method of attack made visible, background of reading. . . . Something of this is seen in Nettie Palmer's *Talking It Over* (1932), a reprinting for the most part of articles contributed to newspapers. They are all much of a length, they are very varied in theme, they are deft and readable, and they all have the faint air of being written to order. This last is probably unavoidable unless the essayist is superlative. But if one is not a Lamb or a Hazlitt what is one to do? One can do a lot worse, the answer might run, than write like Nettie Palmer. These are the extremely competent essays of their kind, putting a point of view, possessing some originality, and never boring a reader.

The best essays this century have been literary criticism. In bulk, influence, and breadth of interest, though less certainly in penetration and sureness, A. G. Stephens remains the most significant figure. Since his *Bulletin* period literary criticism of Australian writing has fallen more into the hands of the academics. The introduction into the universities of courses in Australian literature and the proliferation of theses on aspects of the subject have played a part here. There are critics who would indignantly repudiate the term *academic* as stifling, and certainly some of our best critics are not university lecturers; but as in

America the emergence of the universities as the chief source of such criticism seems inevitable. It is unlikely that we shall again have a critic as influential and competent, and yet so largely self-made, as Stephens.

The literary journals in which criticism appears are few. *Southerly* (ed. Kenneth Slessor) is the organ of the English Association in Australia. It is the most scholarly publication in the literary field. The charge that it is too academic may be countered by pointing to the stories and poems that each issue contains. Reviews, chiefly of books of Australian interest, occupy much of its space. To its former editor, R. G. Howarth, now professor of English at Cape Town, modern Australian criticism owes a considerable debt. His book of essays, *Literary Particles* (1946), bears witness to his learning and his breadth of interest. The most sophisticated periodical in the country is *Meanjin*, founded by C. B. Christesen in 1941 and edited by him since. It is wider in content and contains articles on music and art as well as criticism, fiction, and poetry. Both these publications are quarterlies. *The Australian Quarterly*, though mainly concerned with economics, sociology, and politics, prints a few literary articles as well. The best-known weekly in Australia is *The Bulletin*, which with its Red Page, edited by Douglas Stewart, preserves the Stephens tradition of criticism of current works both Australian and overseas. This page, formerly more open to contributors than now, is mainly written by its staff. Some of the great daily newspapers contain once a week reviews of books. The influence these exert depends on the reviewer. Nearly all these reviews are competent and occasionally one is brilliant.

Our literary criticism of this century falls into three classes—surveys, discussions of individual writers, and collected critical essays on various aspects of our literature. Only criticism of Australian writing is here mentioned.

It was not until 1940 that a really comprehensive survey, encyclopedic in scope, appeared. Before that we had two works (one limiting itself to a period, the other to an area) and a short survey of the whole field.

In 1924 Nettie Palmer won the Lothian Prize Essay with her *Modern Australian Literature*, which covered the period 1900–23. She felt apparently that the survey had to be inclusive, and so in fifty-five pages she dealt with nearly twice that number of writers. The consequence is necessarily a comment on rather than a treatment of all but about a dozen writers. This is not intended as censure, for indeed, given the conditions and the length, nothing else was possible. If the reader turns to the pages dealing with writers who have increased in stature since then, he finds judgments which, except in a few passages of enthusiasm, have been uniformly confirmed. This almost prophetic insight is the mark of an intuitive perception.

In 1930 H. A. Kellow published his *Queensland Poets*. This regional survey is not a cursory account but in many sections a detailed analysis. And yet of all the figures in the book only three—Essex Evans, Brunton Stephens, and William Baylebridge —are likely to be familiar to most readers. So it may seem that Kellow incurs the danger of overestimating minors. He recognises this, however, and prefixes a line from *Midsummer Night's Dream*: The best in this kind are but shadows. It is not difficult to make out a case for Kellow, to claim that this is the most distinguished single volume bearing on our literature, the grounds of assessment being style, penetration, luminous presentation, and a general comprehensiveness of view. It is true that the figures are minors; but a zoologist reveals his calibre in dealing with a mouse as well as with a mastodon.

The doyen of Australian critics is H. M. Green, whose *Outline of Australian Literature* (1930) is the first of its kind and the best. Green worked under great difficulties, for any ordered bibliography was not available to him. So that he had to gather and arrange material and set it in perspective. His little book, long out of print, covers the whole field of creative writing in Australia up to 1928. On many authors Green was the first to pass judgment. This is always a severe handicap, for a previous estimate, even if one disagrees with it, does serve as something to measure one's opinions by. The critical evaluations that Green made still stand without much need of qualification. This volume is the prelude to a much larger and more comprehensive work still to come. His *Fourteen Minutes* (1944) is a reprint of broadcast talks on various authors, and allows him space for quotation and more elaborate discussions. *Australian Literature, 1900–1950* is a brilliant sketch and compares with Nettie Palmer's.

The standard work on our literary history appeared in 1940 in two large volumes. Morris Miller's *Australian Literature* is an exhaustive work, with biographies, criticism, and bibliographies complete almost to that date. A student at first may find it awkward to use and must learn its arrangement and method of reference. And he will discover that, perhaps inevitably, a work of this size contains errors. If he finds that the summary of a novel, for instance, differs from his memory of it, then he will do well to trust his memory. The work has been out of print for years and copies are not easy to come by, a state of affairs very characteristic of us. Despite a certain garrulity and some inaccuracies, the work remains quite indispensable for any serious student of our literature, an unrivalled source of information on a very wide range of related subjects.

In 1956 F. T. Macartney issued a revised edition (brought up to 1950) that was really a new work. Much of the discussion and criticism was condensed and biographical sections were pruned. It is in consequence a shorter work. Its arrangement is alphabetical, and so it serves as a literary dictionary. Many find it no substitute for the original, but for easy and quick reference it is far superior.

A short survey, making use of the work of predecessors, appeared in 1945 and, still in print, is in wide popular use. This is *Creative Writing in Australia*, by John K. Ewers.

One survey, *An Introduction to Australian Fiction* (1950), represents only partly the varied interests of its author, Colin Roderick. Two other volumes, *The Australian Novel* (1945) and *Twenty Australian Novelists* (1947), serve as selected reading material, being anthologies with introductions and summaries that link the extracts. The *Introduction* is the history of our fiction from the beginnings. It is unusual in arrangement, for the most part chronological, but with sections sub-divided into types. One can thus trace the course of any particular genre of novel through its development. For many students the most valuable and startling contribution made by Roderick was his discovery of James Tucker. (This has been mentioned under Tucker.)

The major figures in any literature invite fuller and more elaborate analysis than any survey can provide. Last century in our literature Gordon was the subject of discussion and generally adulatory comment. This century it is Brennan. The volume on him by A. G. Stephens has been mentioned already. Other volumes stressing different aspects have appeared.

A discussion of him as man and poet, especially as symbolist poet, is the theme of *C. J. Brennan. An Essay in Values* (1934). Its author, Randolph Hughes, had been a student of Brennan's at

Sydney and like many others had fallen willing victim to his mentor's talk. This is a very angry little book, full of fierce asides and thumping sarcasms and vehement denunciations of the multitude. It is at the same time extremely readable, couched in a sort of eloquent fluency, so that the technical polysyllables like rocks are submerged in the current. A. R. Chisholm contributes a slightly cautionary Foreword.

Other aspects appear in two public lectures delivered by H. M. Green and printed as *Christopher Brennan* (1939). The basis of the Brennan legend is discussed and Brennan's appearance and habits and some anecdotes are described in an easy natural prose that reflects the lecturer. The critical sections deal with the metre and part of the content of the poems. Green's booklet is a balanced and deliberated comment.

A further two lectures on Brennan delivered by A. R. Chisholm appeared in 1946 as *Christopher Brennan. The Man and His Poetry*. The first part, in somewhat the same fashion as Green's account, deals with Brennan's appearance and the things he did that impressed friends and observers. In the second half Chisholm analyses the symbolism in Brennan and its relation to that of Mallarmé. In this field Chisholm speaks as an authority.

These books are general and only in part analytical discussions of particular qualities or themes in Brennan. But with a figure so striking it was obviously only a matter of time before the research thesis should appear. The first of its kind was by G. A. Wilkes, *New Perspectives on Brennan's Poetry* (1952). (It has been summarised earlier in the discussion of Brennan's poetry.) It is chiefly explicatory, an analysis of the philosophy beneath the verse. Disagreement among critics of Brennan was rife before this monograph appeared. The authority of its analysis has since silenced conflict. In addition, parts of the monograph glance at Brennan's technique, and here Wilkes reveals an unusual and subtle power of appreciation. This essay is a landmark in Brennan scholarship.

From the nineties on young writers have often had critics willing to advise. A. G. Stephens was one such formidable patron. Since then there has probably been no more sympathetic adviser to the literary aspirant than Vance Palmer, and to him a number of younger writers have owed a debt. In his public pronouncements, such as his broadcast reviews of current books, he has managed whenever possible to comment on Australian productions.

T

If an Australian writer comes up before Palmer, then he may be given a yard or two start. If he comes before A. D. Hope, one feels that he may be put a yard or two behind scratch. That stern handicapper is not going to favour local talent just because everybody knows them and wishes them well. Something of course can be said for both attitudes; and both are characteristic. Hope is the most sardonic and penetrating critic in the country. He has probably felt, as others have, that Australian critical paternalism has given us some false values, and he is determined that he will not be a party to the agreement. This is not to say that Palmer is in any way jingoistic: it merely means that he believes in a different kind of literary influence. His own criticism is extensive in scope and bulk and he is probably not sufficiently appreciated for the judgment and competence he manifests in it.

His earliest book on a writer is his *Frank Wilmot (Furnley Maurice)* (1942). It is the tribute of a friend and critic, briefer than F. T. Macartney's book and a little more deft, a result possibly to be expected in view of Palmer's very considerable experience in prose. There are a few points of variance between these two memoirs, but the differences are not fundamental.

Macartney's biography and critical study, *Furnley Maurice* (1955), is an example of devoted but unbiased treatment. The author knew his subject in life. This makes for an intimacy that no reliance on documents can afford. The danger of course is that judgment will yield to friendship. It is a danger that this volume gives little sign of. Not the least of its value derives from the accounts of literary figures and the literary background in the early decades of this century.

One handbook to an author was written by Miles Franklin— *Joseph Furphy* (1944)—with the help of Furphy's friend Kate Baker and her unrivalled collection of material bearing on Furphy's life and writing. The book is full of Miles Franklin's characteristic views on Australianism and Australian literature. The letters, often given *in extenso*, and the anecdotes and memories make this a book that is required reading for any student who wants to know about the inception and production of that classic, *Such is Life*. And if he should want an analysis and criticism of it as well, then he will find that also.

This interest in background, in the literary atmosphere of a period in which a writer grows, reveals itself also in *Louis Esson and the Australian Theatre* (1948). It contains personal reminiscences of the period from 1911 to the death of Esson in 1943, an account of Esson, and perhaps most revealing and important, a selection of letters from Esson. Its author, Vance Palmer, knew Esson well and shared his sympathies and hopes. Both he and Esson wrote plays, and both were deeply concerned with the prevalent discouragement that the Australian playwright endured in the period between the wars.

An unusual treatment of a novelist is *In Mortal Bondage* (1948). In this Colin Roderick gives an imaginative reconstruction of the life of Rosa Praed. It is based on documentary evidence, but the attempt to make it read vividly has given it the appearance of fiction. A great amount of research supports the picture and can be overlooked by a reader simply because he may misinterpret the accessories. Where so much work has been expended on an author, there is a temptation to believe the author important. Some readers consider that Roderick has not completely escaped this danger.

Probably the best of all these books on individual Australian authors is that by Nettie Palmer. Her *Henry Handel Richardson* (1950), partly biographical, concerns itself chiefly with Richardson's novels. The analysis and the estimation were aided by a friendship that extended over twenty years, during which a correspondence went on. Since the appearance of this book there have been investigations into aspects of Richardson that Nettie Palmer from considerations of space forbore to undertake. And probably another full-length analysis of Richardson remains to be written. But as it stands, despite a considerable tact in its treatment, this book is certainly a very satisfying discussion of that novelist. Apart from its critical insight, it has the advantage of being written with a maturity of style.

A novelist as considerable as Richardson invites specialised investigation as well as general biography and criticism. Leonie Gibson in *Henry Handel Richardson and some of her sources* (1954) deals with an implicit theory of fiction. (Reference has been made to this book in the account of Richardson.) Gibson's phrase, "This particular failure of the factual method", epitomises her conclusions. This essay is an original and penetrating piece of research that may well be applied to the fiction of other novelists as well.

Another book on a literary figure is *Bernard O'Dowd* (1954), which Nettie Palmer took over and completed after the death of

Victor Kennedy. She used the outline already drawn and the materials collected and, so it seems, some of the written sections. It is more pedestrian in style than her work on Richardson, but as thorough. The influences on O'Dowd, the background of the period, the changes in his work, its significance and value—these render it a valuable handbook for students of that poet.

The critical essay or collection of critical essays is something of a phenomenon of this century, especially of the last thirty or forty years. In Australia the themes have been writers, background, Australianism in literature, and the literary situation.

Incidental reference and comment have always been made concerning culture and the arts in Australia, but a direct analysis of the situation waited until P. R. Stephensen published his seminal and pioneer work in 1936. This was the controversial *The Foundations of Culture in Australia*. The early history of the country he tends to play down: "The seven decades from 1850 to 1920 are the foundation decades of the Australian nation." The strength and value of the book reside in the analysis of the situation. When he states things as facts and evaluates Australian writers, then some will find it hard to accept his verdicts. He overstresses the literary value of the nineties, for instance, and here he should be read in the light of Vance Palmer's analysis of that period. But the book is instinct with enthusiasm and indignation and is in consequence one of the liveliest of its kind. The definition of culture sets the tone: "Nothing is permanent in a nation except its culture—its ideas of permanence, which are expressed in art, literature, religion, philosophy; ideas which transcend modernism and ephemerality, ideas which survive political, social, and economic changes." It is a loud and vivid protest and an appeal for "an act of intellectual self-consciousness". Other writings on the theme have appeared since then, but this still retains its force, its freshness, and its relevance.

The modern novelists are the subjects of *Essays in Australian Fiction* (1938) by Barnard Eldershaw, the two collaborators themselves being novelists. The subjects are Richardson, Prichard, Davison, Leonard Mann, Boyd, Stead, Dark, and Palmer. These accounts are among the earliest extended treatments this century, and are notably balanced in judgment.

In the same year appeared a landmark in our literary criticism. This was a revaluation of Australian poetry in the figures of McCrae, Neilson, O'Dowd, Baylebridge, Brennan, and

FitzGerald. Tom Inglis Moore in *Six Australian Poets* corrected the widespread over-estimation of some nineteenth-century Australian poets and the under-estimation or neglect or even ignorance of our twentieth-century poets. After its appearance there remained no excuse for any literate person to be in doubt about the relative values formerly confused or reversed. This volume, the first attempt at establishing a canon, speaks with authority, and its influence has been salutary and considerable. Its value lies, moreover, not only in its pronouncements but in its techniques of interpretation and evaluation. It marks a great advance, that is, in critical method and approach. The danger in such a volume, whose aim is to praise poets not fully recognised, is that the praise may be too great for the stature of the poets: they may be accorded the status of major writers. This danger, subtle and pervasive, Moore has escaped; it is not the least of his achievements. A revised and expanded edition, probably dealing with ten poets, is in preparation.

A reappraisal of some earlier poets was made by A. J. Coombes, who won first prize in the Long Essay section of the literary competitions that accompanied the Sesqui-Centenary celebrations. His *Some Australian Poets* (1938) deals with Harpur, Kendall, Gordon, Lawson, and Paterson of last century, and with McCrae and a few lesser poets of this. Coombes writes with ease and has some perceptive things to say, often amusingly ("it is Gordon principally whom we have to thank for the poetical yarding of so many horses in our literature"). It is to his credit —especially when we remember the occasion—that he does not find his geese swans.

The war years discouraged critical essays, and the next volume did not appear until 1947. This was Brian Elliott's *Singing to the Cattle*, which reprints eleven lectures delivered under the auspices of the Commonwealth scheme to foster the study of Australian literature. About half are on poets and novelists, the rest on movements and conditions. Elliott's presentation preserves something of the informality of the lecture. Probably the most original is the essay on the historical novel in Australia, where he makes points that needed to be made.

The most sensitive critic we have is Douglas Stewart, but not the most reliable. Articles and reviews that he wrote for the Red Page of *The Bulletin* he collected in *The Flesh and the Spirit* (1948). Few things date like the review of the latest novel or of the latest book of verse; but this volume is almost as fresh as when first written. One reason is that Stewart is a good critic, and what he said years ago is still true and just. Another point is that, when he reviews a particular book or deals with a particular field of writing, he always offers general comment and critical sugges- tions that are not limited to that field.

One cannot expect him to be always wise. He can make assessments that revolt the right-thinking (that is, those who disagree). His evaluation of Paterson, though he is careful to indicate that other things than literary value are concerned, seems too high, for instance. The most bruited example, of course, is his *Letter to William Shakespeare*, where he raises Eve Langley's *Peapickers* to a height where even his critical authority has not been able to maintain it. And he is quite unrepentant. In three other essays later he uses it as a sort of accepted norm against which examples of humour or description may be measured. It is, we must suppose, one of the crotchets that we have to allow our critics, like a squint.

Stewart is a most refreshing critic, and he has what modern criticism often lacks, a style that is clear and fluent and distinc- tive. He always rewards a reader. His greatest capacity, and the quality that gives him his position, is the ability to go to the heart of the matter. Most of us can write tolerable reviews, saying apposite things about a number of relevant things. But Stewart quite often puts these aside and deals with the one essential point that makes a writer or a book individual.

The most considerable analysis of a period, of the ideals and thoughts that actuated people, is Vance Palmer's *The Legend of the Nineties* (1954). He first discusses and then qualifies the widely held belief that the literature of the period was an idealistic and forward-looking thing. "What becomes then of the theory of the nineties as a golden period when all the creative forces of the country were simultaneously in flower . . . ?" And again: "It is likely that, in our search for a literary tradition, we have made too much of one narrow period." He then goes on to give a reconstruction of the ethos, the attitudes and habits of mind, and the forces that gave rise to these. It is admirably done. Most persons interested at all in our literature and history know some or many of the facts that Palmer sets out. But the relation- ships and implications under Palmer's analysis afford fresh significance and greater depth. There are perhaps some repetition and overlapping; but all in all this book is a most important discussion of the background of the literature and thought of a period that has been often written about and much misunderstood.

Crystal Ball

AUSTRALIAN literature, like English literature and unlike American literature, is as yet greater in its poetry than in its fiction. Its poetry came of age about the turn of the century when Brennan completed the verse he was to publish later. Its fiction came of age, one may reasonably say, with Richardson's trilogy. The Australianism in neither, as it happens, is very important: Brennan could easily not have lived in this country for any debt his verse owes to it; while in Richardson the greatness derives not from the pictures of the background but from the creation of two characters, a man and his wife. This is not to deny the value of Australia for an Australian writer, but merely to indicate what the facts were.

In both fiction and poetry the continent will continue inevitably to influence those who write in it. In fiction, if concerned with the contemporary scene, idiom will play its part and the much-discussed national outlook and character will modify the stress in plot and pattern. If the scene is not contemporary, then we may expect some development along lines already laid down. From Marcus Clarke to Eleanor Dark there are a greater sophistication and a widening; from Eleanor Dark to Patrick White a deepening of implication and an assumption of background rather than an emphasis. Characters replace forces. But how much longer we are to have Australian historical novels is uncertain. More than one critic has suggested that this preoccupation with origins and development may merely indicate immaturity. A growth of the urban novel, dealing with Australian social types, seems inescapable. But it will need to be written better, in a style at least as good as some of our modern short stories.

It will need also to be less instructive and less hortatory than some of it has been. Though our fiction this century has strangely neglected some periods like the depression—except for Kylie Tennant—it has covered parts of the changing scene. But the aim has been in addition reformatory, and this has been so marked as to be distasteful. Last century's dream has dissolved: the fight is on. But very few sermons on the evils of modern society are likely to be literature.

Reaction against Australianism in poetry was to be expected after the bush ballad crop. The twenties saw a more or less extreme example of this in the outbursts of the Lindsay group in *Vision*. FitzGerald indicated that the West is not something that has to find its way into our verse:

> The great gaunt ringbarked trees hiss: "Danger!
> Here's a new face to scan."
> Wherever I go I am a stranger
> Under the stranger's ban.

Since then our poetry, though still rooted in this country, has become more cosmopolitan and, despite the too easy dismissal of it by most overseas critics, has shown some awareness of modern changes of technique.

Australian poetry at the moment seems more rosy in prospect than in performance. Our three best living poets—Slessor, FitzGerald, and Judith Wright—one may conjecture, have written their finest work. But the Australian poet still has advantages. If an English poet, for example, thinks of a bird or a flower or a tree, then he must be almost oppressed by what earlier poets have already written about them. But such a weight of associations does not burden the Australian poet. He is familiar, as we all are, with the Australian background, but he does not know it in terms of good poetry. It took about a century and a half before an Englishman, D. H. Lawrence, for the first time showed us a kangaroo, its quiddity, its kangaroo-ness. He was able to do so not only because he was Lawrence but because there was no corpus of good kangaroo poetry already existing. An Australian poet, then, can still be an Adam. He is lucky: he does not have to have genius—talent will suffice for a time.

This is not to say, of course, that anyone in his senses would advocate an age of nationalistic nature poetry. The mind recoils from the contemplation of a plague of horticultural and ornithological counterparts to the horse and stockman. But poetry derives so often from the image as from a seed, and the image is part of what is experienced.

Encouragement will probably best be found in criticism that is searching rather than paternalistic or cultish. Last century it was the third type, concentrating on Gordon. At the turn of the century, with Stephens, it was the first with a dash of the second.

T*

Today all three types exist. Proletarian novelists changing to naïve criticism find a congenial theme in a work is sufficient warrant for adulation. Right-wingers, though more sophisticated, still are open to the same charge. There are still cults, with Brennan the chief subject, though not the only one. There are cliques with very strict entrance requirements, groups where some odd compromises of religion and politics and literary themes and treatment have been effected. It appears very diversified. Perhaps a settling-down will take place as the increased number of literary and critical periodicals makes its weight felt and gives direction. But whatever the oddities there is plenty of vigour. Indeed a spectator of the scene is tempted to think that, even more than poetry, criticism is sitting pretty.

Acknowledgments

The author and the publishers are grateful to the following for permission to reproduce copyright material. It has proved impossible in some cases to trace the present copyright holders, and we apologise to any who have been inadvertently omitted. In such cases we have listed the sources from which the material was taken.

A. H. Adams: *Maoriland*, "The Bulletin", Sydney.

Marjorie Barnard: *The Persimmon Tree*, Clarendon Publishing Company, Sydney, by permission of Mr. B. G. White.

Djuna Barnes: *Nightwood*, Faber and Faber, London.

A. A. Bayldon: *Collected Poems*.

William Baylebridge: *Selected Poems* and *Love Redeemed*. By permission of P. R. Stephensen and Perpetual Trustees.

Barbara Baynton: *Human Toll*, Duckworth, London.

Martin Boyd: *The Cardboard Crown*, Cresset Press, London.

E. J. Brady: *The Ways of Many Waters*, "The Bulletin", Sydney.

Christopher Brennan: *Poems*, Angus and Robertson, Sydney.

"Brent of Bin Bin": *Up the Country* and *Ten Creeks Run*, Blackwood, Edinburgh.

Vincent Buckley: *The World's Flesh*, F. W. Cheshire Pty. Ltd., Melbourne.

Ada Cambridge: *A Marked Man*, Heinemann, London.

David Campbell: *Speak with the Sun*, Chatto and Windus, London.

"Tom Collins" (Joseph Furphy): *Such is Life*, Angus and Robertson, Sydney.

Peter Cowan: *Drift*, Reed and Harris, Melbourne. By permission of Mr. Max Harris.

Eleanor Dark: *Prelude to Christopher*, *The Timeless Land*, and *No Barrier*, Collins, London.

Norma Davis: *Earth Cry*, Angus and Robertson, Sydney.

Rosemary Dobson: *Child with a Cockatoo*, Angus and Robertson, Sydney.

Albert Dorrington: *And the Day Came*, Hutchinson, London.

Edward Dyson: *Fact'ry 'Ands*, G. Robertson, Melbourne; *Rhymes from the Mines and Other Lines*, Angus and Robertson, Sydney.

"Barnard Eldershaw" (Marjorie Barnard and Flora Eldershaw): *A House is Built*, Harrap, London.

Velia Ercole: *Dark Windows*, T. Butterworth, London, by permission of Messrs. John Farquharson.

R. D. FitzGerald: *Moonlight Acre* and *This Night's Orbit*, Melbourne University Press; *Between Two Tides*, Angus and Robertson, Sydney.

Miles Franklin: *My Brilliant Career*, Blackwood, Edinburgh; *All That Swagger*, "The Bulletin", Sydney. (Now published by Angus and Robertson, Sydney.)

Mary Gilmore: *Selected Poems*, Angus and Robertson, Sydney.

William Hay: *Stifled Laughter*, Macqueen, London; *The Escape of the Notorious Sir William Heans*, Melbourne University Press.

Thomas Heney: *In Middle Harbour*, Routledge and Kegan Paul, London.

Xavier Herbert: *Capricornia*, Angus and Robertson, Sydney.

A. D. Hope: *The Wandering Islands*, Edwards and Shaw, Sydney.

Peter Hopegood: *Circus at World's End*, Angus and Robertson, Sydney.

Rex Ingamells: *Selected Poems*, Georgian House, Melbourne.

"Brian James" (John Tierney): *Cookabundy Bridge*, Angus and Robertson, Sydney.

Nancy Keesing: *Imminent Summer* and *Three Men and Sydney*, Angus and Robertson, Sydney.

Henry Lawson: *Prose Works*, Angus and Robertson, Sydney.

F. J. H. Letters: *In a Shaft of Sunlight*, Shakespeare Head Press, Sydney.

Frederick Macartney: *Something for Tokens*, Endacott, Melbourne; *Tripod for Homeward Incense*, Angus and Robertson, Sydney.

James McAuley: *Under Aldebaran*, Melbourne University Press.

George Gordon McCrae: *The Man in the Iron Mask*, Robertson, Melbourne; *The Fleet and Convoy*, Lothian, Melbourne.

Hugh McCrae: *Poems*, Angus and Robertson, Sydney.

Kenneth Mackenzie: *The Young Desire It*, Cape, London; *Our Earth* and *The Moonlit Doorway*, Angus and Robertson, Sydney.

John Manifold: *Selected Verse*, Dobson, London.

Leonard Mann: *Flesh in Armour*.

"Furnley Maurice" (Frank Wilmot): *Poems*, Lothian, Melbourne.

John Shaw Neilson: *Collected Poems*, Lothian, Melbourne.

John Henry Nicholson: *Halek*, Edwards, Dunlop, Brisbane.

W. H. Ogilvie: *Fair Girls and Gray Horses*, Angus and Robertson, Sydney; *Saddle for a Throne*, R. M. Williams, Adelaide.

Bernard O'Dowd: *Poems*, Lothian, Melbourne.

Vance Palmer: *Let the Birds Fly* and *The Rainbow-Bird*, Angus and Robertson, Sydney.

A. B. Paterson: *The Collected Verse of A. B. Paterson*, Angus and Robertson, Sydney.

Brian Penton: *Landtakers*, Endeavour Press, Sydney.

James Picot: *With a Hawk's Quill*, Meanjin.

Hal Porter: *Act One, Scene One*, Angus and Robertson, Sydney.

Rosa Praed: *Lady Bridget in the Never-Never Land* and *Sister Sorrow*, Hutchinson, London.

Katharine Prichard: *Black Opal*, Heinemann, London; *Coonardoo* and *Haxby's Circus*, Cape, London, by permission of Messrs. Curtis Brown.

Roderic Quinn: *Poems*, Angus and Robertson, Sydney.

"Henry Handel Richardson" (Ethel Florence Richardson): *Maurice Guest*, Heinemann, London.

Roland Robinson: *Tumult of the Swans*, Edwards and Shaw, Sydney.

David Rowbotham: *Ploughman and Poet*, Edwards and Shaw, Sydney.

Helen Simpson: *Under Capricorn*, Heinemann, London.

Frederick Sinclaire: *Annotations*, Fellowship Publications, Melbourne.

Kenneth Slessor: *One Hundred Poems*, Angus and Robertson, Sydney.

Christina Stead: *The Salzburg Tales* and *Seven Poor Men of Sydney*, Peter Davies, London.

A. G. Stephens: *Chris Brennan: A Monograph*, Bookfellow, Sydney.

Douglas Stewart: *The Green Lions*, Whitcombe and Tombs, N.Z.; *The Dosser in Springtime*, *The Birdsville Track*, *Fire on the Snow*, and *The Golden Lover*, Angus and Robertson, Sydney.

Harold Stewart: *Phoenix Wings* and *Orpheus*, Angus and Robertson, Sydney.

Archibald Strong: *Peradventure*, Lothian, Melbourne.

"Price Warung" (William Astley): *Tales of the Early Days*, "The Bulletin", Sydney, and Robertson, Melbourne.

Francis Webb: *A Drum for Ben Boyd* and *Leichhardt in Theatre*, Angus and Robertson, Sydney.

Patrick White: *The Aunt's Story*, Routledge and Kegan Paul, London; *The Tree of Man*, Eyre and Spottiswoode, London.

"Judith Wright" (Judith Wright McKinney): *The Moving Image*, Meanjin, Melbourne; *Woman to Man*, *The Gateway*, and *The Two Fires*, Angus and Robertson, Sydney.

Index